Neuropsychological Rehabilitation and People with Dementia

Rehabilitation provides a core concept around which to organise support, intervention and care for people with impairments in memory and other cognitive functions. This book introduces a conceptual framework and rationale for the application of a neuropsychological rehabilitation approach for people with dementia, helping them to manage, bypass or overcome these problems and experience optimum well-being.

Methods and techniques of cognitive rehabilitation are described and the process of goal-setting is discussed in detail, showing how effective strategies may be linked to form an individualised, goal-oriented approach to intervention. The application of a rehabilitation approach in real-life contexts is explored, demonstrating the role and value of neuropsychological rehabilitation within a holistic, psychotherapeutic framework of care and support.

This overview of the neuropsychological rehabilitation approach to dementia care will be of great interest to psychologists as well as to those studying or practising in the area.

Neuropsychological Rehabilitation: A Modular Handbook
The *Neuropsychological Rehabilitation: A Modular Handbook* series covers a wide range of cognitive deficits and will prove an invaluable resource for the neuropsychologist and others working with neurologically impaired people. The series editors, Barbara A. Wilson and Ian H. Robertson, are also editors of the international journal *Neuropsychological Rehabilitation*.

Linda Clare is a chartered clinical psychologist and clinical neuropsychologist. She is currently Reader in Psychology in the School of Psychology, University of Wales Bangor. In 2003 she received the May Davidson Award from the British Psychological Society for her contribution to the development of clinical psychology.

Neuropsychological Rehabilitation and People with Dementia

Linda Clare

Psychology Press
Taylor & Francis Group
HOVE AND NEW YORK

First published 2008 by Psychology Press
27 Church Road, Hove, East Sussex BN3 2FA

Simultaneously published in the USA and Canada
by Psychology Press
270 Madison Avenue, New York, NY 10016

Psychology Press is an imprint of the Taylor & Francis Group, an Informa business

© 2008 Psychology Press

Typeset in Times by Garfield Morgan, Swansea, West Glamorgan
Printed and bound in Great Britain by TJ International Ltd, Padstow,
Cornwall
Cover design by Hybert Design

This publication has been produced with paper manufactured to strict
environmental standards and with pulp derived from sustainable
forests.

British Library Cataloguing in Publication Data
A catalogue record for this book is available from the British Library

Library of Congress Cataloging in Publication Data
Clare, Linda.
  Neuropsychological rehabilitation and people with dementia /
Linda Clare.
      p. ; cm.
  Includes bibliographical references.
  ISBN 978-1-84169-676-8 (hardcover)
  1. Dementia—Patients—Rehabilitation. 2. Clinical
neuropsychology. I. Title.
    [DNLM: 1. Dementia—rehabilitation. 2. Memory Disorders—
rehabilitation. 3. Rehabilitation—methods. WM 220 C591n 2007]
  RC521.C52 2007
  616.8'3–dc22
                                                    2007004668

ISBN 978-1-84169-676-8
(Neuropsychological Rehabilitation: A Modular Handbook
ISSN 1466-6340)

Contents

Series preface

Rehabilitation is a process whereby people who have been impaired by injury or illness work together with health service staff and others to achieve their optimum level of physical, psychological, social and vocational well-being (McLellan, 1991). It includes all measures aimed at reducing the impact of handicapping and disabling conditions and at enabling disabled people to return to their most appropriate environment (WHO, 1986; Wilson, 1997). It also includes attempts to alter impairment in underlying cognitive and brain systems by the provision of systematic, planned experience to the damaged brain (Robertson & Murre, 1999). The above views apply also to neuropsychological rehabilitation, which is concerned with the assessment, treatment and natural recovery of people who have sustained an insult to the brain.

Neuropsychological rehabilitation is influenced by a number of fields both from within and from without psychology. Neuropsychology, behavioural psychology and cognitive psychology have each played important roles in the development of current rehabilitation practice. So too have findings from studies of neuroplasticity, linguistics, geriatric medicine, neurology and other fields. Our discipline, therefore, is not confined to one conceptual framework; rather, it has a broad theoretical base.

We hope that this broad base is reflected in the modular handbook. The first book was by Roger Barker and Stephen Dunnett, which set the scene by talking about "Neural repair, transplantation and rehabilitation". The second title, by Josef Zihl, addressed visual disorders after brain injury. The most recent book by Barbara Wilson, Camilla Herbert, and Agnes Shiel focused on behavioural approaches to rehabilitation. Future titles will include volumes on specific cognitive functions such as language, memory and motor skills, together with social and personality aspects of neuropsychological rehabilitation. Other titles will follow as this is the kind of handbook that can be added to over the years.

Although each volume will be based on a strong theoretical foundation relevant to the topic in question, the main thrust of a majority of the books will be the development of practical, clinical methods of rehabilitation arising out of this research enterprise.

The series is aimed at neuropsychologists, clinical psychologists and other rehabilitation specialists such as occupational therapists, speech and language pathologists, rehabilitation physicians and other disciplines involved in the rehabilitation of people with brain injury.

Neuropsychological rehabilitation is at an exciting stage in its development. On the one hand, we have a huge growth of interest in functional imaging techniques to tell us about the basic processes going on in the brain. On the other hand, the past few years have seen the introduction of a number of theoretically driven approaches to cognitive rehabilitation from the fields of language, memory, attention and perception. In addition to both the above, there is a growing recognition from health services that rehabilitation is an integral part of a health care system. Of course, alongside the recognition of the need for rehabilitation is the view that any system has to be evaluated. To those of us working with brain-injured people including those with dementia, there is a feeling that things are moving forward. This series, we hope, is one reflection of this move and the integration of theory and practice.

References

McLellan, D. L. (1991). Functional recovery and the principles of disability medicine. In M. Swash & J. Oxbury (Eds.), *Clinical neurology*. Edinburgh: Churchill Livingstone.

Robertson, I. H., & Murre, J. M. J. (1999). Rehabilitation of brain damage: Brain plasticity and principles of guided recovery. *Psychological Bulletin, 125*, 544–575.

Wilson, B. A. (1997). Cognitive rehabilitation: How it is and how it might be. *Journal of the International Neuropsychological Society, 3*, 487–496.

WHO. (1986). *Optimum care of disabled people. Report of a WHO meeting*, Turku, Finland. Geneva: World Health Organization.

Barbara A. Wilson
Ian H. Robertson

Other titles available in the series:

Neural Repair, Transplantation and Rehabilitation
by Roger A. Barker & Stephen B. Dunnett

Rehabilitation of Visual Disorders After Brain Injury
by Joseph Zihl

Behavioural Approaches in Neuropsychological Rehabilitation: Optimising Rehabilitation Procedures
by Barbara A. Wilson, Camilla M. Herbert, & Agnes Shiel

Figures and tables

Acknowledgements

My thanks must go first to the research participants – people with dementia and their family members – who showed me that it was possible to make a difference and inspired me to continue working in the field of dementia. I am very fortunate that doing research and clinical practice in this area has provided me with a tremendous group of colleagues and collaborators who have encouraged and supported me both professionally and personally. Many of them are mentioned in the text, but I am grateful to all of them. I am also grateful to the co-workers, PhD students and clinical psychology trainees who have contributed in various ways to the work described here, and to the faculty and staff at the School of Psychology, University of Wales Bangor. Finally, I would like to acknowledge the financial support for my research provided by the Alzheimer's Society (UK) and the Economic and Social Research Council.

1 Introducing neuropsychological rehabilitation and people with dementia

This chapter introduces the concept of neuropsychological rehabilitation for people with dementia and presents an overview of the book.

The way we think about dementia has undergone significant changes in recent years. There is a new emphasis on living with, and managing, the effects of dementia, in order to maintain and support well-being and quality of life. This emphasis reflects the aims of rehabilitation and has relevance right across the spectrum of dementia severity. Rehabilitation has the potential to contribute to quality of life for people with dementia and their families. Because neuropsychological change is central to dementia, a neuropsychological focus is important when considering rehabilitation for people with dementia. At the same time, dementia is about much more than neuropsychological change, and rehabilitation for people with dementia should take account of the whole person, with an understanding of subjective experience and needs. In this book, I consider what we know about the experience of dementia at a neuropsychological and also at a psychosocial level, and I attempt to integrate these elements to provide a comprehensive and holistic framework for neuropsychological rehabilitation in this context.

At present, we have no cure for the dementias, and although some pharmacological treatments offer modest benefits for a proportion of individuals with dementia, there are no effective medical interventions to reverse decline or prevent progression of impairments. In this context, rehabilitative approaches are especially important. Rehabilitative approaches, most commonly thought of in relation to non-progressive problems, for example following brain injury, can also be applied to the whole range of progressive neurological disorders. Much of the research in this area, including my own, has focused on people in the early stages of a primary progressive dementia, most commonly Alzheimer's disease (AD). The focus taken in this book will reflect this emphasis, referring mainly to work with people who have early-stage AD. Nevertheless, many of the principles discussed here might be applied to assist people experiencing other forms of dementia, and indeed other progressive neurological disorders that may result in cognitive impairment.

In preparing this book I have attempted to do two things. First, I have aimed to review the research literature relevant to neuropsychological rehabilitation in dementia and to present a concise and helpful account of the foundations and rationale for the approach, the methods and techniques involved, the application of the approach and how it might develop in the future. Second, I have drawn on experience gained in my own research studies and clinical practice to describe aspects of the practical application of cognitive rehabilitation in early-stage AD, and I illustrate these with real-life examples. While the focus here is on 'neuropsychological' rehabilitation, I hope that this volume will be of value not just to psychologists, but also to other health professionals working in dementia care who are keen to offer a constructive, practical intervention approach.

Overview of the book

In attempting to introduce the concepts of neuropsychological rehabilitation for people with dementia, I begin with a discussion of how dementia is understood and the relevance of rehabilitation, and consider the psychosocial impact of dementia. I then go on to address the neuropsychological aspects and the way in which cognition-focused interventions have developed. These early chapters provide the background and rationale for applying neuropsychological rehabilitation with people who have dementia in clinical settings. This sets the scene for chapters focusing on the current application of neuropsychological rehabilitation, and addressing assessment, specific rehabilitation strategies, and clinical applications. Finally, I present an holistic model of neuropsychological rehabilitation for people with dementia. Here I briefly outline the content of each of the chapters.

Chapter 2 begins with an overview of dementia, considering how it is currently defined and categorised into various sub-types, how it relates to other conditions, and how frequently it occurs in different age-groups. This leads into a discussion of how dementia may best be understood. Recent developments in our thinking about dementia have made a powerful case for moving beyond a standard disease model to consider dementia within a biopsychosocial framework and place the person with dementia in context. The application of a biopsychosocial framework is discussed, showing how dementia may usefully be viewed in terms of disability, and how this points to the relevance of a rehabilitation approach. I suggest that rehabilitation interventions that aim to impact on the disability and handicap resulting from the underlying neurological impairments, and in particular to reduce excess disability, have the potential to benefit people with dementia and their families.

Adopting a biopsychosocial framework encourages us to address the psychosocial impact of dementia, and I discuss this with a particular emphasis on people with early-stage AD. Chapters 3 and 4 consider current knowledge in this area and what it tells us about the potential for rehabilitation. Chapter 3 focuses on the subjective experience of AD. Models of the subjective experience of the person with early-stage AD, and how people with AD make sense of their condition, are reviewed. In order to place the person with dementia in context, the nature of interactions with family caregivers is discussed, aspects of the experience of family caregivers are outlined, and recent work focusing on social participation in dementia is introduced. Finally, implications for intervention are described, and the role of rehabilitation in this context considered. Following on from the account of subjective experience, Chapter 4 introduces the related issue of awareness. The extent to which the person with AD is aware of the developing difficulties and changes has important implications for the potential to engage in rehabilitation. This chapter reviews the theoretical frameworks that are available to help in making sense of changes in awareness, and the methods that are currently used to assess awareness. Practical implications of variations in awareness, and the relationship between awareness and outcome of rehabilitation interventions, are discussed.

Having explored the psychological and social experience of AD, in Chapter 5 I discuss the neuropsychological changes that dementia brings, again with particular reference to AD. Chapter 5 explores how theoretical models from neuropsychology combine with experimental evidence on learning, behaviour change and neural plasticity to provide a basis for cognitive rehabilitation interventions in early-stage Alzheimer's disease. I introduce a range of evidence suggesting that people with early-stage AD may benefit from such approaches, provided they are appropriately targeted and based on a sound understanding of the profile of cognitive change and its implications for everyday functioning.

Before considering how neuropsychological rehabilitation can best be put into practice in dementia care, it is useful to reflect on the history of psychological interventions in dementia, to consider how neuropsychological rehabilitation relates to other approaches, and to review some of the available methods and techniques. Chapter 6 provides a brief history and overview of cognition-focused interventions for people with dementia in order to help clarify the distinctive aspects of neuropsychological rehabilitation in this context and how it differs from other forms of cognition-focused intervention. This chapter sets the scene for a comprehensive discussion of the application of cognitive rehabilitation in the following chapters.

The starting point for effective cognitive rehabilitation interventions is a comprehensive assessment. Chapter 7 provides a brief overview of the diagnostic assessment of dementia, followed by a longer discussion of assessment for cognitive rehabilitation, outlining the areas to be considered in an assessment and the way in which information from the assessment contributes to planning and conducting the intervention. In Chapter 8 I review a range of methods that can be used as the building-blocks of memory rehabilitation interventions. Methods that have been used to assist people with early-stage dementia in learning or relearning information include principles such as effortful processing and errorless learning, along with specific techniques such as spaced retrieval and mnemonic methods. The relevance and effectiveness of these methods are considered. Methods for maintenance or development of practical skills of everyday living are discussed along with methods of familiarising people with dementia with new memory aids and teaching the use of memory aids. In Chapter 9 I explore how the various specific methods and techniques described in earlier chapters can be linked to form a comprehensive, individualised clinical intervention for the person with early-stage AD. The concept of personal goal setting provides a central focus for applying the available techniques creatively in a way that has the potential to enhance the person's functioning in everyday life.

Drawing together the many themes discussed throughout the book, Chapter 10 describes an holistic approach to neuropsychological rehabilitation for people with dementia. Interventions are considered in relation to psychotherapeutic and systemic perspectives. Service and policy contexts are briefly discussed, and methods for evaluating treatment outcome are considered. The chapter concludes by outlining current evidence for the efficacy of cognitive rehabilitation and suggesting some future directions for the further development of this approach.

Conclusions

In this book I hope to stimulate a greater understanding of what it is like to experience dementia, to convey the importance and relevance of applying the concept of rehabilitation to assist people with dementia and progressive neurological disorders, and to encourage readers to incorporate the principles of rehabilitation into their work with people who have dementia. As later chapters show, there are many possible ways of doing this, and therefore I hope that all readers will be able to gain some useful ideas that they can apply in their own work settings.

2 Dementia, disability and rehabilitation

A brief overview of dementia leads into a discussion of how this condition may best be understood. The application of a biopsychosocial model to AD is discussed, showing how dementia may usefully be viewed in terms of disability. This points to the relevance of a rehabilitation approach. Rehabilitation interventions that aim to impact on the disability and handicap resulting from the underlying neurological impairments, and in particular to reduce excess disability, offer tremendous scope to benefit people with dementia.

In this chapter, I begin by reflecting on current understandings of dementia and the relevance of rehabilitation. As I said in the introduction, the way in which we view and understand dementia has undergone considerable change in recent years, and dementia care focuses increasingly on finding ways of managing disability so as to support or maintain well-being. Through exploration of the biological, psychological and social aspects of dementia I will highlight the relevance and scope of neuropsychological rehabilitation.

Dementia: A brief overview

Dementia is a broad term encompassing a number of different progressive neurological conditions. A general definition describes dementia as 'a clinical syndrome characterised by loss of function in multiple cognitive abilities in an individual with previously normal (or at least higher) intellectual abilities and occurring in clear consciousness' in the absence of any other disease process that could account for the observed cognitive decline (Whitehouse, Lerner, & Hedera, 1993, p. 603). Prevalence estimates vary, but dementia is thought to affect about 2.5 per cent of all people over 65, and prevalence doubles with every 5 years of increasing age, so that about 10 per cent of all people over 75, and 40 per cent of all people over 85, are affected (R. S. Turner, 2003). Thus dementia is associated with increased age, and incidence is most common between the ages of 70 and 90; there is some suggestion that incidence rates may be reduced in those who survive beyond the age of 90 (McKeith & Fairbairn, 2001). Increases in life expectancy lead to an associated increase in the number of people who are at risk of developing dementia. However, dementia does occur in younger people, and dementia with onset before the age of 65 is also a matter of concern (Cox & Keady, 1999). Dementia accounts for a considerable proportion of health care expenditure in developed countries. As rates of population growth for older people increase in developing countries, so concern about dementia is likely to rise in these societies as well (Pollitt, 1996). Recent years have also seen a growing awareness of the prevalence of dementia among people with intellectual disability as they age (C. Oliver, Adams, & Kalsy, in press).

Dementia needs to be distinguished from other psychiatric and medical disorders that may produce apparently similar effects, such as depression, as well as from the ill-effects of nutritional deficiencies, exposure to toxins or iatrogenic consequences of taking prescribed medications (Christensen, Griffiths, MacKinnon, & Jacomb, 1997). Some of these conditions are treatable, although depression in particular may still represent a risk factor for later development of dementia (J. O'Brien, Ames, Chiu, Schweitzer, Desmond, & Tress, 1998). All of these possibilities must be excluded before arriving at a diagnosis of dementia.

There are numerous possible types of dementia (McKeith & Fairbairn, 2001). The most frequent dementia diagnosis is Alzheimer's disease (AD), accounting for approximately 50–60 per cent of all dementia diagnoses. Vascular dementia on its own accounts for about 10 per cent of all dementia diagnoses, but is often present alongside other forms of dementia. Dementia with Lewy bodies accounts for about 15–20 per cent of diagnoses and may often co-exist with Alzheimer's disease. Less common sub-types of degenerative dementia include fronto-temporal dementia, encompassing the subcategories of frontal dementia and semantic dementia, which accounts for 10–20 per cent of dementias with age of onset between 45 and 70 years, and Huntington's disease, with a prevalence of 4–7 cases per 100,000 people. Dementia may also arise in Parkinson's disease, affecting 10–80 per cent of those diagnosed, in multiple sclerosis, affecting 50–66 per cent of those diagnosed, and in other very rare progressive neurological disorders, such as progressive supranuclear palsy (PSP), Creutzfeld-Jakob disease, limbic encephalitis, progressive multifocal leucoencephalopathy and sub-acute sclerosing panencephalitis. Dementia may also result from trauma, for example following head injury or anoxia, from toxic exposure, as in alcohol-related dementia, from infection, as in AIDS dementia complex, or from space-occupying lesions, metabolic problems or other causes such as normal pressure hydrocephalus. A distinction is commonly made between cortical and subcortical dementias. Cortical dementias, of which AD is one, primarily affect cortical areas of the brain. In subcortical dementias, such as PSP or Huntington's disease, the normal regulatory effect that subcortical structures exert on the cortex is diminished or lost. All these various forms of dementia have different neuropsychological profiles, particularly in the earlier stages, and consequently different implications for intervention (Brandt & Rich, 1995). Since the application of neuropsychological rehabilitation approaches to date has focused on the most commonly diagnosed forms of dementia, and especially Alzheimer's disease, this focus is also reflected in the chapters that follow, although where appropriate, mention is made of potential relevance to other groups. Many of the principles discussed have some relevance to people with other forms of dementia.

Although several different sub-types of dementia have been identified, it is important to note that diagnosis and classification are not always straightforward. A diagnosis of AD can only be confirmed fully where post mortem examination makes it possible to clarify the precise nature of the brain pathology (R. S. Turner, 2003). Some forms of dementia may coexist, and in such cases it is hard to be sure about the relative contribution of each to the observed difficulties. For example, some individuals may have a mixed type of dementia with features of both AD and vascular dementia (Norris, MacNeill, & Haines, 2003). AD itself may represent a heterogeneous category, encompassing multiple aetiologies and presenting with different profiles of neuropsychological change and progression (R. G. Morris & Becker, 2004).

The main sets of diagnostic criteria for AD and vascular dementia (American Psychiatric Association, 1995) require impairment in at least two domains of cognition, of a degree that affects everyday functioning. Thus, at the point of diagnosis, the level of impairment is already significant. Recently, interest has focused on detecting those with very early signs of dementia and those most at risk of developing dementia. Again, this is not always straightforward. Most, though not all, older people experience some decline in cognitive functioning with age, and there is wide variation in what might be considered 'normal' performance (Kester, Benjamin, Castel, & Craik, 2002). Some individuals fall into the area between 'normal' cognition and dementia, with difficulties that are more extensive than the norm but do not impact significantly on functioning and are not of such an extent as to meet criteria for a dementia diagnosis. Various terms and definitions have been applied to this group, such as 'benign/malignant senescent forgetfulness' (Kral, 1962), 'age-associated memory impairment' (Crook, Bartus, Ferris, Whitehouse, Cohen, & Gershon, 1986) or 'age-associated cognitive decline' (American Psychiatric Association, 1995); currently, they are most likely to be described as experiencing 'mild cognitive impairment' (MCI; Petersen, 2004). Individuals with MCI are at increased risk of going on to develop dementia, and some researchers have argued that MCI represents a very early stage of AD (J. C. Morris et al., 2001). The approaches to intervention for people with dementia described in this book are likely to have considerable relevance to people who meet criteria for MCI (Woods & Clare, 2006).

Diagnostic assessment requires a comprehensive multidisciplinary evaluation. The process of diagnostic assessment, and the role of neuropsychological assessment in particular, is discussed in more detail in Chapter 7, leading on to consideration of assessment for cognitive rehabilitation. The multidisciplinary approach to diagnostic assessment highlights the importance of considering a number of areas and viewing the person in context.

Conceptual frameworks for understanding dementia

The 'standard paradigm' for understanding dementia (Kitwood, 1997) has been a medical or disease model (Roth, 1994). Research based on this model has emphasised the need to understand causal mechanisms leading to pathological changes in the brain that produce the observed features of dementia. This has resulted in valuable advances. However, a number of findings indicate that causal mechanisms are far from straightforward, and a broader focus may be needed. For example, the key forms of neuropathology associated with AD are also found in the brains of some older people with no cognitive impairment, and conversely some older people may appear to show all the symptoms of AD yet have no observable abnormal brain pathology at post mortem (Snowdon, 2003). One possible explanation lies in the cognitive reserve hypothesis (Stern, Zarahn, Hilton, Flynn, De La Paz, & Rakitin, 2003), which proposes that people who benefit from greater education, engage in more cognitive and physical activities and have wider social networks build up a degree of cognitive reserve that protects them from the effects of this brain pathology, such that more extensive pathology is required for impairments to become evident. This highlights the relevance of psychosocial factors. A simple disease model assuming a causal relationship between disease process and pathology cannot account for 'excess disability' whereby functioning is worse than the degree of impairment would predict (Reifler & Larson, 1990), for periods of 'rementing' where functioning improves or stabilises following environmental changes (Sixsmith, Stilwell, & Copeland, 1993), or for the rapid deterioration that often follows adverse events such as temporary hospitalisation (Kitwood, 1996). A complete explanation requires consideration of psychological and social factors.

An 'alternative paradigm' has been most clearly articulated by Kitwood (1996, 1997), although related ideas have been presented by others (Sabat, 1994, 1995; Sabat & Harré, 1992; Sabat, Wiggs, & Pinizzotto, 1984). Kitwood (1996, 1997) proposes a dialectical model of dementia, which is summarised in Figure 2.1. The term 'dialectical' reflects the emphasis on interactions between variables operating at the biological and psychosocial levels. The aim of this 'alternative paradigm' is to develop an account of the process of dementia that bridges these two levels. Kitwood suggests that the manifestation and progression of AD in any one individual are influenced by the interplay of neurological impairment, physical health and sensory

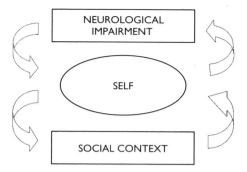

Figure 2.1 Dialectical model of dementia (based on Kitwood, 1997).

acuity, personality, biographical experience, and social psychology, in terms of environment, communication and interaction. Where the social psychology is 'malignant', the result is a spiral of deterioration. Social interactions and care processes that are undermining and discouraging, and fail to take account of personality and life history, lead to a reduction in self-efficacy, which in turn increases the likelihood of further damaging interactions (Sabat, 1994). According to Kitwood, events or states experienced at the mind or psychological level are also brain events or states (Kitwood, 1997, pp. 17–18, 50–53, 67–69). The brain has considerable potential for change (plasticity), some of which is retained in dementia, and brain structure is shaped by a lifelong process of development in response to experience and environment. Psychological experience may affect brain structure just as brain structure may affect experience. While a malignant social environment might contribute to excess disability and speed up decline, Kitwood believed that a benign social psychology coupled with an enriched environment might facilitate some regeneration, or at least the maintenance of function for a period of time, and there is some evidence to support this (Bråne, Karlsson, Kihlgren, & Norberg, 1989; Karlsson, Bråne, Melin, Nyth, & Rybo, 1988), albeit as yet rather limited in extent. The interaction of these factors will depend crucially on the individual psychological profile as the person copes with and adjusts to the changes dementia brings. This has clear implications for care provision, indicating a requirement for care that meets people's psychological needs and affirms personhood, sense of self and social value, thus impacting on quality of life (Brooker, 2004) – this is termed 'person-centred' care.

Acknowledging that dementia involves changes and needs at the biological, psychological and social levels and is experienced within the context of social and cultural beliefs and practices (Downs, Clare, & Anderson, in press) indicates that a comprehensive explanatory framework can be encompassed within a biopsychosocial approach (Engel, 1977). The biopsychosocial framework for understanding disability (World Health

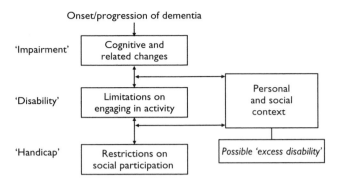

Figure 2.2 Disability model of dementia (based on WHO, 1980, 1998).

Organisation, 1980, 1998) is helpful in this regard, because it makes the important distinction between underlying impairment at the neurological or physical level, activity (disability) and participation (handicap), as summarised in Figure 2.2. Activity and participation are influenced by the personal and social context and do not follow directly or straightforwardly from impairment. Negative contexts can contribute to producing unnecessary excess disability (Reifler & Larson, 1990). Conceptualising dementia within a disability framework encourages us to consider each of these levels and the interactions between them, in order to maximise well-being. Kitwood's dialectical model is consistent with this approach.

Applying a biopsychosocial framework to AD

Adopting a biopsychosocial framework encourages us to view dementia in terms of disability, and this in turn has significant implications for intervention. Here, taking AD as an example, I consider in detail how using a biopsychosocial approach expands our conceptualisation of dementia and provides pointers for intervention. I review each of the three levels of the framework in turn, and consider possible interactions between them. Since interventions at different levels may have an interactive effect (Koltai & Branch, 1999), the benefits derived from any single intervention may be evident across several domains. Table 2.1 provides an overview of the range of issues that can be considered at each level.

Biological aspects

At the biological level, we can consider developmental factors, pathology, and the physical health of the individual. With regard to genetic influences, two main categories of AD are distinguished (R. S. Turner, 2003). In the

Table 2.1 Areas to consider in formulating a comprehensive intervention approach for people with AD and their families

Level	Areas to assess	Possible interventions
Biological level	Genetic vulnerability	None available
	Possible reversible causes	Treat any reversible causes
	Brain changes; neurological signs	Medication aimed at slowing progression
	Physical health problems, mobility and sensory impairments	Treatment for physical health problems, chronic pain, etc.; promote mobility
	Medication effects and interactions	Monitor/reduce medication
Psychological level	Neuropsychology – full range of cognitive functioning; everyday functioning and task performance in the home setting	Interventions to assist with effects of cognitive impairments, e.g. strategies for managing memory problems; interventions to develop adaptive behaviours
	Individual psychological needs, including the life history, recent changes in personality and behaviour, anxiety and depression, catastrophic reactions, coping and defensive mechanisms	Support groups, psychotherapy, counselling; life review, reminiscence, identity maintenance; strategies for dealing with anxiety or depression
	Richness of environment and level of stimulation	Environmental adaptation and enrichment
Social level	Social interactions and communication; social networks	Caregiver training to promote communication and positive interactions
	Needs of primary caregiver; dyadic communication	Interventions for caregiver, e.g. psychoeducation; support groups; individual therapy or counselling; couple or family therapy
	Needs of other family members	Support; family therapy
	Care practices, interactions and attitudes in formal settings	Staff training and environmental enrichment
	Experience of societal discrimination and stigma	Approaches to counter discriminatory attitudes
	Social circumstances and financial situation; access to services and resources	Equitable access to services; assistance with benefit claims

rare, familial form of AD, faulty genes on chromosomes 1, 14 and 21 may be inherited from a parent in an autosomal dominant pattern; anyone who inherits a copy of the faulty gene will develop the disorder, usually at a relatively early age. In the more common non-familial form of AD, the apolipoprotein E-4 (Apo E-4) allele on chromosome 19 is associated with increased risk for developing the disorder, while some cases of later onset AD have been linked to chromosome 12 abnormalities. However, it remains unclear why some people with the higher risk combinations go on to develop AD while others do not; this clearly has to relate to epigenetic factors and the biological effects of outside influences on lifespan development. For example, stress resulting from adverse life events may affect the hypothalamic–pituitary–adrenal axis and thus contribute to neuronal damage and the development of AD (O'Dwyer & Orrell, 1994). Understanding more about these factors could open possibilities for preventive intervention in the future; this is discussed further in Chapter 4.

An extensive range of neuropathological features has been observed in AD, although as noted above these are not found in all individuals showing symptoms of AD. A comprehensive review of these features and their impact on cognitive functioning is provided by Morris (R. G. Morris, 2004). Key aspects include generalised atrophy, cell loss, structural changes resulting from abnormalities in protein metabolism, and neurochemical changes. Many people with AD also have vascular changes and white matter lesions, and it is increasingly acknowledged that AD and vascular dementia often co-exist, a situation referred to as 'mixed dementia' (Norris et al., 2003). Risk factors for the two conditions are very similar, and vascular risk factors appear to also increase risk of AD. Neurological examination of the person with AD may indicate abnormalities in reflexes, thought to result from deterioration of the frontal lobes. Abnormalities may also be detected on EEG.

Treatments that target the neurobiological level are now available (Lopez & Bell, 2004), although there is no treatment that can either prevent the onset of AD or provide a cure. The aim of the pharmacological treatments presently available is to mitigate the symptoms of AD, albeit for a limited period. Dysfunction in the cholinergic system provides the strongest association between AD and neuronal loss, and acetylcholinesterase inhibitors (AChEIs), aimed at enhancing cholinergic function, have been a major focus of research. These may offer modest improvements in verbal learning and memory, psychomotor functioning, and attention (Rogers, Doody, Mohs, Friedhoff, & the Donepezil Study Group, 1998). Such improvements might be reflected, for example, in a change of 2 to 3 points on a cognitive screening test such as the Mini-Mental State Examination (MMSE; Folstein, Folstein, & McHugh, 1975), which has been interpreted as representing a saving of approximately 6 months of deterioration. However, findings of this kind must be viewed with some caution as repeated administration of the MMSE can lead to practice effects, and taking into account limitations on test–retest reliability, only changes of the magnitude of at least 4 points should be regarded as significant (Clarke et al., 1999).

A significant proportion of people with AD will also have other physical health problems, which may be treatable (J. C. Morris, 1996). If untreated, such conditions are likely to have an adverse effect on cognitive functioning and thus to contribute to excess disability. Similarly, people with dementia may have sensory impairments that, if unrecognised, will adversely affect their functioning (Kitwood, 1996). Functioning may be affected by iatrogenic factors, such as the effects of multiple prescribing and drug interactions. Physical health problems need to be targeted in any comprehensive intervention plan for the person with AD, in order to minimise excess disability and enable the person to function at the highest possible level (Cohen & Eisdorfer, 1986). Important aspects include recognising and stabilising chronic conditions such as arthritis, managing pain, maintaining mobility, compensating for sensory impairment and reducing physical discomfort.

Psychological aspects

Changes at the neurobiological level have a direct impact on neuropsychological functioning (R. G. Morris, 2004). In the early stages of AD, specific cognitive functions are impaired while others remain intact. As already mentioned, presentations of AD can vary, and a range of neuropsychological profiles can be observed (R. G. Morris & Becker, 2004). However, memory is usually the first function to be affected, although the impairments are evident only in certain memory systems, particularly episodic memory; for a full discussion, see Chapter 4. Attention (Crossley, Hiscock, & Foreman, 2004), executive function (Collette & Van der Linden, 2004) and word finding (Kertesz, 2004) may also be affected. As the disorder progresses, psychomotor functions become impaired (Kidron & Freedman, 2004), and deficits in memory, attention, language and executive function become more extensive. A decline in global cognitive functioning becomes evident. Visuospatial perception is usually affected only in the later stages, although in some atypical cases it may be observed as one of the earliest symptoms (R. G. Morris & McKiernan, 1994). The level of awareness that individuals have of the changes they are undergoing is variable, and is likely to be determined by an interaction between neuropsychological impairments and psychological reactions; this is discussed in full in Chapter 3.

Changes in the ability to perceive, process and experience emotion may result from neurological changes affecting emotional responsiveness (Zaitchik & Albert, 2004). Emotional changes may also follow from a psychological reaction, for example to perceived losses (Wands, Merskey, Hachinski, Fisman, Fox, & Boniferro, 1990), or from an interaction between these two factors. The prevalence of anxiety and depression is high, although estimates vary (Ross, Arnsberger, & Fox, 1998). For example, Wands et al.

(1990) found rates of 38 per cent for anxiety and 28 per cent for depression in a sample of 50 people with early-stage dementia. Reifler and Larson (1990) comment that depression is the most common cause of excess disability in people with AD. Emotions may also play a positive role for the person with dementia, influencing experiences and reactions more and more directly as cognitive abilities decline, in line with theoretical models of the relationship between cognition and emotion (Teasdale & Barnard, 1993).

The subtle changes in behaviour and personality that occur in early-stage AD may also result from an interaction of neurological and psychological factors (Petry, Cummings, Hill, & Shapira, 1989). From a psychodynamic perspective, Hagberg (1997) suggests that the organisation of personality is affected, resulting in a reduction in ego resources, regressive behaviour, use of more primitive defence mechanisms to stave off painful emotions, and reactivation in conscious awareness of previously unconscious material. In the early stages of dementia, defensive mechanisms may be used to protect the self from acknowledging losses, including denial, withdrawal or blaming others for difficulties (O'Connor, 1993). Additionally, as dementia progresses, attachment may re-emerge as a key issue (Miesen, 1992). Patterns of attachment developed within intimate relationships early in life influence internal working models of relationships that guide the individual's behaviour towards others and affect the quality of relationships. Attachment styles remain relevant in later life, affecting attitudes towards support received from others and satisfaction with interactions (Bradley & Cafferty, 2001), and may be particularly salient as cognitive impairments develop (Browne & Shlosberg, 2005). It can be surmised that for the person with dementia there is a continual experience of being in a seemingly strange situation, which activates attachment needs and a desire for safety and security. A preoccupation with early relationships with caregivers, in which these needs were originally worked through, may develop. People who had problems in early attachment may become correspondingly emotionally distressed as their need for care increases.

Behavioural changes are frequently reported in AD and are likely to constitute a particular problem for carers (Camp & Nasser, 2003). These may include agitation, aggression, apathy and lack of attention to personal hygiene. Many behavioural disturbances, especially shouting, aggression, incontinence and wandering, cannot be explained purely in terms of cognitive impairment, and therefore may be regarded as excess disabilities (Bleathman & Morton, 1994). Funtional analytic approaches can help in determining the function that such behaviours serve for the individual, and thus assist in identifying appropriate intervention approaches (e.g. Bird, 2001). Lack of social contact and environmental stimulation, perhaps resulting from loss of confidence, may contribute to lowered well-being and consequently to behavioural difficulties (Woods & Britton, 1985).

At a psychological level, the onset of dementia can be understood as constituting a threat to self (Pearce, Clare, & Pistrang, 2002). This is true of many forms of serious illness or disability, but is particularly salient in dementia given that representations of dementia expressed by those who know their diagnosis typically incorporate the sense that at a certain point self-awareness will be diminished or lost. Thus, for the person with early-stage dementia, the sense of continuity that characterises the experience of self is challenged, and the nature of future experience of self becomes uncertain. Similarly, the central role of memory in the experience of self can lead people to question what will be the nature of their experience when memory is severely affected. Alongside these issues of the changing experience of self, there is a major impact on relationships, and a sense of loss of future possibilities, such as seeing one's grandchildren grow up. At the same time that people with early-stage dementia are challenged to consider these fundamental issues, they also face the immediate impact of developing memory and cognitive difficulties. In addition to the practical consequences, they may experience adverse reactions from others in response to memory lapses, which can lead to loss of confidence and withdrawal from activities, thus exacerbating the sense that one's very identity is under threat.

Consideration of how the individual copes with the changes resulting from AD is integral to a psychological understanding of this disease. The development of adaptive coping strategies is important in maximising well-being and minimising excess disability, but the onset of AD places major demands on coping resources. Furthermore, AD most commonly arises at a time when the individual is negotiating development into later life, and is superimposed onto the normative developmental tasks faced by the individual and family in relation to growing older, which may include reviewing one's life, achieving resolution of important themes or issues, accepting losses, and coming to terms with approaching death (Coleman & O'Hanlon, in press). Recent studies of the phenomenological experience and coping strategies of people with early-stage AD (Clare, 2003a) have demonstrated two key dimensions – the attempt to protect or maintain an existing or prior sense of identity, and the attempt to acknowledge and integrate the changes experienced in order to facilitate the development of a modified sense of identity. These are discussed in detail in Chapter 3. Understanding the current needs of each individual with respect to these tasks, and the way in which the individual perceives his or her situation, is invaluable in helping to determine what kinds of interventions may be appropriate at any given stage.

The range of psychologically based interventions that has been attempted with individuals with AD and their caregivers is considerable (for reviews, see Kasl-Godley & Gatz, 2000; Zarit & Edwards, in press). However, the likelihood is that in reality most people with AD are offered little in the way of psychological support. Approaches described in the literature include, for example, life review (Woods, Portnoy, Head, & Jones, 1992), reminiscence (Bender, Bauckham, & Norris, 1998), self-maintenance therapy (Romero & Wenz, 2001), psychotherapy (Cheston, Jones, & Gilliard, 2003), systemic family therapy (Curtis & Dixon, 2005), cognitive behaviour therapy (Marriott, Donaldson, Tarrier, & Burns, 2000), behavioural and functional analytic approaches (Bird, 2000, 2001), psychoeducational and support groups (Yale, 1995), and environmental modifications (Woods & Britton, 1985) as well as approaches that specifically target memory functioning. The latter are discussed in full in Chapter 8. Since memory impairments are a central feature of early-stage AD, and impact extensively on daily life and well-being (Bieliauskas, 1996), interventions targeting coping with memory difficulties are likely to have particular relevance and are clearly indicated within the framework of a biopsychosocial understanding of AD.

Social aspects

The social or systemic level encompasses interactions between individuals, the way these are expressed in care practices, wider social attitudes, and the impact of social advantage or deprivation. The experience of the person with AD and his or her social network arises in the context of broader social attitudes and practices in relation to ageing in general (Bond, Coleman, & Peace, 1993), which in Western society are often negative. Greater public awareness and better education of both professionals and public are needed to counteract these influences (Reifler & Larson, 1990).

Social models of disability focus on the disabling effects of attitudes, environments, practices and policies (M. Oliver, 1990). The attitudes and interactions of others can disempower those with some form of difference, resulting in increased disablement (Kitwood, 1997). Sabat (2001) argues that having dementia affects the possibilities available for the social presentation of self in the context of relationships, and that people with dementia are often positioned negatively by others. This may be compounded by a sense of shame and embarrassment on the part of the person with dementia, with implications for sense of self and identity (Cotrell & Schulz, 1993). Equally, family carers, care workers and others who come into contact with people who have AD may distance themselves emotionally and adopt a 'them and us' stance as a protective strategy (Hausman, 1992). The effects of stigma can extend throughout the person's social network (Shifflett & Blieszner, 1988). Interventions may be directed at enhancing communication (Bourgeois, 1991) and choice (Allan, 2001) through providing training, advice and support for carers and care staff.

With the onset of AD, family members – typically spouses or adult daughters – and sometimes close friends find themselves in the role of caregiver. There is an extensive literature on the experiences and needs of family caregivers (Zarit & Edwards, in press), and a number of models have been proposed to assist in understanding the caregiving process. Pearlin's stress process model (Pearlin, Mullan, Semple, & Skaff, 1990) views caregiving as a developmental process, in which a delicate balance between stressors and coping resources must be continually negotiated. Although this model does not directly incorporate the perspective of the person with dementia, quality of caregiving clearly has implications for the person with dementia, and is closely related to carer well-being. Negative interactions are particularly likely to occur where the carer is experiencing stress. Equally, the person with dementia may be less able to respond as before, and mutuality in the relationship is likely to diminish, with important consequences for dyadic communication (Clare & Shakespeare, 2004). It is important to note that there may be positive aspects to the experience for some caregivers that mitigate levels of stress, especially where some continuation of meaningful shared activity is possible. Being a caregiver can be a positive experience. Andrén and Elmståhl (2005) found that, while experiencing some feelings of burden, a high proportion of caregivers expressed great satisfaction in their role. Although there may be positive dimensions of caregiving, however, investigations of health outcomes for caregivers suggest that caring is frequently linked to reduced well-being, low morale and depression (Zarit & Edwards, in press) and perhaps to physical ill-health (Kiecolt-Glaser, Dura, Speicher, Trask, & Glaser, 1991). Distress is critically determined by the caregiver's appraisal of the situation (Gatz, Bengtson, & Blum, 1990). This includes both the appraisal of specific problems, in terms of how upsetting or difficult to manage they are, and the appraisal of the extent to which the changes in lifestyle are acceptable, and the role of carer manageable. Personality characteristics of the carer influence the way in which the person approaches the task of caring and the coping styles adopted (Hooker, Frazier, & Monahan, 1994). Related to coping may be the sense of having control over events as opposed to feeling helpless or powerless.

The most common form of dementia caregiving relationship arises where a person is caring for his or her spouse. Wives caring for husbands with dementia constitute the majority of dementia caregivers. The closer the relationship between the carer and the person with dementia, the more stressful caring becomes and the greater the effects on carers' mental health (Gilhooly, 1984). The carer has to face not only the need to give care to the dependent partner, but also the loss of a companion, confidante and supporter. People with early-stage AD living as part of a couple themselves acknowledge an increasing reliance on their spouses. Indeed, this is one of the most commonly described coping strategies in early-stage AD (Clare, 2002c). Factors such as the pre-existing quality of the relationship are likely to influence the quality of caregiving. Caregiving may intensify pre-existing family problems, and a poor prior relationship between husband and wife has been shown in some studies to contribute to negative outcomes for the carer's well-being (Samuelsson, Annerstedt, Elmståhl, Samuelsson, & Grafström, 2001), while a strong prior relationship is related to lower stress levels, perhaps because where the relationship has been strong carers undertake the caring role more out of affection than duty. Wives caring for their husbands generally report higher levels of distress than husbands caring for their wives, when severity of dementia is controlled for (Collins, 1992). Kahana and Young (1990) emphasise the importance of a dyadic model of the caregiving relationship, and the need for a detailed analysis of the cycles of interaction between caregiver and care-recipient. For example, Cavanaugh et al. (1989) investigated the way in which carers support care-recipients in a problem-solving activity as a way of gaining insight into the nature of a cognitively supportive environment for the person with dementia. Recent formulations have proposed a relationship-centred focus that considers the caregiving dyad (Keady & Nolan, 2003). De Vugt et al. (2004) identified three caregiver management styles, termed 'supporting', 'nurturing' and 'non-adapting', and demonstrated a circular interactive relationship between carer management style and level of behavioural problems in the person with dementia.

It has been suggested that caregiving is best viewed as a family systems issue (Fisher & Lieberman, 1994). Clinical interventions with family care-givers target areas of the stress process where change may be possible, and aim to provide information, assist in managing stress, facilitate expression of emotional responses, encourage practical problem-solving, and strengthen coping resources (Brodaty, Green, & Koschera, 2003; Mittelman, Roth, Coon, & Haley, 2004). Interventions may take the form of psychoedu-cation, support groups, individual counselling or therapy, and family or couple therapy. Psychoeducational interventions might include specific skills for managing behavioural problems, communicating effectively, providing cognitive stimulation, or carrying out practical nursing tasks, along with the provision of information about medical, psychological and social aspects of dementia, financial and legal implications, and services available (Bourgeois, Schulz, Burgio, & Beach, 2002). Support groups may also focus on some of these areas, while aiming to increase the social support available to members through sharing of experiences, development of relationships within the group, and encouraging identification of other potential sources of support (Hettiarachty & Manthorpe, 1992). Individual therapy or counselling might encourage discussion of emotional responses, adjustment to role changes, problem-solving and self-care (Brodaty, 1992), and specific therapeutic paradigms such as cognitive behavioural therapy or psychodynamic therapy (O'Connor, 1993) may be employed. Family therapy or counselling might aim to help families develop skills for solving some of the problems arising from the situation they are in and to enhance their sense of being in con-trol (Gatz et al., 1990). Support provided by community-based services such as specialist nursing teams who focus on the caregiver (known as 'Admiral Nurses' in the UK) is helpful in reducing caregiver distress (Woods, Wills, Higginson, Hobbins, & Whitby, 2003). Reflecting the importance of appraisals and attributions, Mittelman et al. (2004) demonstrated that a multicomponent support and counselling intervention was successful in altering caregiver appraisals of behavioural problems exhibited by the person with dementia.

In formal care settings, interactions between care staff and people with dementia can all too often reflect a 'malignant social psychology' in which many negative elements are evident. This can be the case even for well-intentioned interactions. Components of this 'malignant social psychology' observed in interactions with people who have AD within formal care settings include a range of behaviours described by Kitwood as 'personal detractions', such as intimidation, ignoring, mockery, disparagement and stigmatisation of the person with dementia. 'Personal detractions' of this kind can be further disabling for the person with dementia (Pollitt, 1996). Kitwood (1997) argued for a 'new culture of care' emphasising positive interactions that would enable the person with AD to experience optimal security and well-being and to engage with carers in shared, enjoyable activity. This is what effective person-centred care can achieve (Brooker, 2004). It has been suggested that providing this kind of care could in some cases produce a degree of 'rementia', reflecting the beneficial impact of a more positive and benign environmental context (Sixsmith et al., 1993), and could have effects at a physical and a neurobiological level (Bråne et al., 1989) as well as enhancing psychological well-being.

The relevance of rehabilitation

Conceptualising dementia in terms of disability, within a biopsychosocial framework, points to a range of possibilities for intervention and provides a strong rationale for psychosocial intervention in the broadest sense. In recent years a 'quiet revolution' has been taking place in dementia care (Clare, Baddeley, Moniz-Cook, & Woods, 2003), with the emergence of the concepts of personhood and person-centred care, the increasing focus on relationships and interactions, and the developing emphasis on living with and managing dementia. The perspective of the person with dementia, previously largely neglected (Cotrell & Schulz, 1993), is now being explored and valued (Sabat, 2001) alongside that of the family member or caregiver. Psychosocial models of dementia (Sabat et al., 1984) highlight the importance of the unique set of life experiences and coping strategies that each individual brings to the challenge of living with dementia, and the impact of the social environment on the expression and course of neurological impairment.

In order to meet the needs of people with AD and their families, an holistic approach to intervention is proposed, in which assessment and possible interventions encompass all three levels of the biopsychosocial conceptual framework. At the biological level, drug treatments may be offered, and physical health problems can be attended to. At the psychological level, a range of therapeutic and supportive psychological interventions may be offered to maximise functioning and well-being and to assist in the process of adapting and coping with AD. At the social level, carers may be helped in their task of interacting with the person with AD by means of information, support and therapeutic help, care staff can be educated and supported in using a beneficial approach, education for professionals can assist in ensuring that people with AD access the necessary health care and are dealt with appropriately, and advocacy can be provided to ensure that the voice of the person with AD is heard. In addition, work is needed to change societal attitudes, and the person with dementia may need support in coping with negative and stigmatising responses.

The aims of effective intervention, then, include optimising functioning and well-being, minimising excess disability, enhancing self-efficacy and coping skills, combating threats to self-esteem, and preventing the development of a malignant social psychology. These aims reflect the core tenets of a rehabilitation approach (McLellan, 1997). Rehabilitation has been defined as: 'enabling people who are disabled by injury or disease to achieve their optimum physical, psychological, social and vocational well-being' (McLellan, 1991, p. 785). Indeed, Cohen and Eisdorfer (1986) propose that rehabilitation plays an important role, both as a guiding philosophy and as a methodology, in the provision of care for people with AD. The concept of rehabilitation, implying as it does a focus on maximising functioning across a whole range of areas including physical health, psychological well-being, living skills and social relationships, provides a unifying core concept around which to organise thinking about intervention in AD (Clare, 2003b). Recently there has been a growing awareness of the relevance of rehabilitation (Marshall, 2005), and people with a diagnosis of dementia have themselves begun to advocate for a rehabilitation-oriented approach (Friedell, 2002).

Rehabilitation is conducted in the context of a natural trajectory of change over time, which varies according to the individual, the nature of the impairment, and the social context. In a condition such as AD with a trajectory of progressive impairment, rehabilitation goals will necessarily change over time in a way that reflects this trajectory (Clare, 2003b). In the early stages, when impairments are predominantly in the cognitive domain, cognitive rehabilitation (B. A. Wilson, 2002) is particularly relevant, especially with regard to memory functioning. Cognitive rehabilitation has been very broadly defined as:

> Any intervention strategy or technique which intends to enable clients or patients, and their families, to live with, manage, by-pass, reduce or come to terms with deficits precipitated by injury to the brain.
>
> (B. A. Wilson, 1997, p. 488)

This broad definition could encompass a number of different approaches, including the use of cognitive neuropsychological theories and models to identify and address specific deficits, the application of behavioural principles based on learning theory, or holistic programmes that emphasise awareness and emotional adjustment (B. A. Wilson, 1997). Wilson argues that cognitive rehabilitation for people with brain injury should integrate the key elements of each of these approaches. An integrative approach would seem equally, if not more, appropriate for people with progressive disorders such as dementia.

In the early stages of AD, since memory impairments are a defining feature of the disorder, interventions targeting coping with memory difficulties are likely to have particular importance within an integrative approach. As dementia progresses, the emphasis will shift to other areas. In the moderate stages, maintaining practical skills and engagement in conversation, providing an appropriately stimulating and enriching environment, and circumventing behavioural difficulties may provide a focus, while in the later stages the emphasis might be on maintaining mobility or reducing pain. In these later stages the aims of rehabilitation overlap with those of palliative care, with a shared emphasis on optimising well-being and dignity (Froggatt, Downs, & Small, in press).

Rehabilitation interventions focus largely on functioning and on promoting activity and participation (or reducing disability and handicap), and do not claim to remove, reduce or cure the underlying impairments. Nevertheless, the question arises as to whether cognitive rehabilitation could contribute to delaying or preventing the progression of impairments, and leading on from this, whether it could contribute to preventing or delaying the onset of impairments in those at high risk. It remains for further research to delineate the extent of the possibilities that cognitive rehabilitation offers in this respect, and to explore how this approach might be most effectively combined with interventions at the biological level. Interest in this area has been stimulated by increasingly early detection of AD, leading to possibilities for intervening as early as possible in the course of AD once impairments begin to become evident, and concomitantly by the increased interest in identifying people with MCI who will undoubtedly represent an increasingly important target for intervention (Alladi, Arnold, Mitchell, Nestor, & Hodges, 2006). Increased understanding may also, in time, contribute possibilities for primary prevention. Epidemiological studies have suggested that dementia may represent, in effect, one end of a continuum of functioning in the ageing population (Lishman, 1994). If there is indeed a continuous distribution, and people with a diagnosis of AD represent the upper tail of the distribution, then efforts could be made to shift the entire population distribution in a favourable direction (Brayne, 1994) in an attempt at primary prevention. Although the possibility of a preventive approach opens exciting possibilities, it remains unclear how this might operate in practice, as knowledge of risk factors and protective factors remains limited. Nevertheless, what is known about protective factors suggests that lifestyle issues and psychosocial context are relevant, for example social networks (Fratiglioni, Paillard-Borg, & Winblad, 2004), engagement in cognitively stimulating activity (R. S. Wilson, Bennett, et al., 2002; R. S. Wilson, Leon, et al., 2002), and physical exercise (Laurin, Verreault,

Lindsay, MacPherson, & Rockwood, 2001) have all been identified as having the potential to offer some protection against dementia, or to delay its onset. While possibilities for developing preventive measures using a rehabilitation approach are exciting, the current focus in this area remains primarily at the level of intervention for people where a diagnosis has already been established.

Conclusions

Working from a biopsychosocial framework, we can understand dementia in terms of disability. This opens the possibility of a rehabilitative approach to intervention. While possibilities for prevention may emerge in the next few years, the emphasis at present remains primarily on supporting activity and participation in an attempt to optimise well-being, and on understanding how this may best be achieved for each individual. Since people with AD are a heterogeneous group, it is important to develop for each person an individual formulation that can guide the selection of intervention approaches. This requires an understanding not only of the neuropsychological profile but also of the person's subjective experience, context, and awareness. Chapter 3 focuses on understanding the experience of the person with dementia, Chapter 4 gives an overview of awareness and its implications, and Chapter 5 explores the neuropsychology of AD.

3   Understanding the experience of dementia

This chapter focuses on the experience of dementia and the role of rehabilitation within this context. Models of the subjective experience of the person with early-stage dementia, and how people with dementia make sense of their condition, are reviewed. In order to place the person with dementia in context, the nature of interactions with family caregivers is discussed, aspects of the experience of family caregivers are outlined, and recent work focusing on social participation in dementia is introduced. Finally, implications for intervention are described.

In order to provide appropriate psychological and rehabilitative interventions, it is first helpful to try to understand something of the subjective experience of those involved, and how they may adjust and cope. Key issues for rehabilitation with people who have dementia include finding ways to support preferred styles of coping and adjusting, to enhance well-being, and to help maintain a sense of self, identity, and worth. Many, though not all, individuals with dementia are supported by a spouse, family member or other care partner. It is also important to address the needs of family members and carers, which may sometimes be in conflict with the needs or preferences of the person with dementia, and to consider the family system as a whole rather than viewing each individual as a separate unit.

Understanding the experience of the person with dementia

Until relatively recently, little was known about the subjective experience of people with dementia. The person with dementia was viewed more as an object to be studied than as a participant who could contribute directly to understanding the experience of dementia.

Indeed, Kitwood (1988) observed that any attempt to frame dementia in personal terms was completely absent from any official agenda. This neglect of the subjective experience of dementia was so extensive as to be termed a 'flight from intersubjective engagement' (Kitwood, 1997, p. 70).

Goldsmith (1996) suggested we might usefully engage in trying to understand the experience of dementia, and proposed that we should actually talk with people who have dementia about the nature of their experience:

> Hearing the voice of people with dementia is both a challenge and a journey, and we ourselves will be affected in the process. . . . How we hear that voice and how we encourage and interpret it must surely be one of the next areas to be addressed in our research and training programmes.
>
> (p. 24)

At that time the idea was groundbreaking, and the earliest studies in this area were just beginning to appear. Since then, there has been a veritable explosion of research studies and personal accounts. These are complemented by the more extensive literature on the experience of caregiving. Attention is now being given to the experience of relationship for the person with dementia and the carer (Henderson & Forbat, 2002) and to the interrelationships between the person with dementia, family members, and professionals (Fortinsky, 2001). This chapter focuses on the subjective experience of dementia and the role of rehabilitation within this context.

It is increasingly acknowledged that the person with dementia can express views, needs and concerns, even in the later stages of dementia. The quotations in Figure 3.1 show, for example, how participants with early-stage AD in one of my studies described their memory problems and indicate just how devastating the impact of memory difficulties can be. The challenge is to find effective ways of communicating in order clearly to hear the voice of the person with dementia (Goldsmith, 1996). Understanding the perspective of the person with dementia is a valuable prerequisite to improving services and making them more flexible, responsive and individually based. Clearly, there are difficulties in trying to understand the experience of dementia, since 'no-one has returned from this particular journey of cognitive impairment to tell us what it is like' (Kitwood, 1997, p. 71). Nevertheless, there are many ways in which understanding can be attempted, including listening to what people with dementia say in various contexts, reading the personal accounts that are increasingly becoming available (e.g. Lee, 2003), observing the way people with dementia cope and adjust, drawing on accounts of what it is like to experience other terminal illnesses, and engaging in creative interaction using poetry, music or the arts (Killick & Allan, 2001). An extract from the diary of James Thompson, written 1 year after dementia was diagnosed, was used in one early text to provide an effective and moving illustration of what the process of dementia could feel like for the individual:

> No theory of medicine can explain what is happening to me. Every few months I sense that another piece of my brain is missing. My life . . .

Remembering what you said, what you heard, what you are supposed to be doing, suddenly it's not there. (Louis)

Well, everything I like to do has just gone now. I can't do any of it. (Paula)

You can't be alive without a memory . . . (Louis)

Every now and again I just can't remember things and I get a bit frustrated . . . (George)

I feel such a blooming fool myself . . . I feel . . . I'd almost say violent to myself over it. (Neil)

It's the worst experience I've had in my life . . . the memory experience . . . I'm just cut off from everything. (Joel)

If I get really low sometimes . . . I think 'well, you know, if you could snuff it', and I think 'well, I wouldn't mind actually' . . . (Iain)

I think the greatest trouble is largely social, your very close friends you don't . . . you can't really recollect on that information. (Martin)

You get rather cunning . . . It's quite an art really . . . trying to behave socially normally without letting on that you've forgotten that person's name. I'll tend not to do introductions very often, because it's terrible to mess up an introduction. (Martin)

Devices, that's what you do . . . I'll say 'I've had a bad night, I'll tell you another time' . . . I say 'I've had one too many' . . . I usually get away with that. (Iain)

She [wife] has a rough life . . . because of me . . . because of my problems. (Roy)

Figure 3.1 The subjective experience of developing memory problems in early-stage AD.

> my self . . . are falling apart. I can only think half thoughts now. Someday I may wake up and not think at all . . . not know who I am.
> (Cohen & Eisdorfer, 1986, p. 22)

Early models focused on the progression of dementia over time and conceptualised the experience in terms of a sequence of stages involving different responses such as 'suspecting' and 'covering up' (Keady & Nolan, 1995). An interview study with people who had early dementia indicated that emotional reactions of fear, anger and frustration, and a sense of not being in control, characterised the early stages (Keady, Nolan, & Gilliard, 1995). People with dementia tended to try to cover up their difficulties in order to protect both themselves and their families. While experiencing this inner turmoil, they also demonstrated a striking degree of acceptance, and positive coping statements were common. All continued with some valued roles and tasks, and some were actively developing strategies for coping with their memory problems. Another study (Cohen, 1991) identified six components or phases in adjusting to the onset of dementia: recognition and concern ('something is wrong'); denial ('not me'); anger, guilt, sadness ('why me?'); coping ('in order to go on, I must . . .'); maturation ('living each day until I die'); and finally separation from self.

Recent work has moved away from a stage approach. In my own studies I have suggested that the process of making sense of the experience and adapting to changes instead constitutes an ongoing reiterative cycle (Clare, 2003a), and emphasised the need to allow for individual differences in responding. Based on qualitative analysis of interview data, I derived a model of the experience of developing AD, which is summarised in Figure 3.2. This model proposes that people with dementia engage in five inter-related processes in response to the changes that are occurring: registering, reacting, explaining, experiencing and adjusting. First, changes are registered. Second, the person reacts to the changes, deciding how to view them – for example, whether to regard them as potentially serious and seek help, or as minor and insignificant. Third, the person seeks to find an explanation for the changes. Fourth, the person experiences the emotional impact of the changes. Finally, the person seeks ways of adjusting to the changes. As people engage in each of these processes, their responses fall somewhere along a continuum between self-maintaining and self-adjusting stances. A self-maintaining stance consists of attempting to normalise the situation and minimise difficulties, thus maintaining continuity with the prior sense of self, while a self-adjusting stance consists of attempts to confront difficulties head on and incorporate them into an adjusted sense of self. For any individual, at any time, there can be a tension between these two styles of responding. For example, in evaluating the significance of changes, a person may vary between minimising their importance and feeling that they are indicative of major problems. Similarly, in experiencing the emotional impact of changes, there may be a tension between a sense of despair leading to suicidal thoughts on the one hand and a belief that there is sufficient hope to warrant carrying on for a time on the other. The way in which these tensions are managed and resolved on a day-to-day basis will

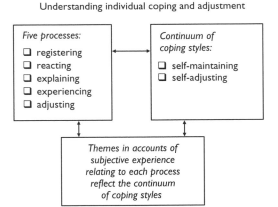

Figure 3.2 Coping styles in early-stage AD (from Clare, 2002c, 2003a).

have implications for how people cope, which in turn will influence the degree to which responses tend to change over time. Self-maintaining coping responses include attempts to 'hold on', for example through the use of medication or simply trying harder, and to 'compensate', for example by relying on others more or implementing practical strategies. Self-adjusting coping responses include the development of a 'fighting spirit' and active attempts to 'come to terms' with the situation at a psychological level. A follow-up study (Clare, Roth, & Pratt, 2005) suggested that coping styles tended to polarise over time, with individuals responding more consistently in either a self-maintaining or a self-adjusting style.

These studies suggested that people with early-stage dementia use a range of coping skills as they try to adjust to the changes they experience (Clare, 2002c). Coping methods typically include practical strategies for managing the impact of memory and other cognitive difficulties in an attempt to maintain functioning and independence and compensate for changes. These strategies may be undertaken irrespective of the attributions made about the reason for the changes experienced. Examples include adapting and extending one's use of lists, calendars and reminder devices. Strategies for managing social situations may be developed, perhaps involving altering social roles to some degree, although there is often a danger of withdrawal as social interaction becomes difficult and negative reactions are elicited from others. At the same time people may look for remedies and try perceived neuroprotective agents like gingko biloba, or they may use acetyl-cholinesterase-inhibiting medication if this is offered following a formal diagnosis. Individuals who adopt a more self-adjusting stance are likely to seek out information about their condition and are often keen to discover new ways of being useful, such as participating in research that may help others in the future. For some, there is a sense of fighting back against the condition and its implications. There may be a renewed search for meaning in life, for example through spiritual development, and for some there can be a sense of having learned from the experience and furthered one's personal wisdom and maturity. Nevertheless, as the condition progresses, the process of coming to terms with dementia and moving towards acceptance of one's condition is likely to be an ongoing process of negotiation aimed at reaching a balance between hope and despair.

It may be helpful to illustrate this with some specific examples from my research. I will describe four individuals with early-stage AD who each took a very different stance. Iain exemplified a self-adjusting stance, while Kath took up a self-maintaining stance. The other two participants, Martin and Steve, fell somewhere in between.

- Iain (aged 68) acknowledged that he had been given a diagnosis of dementia. He had come to accept this through observing the difficulties he was having with his memory and noticing the impact of these on his everyday life. However, he did not accept that this meant he had

Alzheimer's, which he saw as the worst possible fate. Iain had experienced a great deal of depression and sadness as he came to terms with the dementia diagnosis and what it meant. He experienced it as a loss of status and authority. He mourned the anticipated loss of his relationship with his grandchildren, and feared becoming a burden on his family. He had decided that 'when the time came' he would take his own life. Having gone through the depths of despair, he decided to fight the dementia as best he could. He was determined to continue with as many activities as possible, including some volunteer work, even though his memory problems caused him a great deal of embarrassment in social situations. Because he wanted to explore issues of meaning, he started going to church. He wanted to find out about rehabilitation strategies that could help with his memory problems.

- Kath (aged 76) thought that she was perhaps a bit forgetful, but felt that this was to be expected when one got older. She did not think her memory difficulties had any real impact on daily life, and said she was just carrying on as normal. She felt that she had her family around her and knew they would support her, so there was no need for her to worry about anything. She remembered going to the Memory Clinic, but she was sure that since they had not called her back for further tests this meant there was nothing wrong with her.

- Martin (aged 77), although retired, was still involved in professional and charitable activities, and had asked his GP for help when he become concerned about the impact of his increasing forgetfulness in social situations. Having been assessed at the memory clinic, he was given a diagnosis of AD in a very abrupt manner. Subsequently, he insisted that he did not have dementia, and indeed that he had been told the original diagnosis was wrong (the clinic staff denied this). Nevertheless, he was still just as concerned about the effects of his forgetfulness. He had learned some memory strategies in the past, and was very keen to find ways of dealing with the difficulties he was experiencing. He was also thinking about how best to plan for the future and whether it would be advisable to move house.

- Steve (aged 62) accepted that he was forgetful, but felt that this only caused him minor difficulties. He knew that he was taking part in a drug trial, and he acknowledged that he had been told his memory problems were due to what he called 'slight dementia', but he felt this was normal for his age. He belonged to a bowls club, which he enjoyed, but he often got muddled about arrangements and sometimes got lost on his way to and from the club. Despite this, he thought that his strategies for dealing with forgetfulness worked very well.

The model acknowledges that the way in which people understand their condition is also a major contributory factor to the way in which they cope and adjust. My colleagues and I have recently begun to explore this in more detail through applying Leventhal's self-regulation model (SRM) of adjustment to illness (Leventhal, Nerenz, & Steele, 1984). Within the SRM, the cognitive working models people hold regarding their illness, termed 'illness representations', consist of five dimensions (Leventhal et al., 1997): illness identity, or the label ascribed to the illness; cause; course or time-line; means of curing or controlling the condition; and the consequences of the condition.

We interviewed people with dementia attending memory clinics and outpatient services (Clare, Goater, & Woods, 2006), and found that difficulties were most commonly characterised in terms of memory problems or forgetfulness, and terms such as 'dementia' or 'Alzheimer's' were rarely used. This is in line with other recent studies (Gillies, 2000). Practice with regard to disclosing a diagnosis of dementia of course remains variable (Bamford, Lamont, Eccles, Robinson, May, & Bond, 2004), and this is likely to influence the representations people hold, even where they are in receipt of services. Similarly, the most common attribution regarding cause was that the problems are a natural part of ageing, although broad-ranging models including consequences of previous stress or current lack of motivation were frequently proposed. Previous accidents such as falls or head injuries were sometimes cited as reasons, and difficulties were sometimes viewed as inherited, where parents or other family members have been forgetful. Certainly, therefore, participants did hold representations of their condition, but it may not be appropriate to describe these as 'illness' representations. Interestingly, despite the common attribution to ageing, the condition was quite often seen as stable or even likely to improve, with only about half thinking it would get worse over time. As discussed above, participants engaged in a range of coping endeavours, and despite describing a number of negative effects of their difficulties, both for themselves and for their families, many commented that 'you can't complain' and opted to 'take it as it comes'. Importantly, participants who identified fewer coping strategies tended to score higher on a measure of depression and anxiety. Those who scored in the clinical range for depression were also those who believed that nothing could be done to assist with memory problems. This study also provided a preliminary indication of some of the factors that might influence the kinds of illness representations people develop. Younger participants were more likely than older participants to refer to dementia or Alzheimer's, and to refer to brain malfunction or stress as possible causal factors, while older participants were more likely to see their difficulties as part of normal ageing and to feel that nothing much could be done to help. Participants scoring higher on the MMSE and those taking AChEI medication were more likely to refer to dementia or Alzheimer's, perhaps reflecting a greater likelihood of having the diagnosis communicated clearly and discussed with them.

In a subsequent study (Harman & Clare, 2006), we focused on the illness representations of people who had received, and were willing to acknowledge, their diagnosis, and the way in which these related to their daily lived experience. Again, the majority of participants referred to difficulties with memory, and only a few used the terms 'dementia' or 'Alzheimer's'. A range of causes was proposed, including brain damage, genetic inheritance, environmental and lifestyle factors, stress, loneliness, failure to keep sufficiently active, and the ageing process itself. While acknowledging the role of practical strategies to help with memory problems, only half believed medication was helpful, and some explicitly said it did not help them. All described a range of negative consequences, particularly in terms of how others treated them. One interesting feature in this group, however, was that all participants believed the condition would get worse and that they would decline over time, although the exact pattern was unclear. This sense that the condition would get worse contrasted with a strong desire to maintain a sense of self and identity. This in turn gave rise to a number of significant personal and interpersonal dilemmas. Personal dilemmas reflected tensions between wanting to understand more about dementia and wanting to avoid having to think about it, between actively fighting it and passively accepting it, and between carrying on or attempting to put an end to one's life. Interpersonal dilemmas arose because with the onset of dementia an 'invisible line' had been crossed, and suddenly inter-actions with others were no longer the same. Participants felt that people treated them differently, that professionals did not show as much respect, that they were generally excluded, even perhaps betrayed, and that infor-mation about the condition either was not forthcoming or was not available in a form they could understand.

The model of subjective experience in early-stage dementia that I described earlier (Clare, 2003a) was developed on the basis of accounts from both men and women, and further studies explored the experiences of men and women separately. For a group of men with early-stage AD, all of whom lived with their wives, the experience they described was consistent with the model (Pearce et al., 2002). Men attempted to balance the wish to maintain a prior sense of self against the need to reappraise their situation and construct an altered sense of self. A related study explored the experi-ence of a group of women with early-stage AD (van Dijkhuizen, Clare, & Pearce, 2006). A third of the women lived with their partners, and the remainder were widowed, but had support from other family members. This study suggested that, for these women, the position on the continuum of coping styles was related to the level of connectedness – with family, friends and neighbours, social roles and familiar settings – that each woman experienced. A self-adjusting stance was related to a stronger sense of connectedness, while a self-maintaining stance, involving an emphasis on protective strategies such as avoidance or minimisation, was related to a sense of disconnection.

It is now possible, then, to model the subjective experience of early-stage dementia, and the resulting understanding can provide a basis for developing appropriate interventions – we return to this point in Chapter 8, which focuses on assessment. The subjective experience of moderate to severe dementia is less well delineated, although a number of studies provide a valuable insight into the experience of life in long-term care, using either self-report or informant report methods or observational approaches such as dementia care mapping (Cohen-Mansfield, Golander, & Arnheim, 2000). Our own current work in this area highlights themes of loneliness, boredom and loss, reflecting the social and environmental deprivation that institutional life entails even in the best-run settings (Clare, Rowlands, Bruce, & Downs, 2006).

Viewing the person with dementia in context

Our developing understanding of the experience of dementia highlights the importance of viewing the person with dementia in the context of a network of relationships and social roles. Dementia research has focused quite extensively on the family member or carer of the person with dementia (Zarit & Edwards, in press). However, with a few exceptions (Shakespeare, 1993), relatively little consideration has been given to the complex interactional relationship between the person with dementia and the carer, and to the nature of communication in this context. Where the person is part of a couple relationship, the onset and diagnosis of dementia fundamentally affect both partners. The early stages of dementia can be a time of prolonged uncertainty for the caregiver as well as for the person with dementia. However, the way they work within a partnership will have significant implications for their relationship, as they are both attempting to make sense of their experiences (Keady & Nolan, 2003). They may 'work together', sharing an early recognition of the problem, or they may 'work apart'. Alternatively, they may 'work alone', not sharing concerns, or may 'work separately', where the person with dementia hides the difficulties while the caregiver increases vigilance The nature of these processes and interactions occurring in the early stages of dementia can affect how readily people adjust and how quickly they seek help, and is likely to have a significant impact on longer-term outcomes.

Exploration of the shared experience of couples where one partner has dementia (Robinson, Clare, & Evans, 2005) highlights a circular process of trying to make sense of what is happening and reaching a degree of acceptance, in which couples oscillate between a sense that everything has changed and a focus on difficulties and losses on the one hand, and a sense that they can move on from this point and a belief in the ability to adapt and adjust on the other. Changes in the person who was developing dementia were gradually noticed and eventually led to a decision to take them seriously and an attempt to find out what was wrong. Couples engaged in a process of joint negotiation over time, with both partners engaging in self-maintaining and self-adjusting responses, both individually and in relation to the spouse.

This process was explored in more detail by recording and analysing conversations between people with dementia and their partners (Clare & Shakespeare, 2004). People with dementia struggled to retain a voice in these conversations, and to be able to express and discuss their feelings and fears openly and honestly. They also struggled against being positioned negatively and viewed primarily in terms of their difficulties. Perhaps understandably, partners seemed reluctant to acknowledge, at least in front of the person with dementia, the full implications of the dementia diagnosis, and consequently seemed reluctant to support the expression of fears and concerns, or to engage in discussion of these. They tended to avoid potentially distressing topics, positioning themselves instead as collaborators who could help in overcoming practical difficulties, and offering a stance that emphasised positive coping attempts. The problems were rarely referred to in terms of illness, disorder or disease, and the terms 'Alzheimer's' and 'dementia' were never heard in these conversations. However, there were times when partners refused to collude with attempts at face-saving or normalising the situation, which added to the struggle for the person with dementia. Partners carried more responsibility for maintaining the form and structure of the conversation, moving it along and prompting appropriate turn-taking (Shakespeare, 1998), which highlighted the difficulty for both partners in achieving a satisfactory 'voice'. The person with dementia could be positioned, in conversation, as a 'less-than-full member' (Shakespeare & Clare, 2005), while the plight of the carer who had to take full responsibility for making the conversation work while receiving little support or assistance was also evident.

The experience of family caregivers

Initially, family members providing help and support to a person who is developing dementia may not perceive themselves as being 'a caregiver' at all (Pollitt, 1994). Caregiving usually emerges out of existing family relationships in parallel with the gradual onset of the disorder, and over time reciprocity and mutual exchange start to decline as the person with dementia becomes more dependent and requires regular help (Gilleard, 1992). Once it is acknowledged that the person has dementia, relatives may move through a range of responses from denial to acceptance (Robinson et al., 2005). As the dementia progresses, there is typically a growing need for help with 'instrumental' tasks of daily living, such as managing finances or attending appointments, and more effort is required by the carer to support the person with dementia in activities and interactions, and to maintain social relationships (Clare & Shakespeare, 2004). With growing dependency, caregiving becomes an increasingly dominant part of the relationship, and may eventually encompass all of it (Pearlin et al., 1990). The following quotations provide examples of the perspective of people whose partner is developing AD, as described by carers in one of our studies

(Quinn & Clare, 2006), and illustrates the extent to which this impacts on life right from the early stages:

I don't feel we have, if I'm honest, an equal relationship any more.

. . . it creeps its way into all the corners of our life.

. . . we don't get invited in the way we used to be.

I feel more tied, in that I don't like leaving him.

I have to take over a lot of functions that normally [my wife] would . . . you feel rather inadequate.

As outlined in Chapter 1, although the impact for each carer must be considered on an individual basis, and caregiving can be a positive experience in some respects for some people (Andrén & Elmståhl, 2005), overall it appears that caregiving is often linked to reduced well-being, with increased rates of depression and a possible association with poor physical health. The support that carers receive is likely to influence coping and well-being. Informal support from family and friends is a potentially valuable resource (Kiecolt-Glaser et al., 1991). Informal support is particularly important since support from services is often lacking. Caregivers often receive little information at the time of initial diagnosis, either about the condition or about the services and resources available to them (Aneshensel, Pearlin, Mullan, Zarit, & Whitlatch, 1995), and where they are told the diagnosis they may sometimes be left with the responsibility of deciding whether or not to convey this information to the person with dementia. Subsequent to diagnosis, many caregivers have typically had little or no involvement with formal services. However, support groups for carers are widespread and much valued, and some carers benefit from access to specialist services such as those provided by Admiral Nurses in the UK (Woods et al., 2003).

One recent study (J. Perry, 2002) investigated the experiences of wives as they became caregivers, and described this in terms of moving through a process of interpretative caring. This process began with the wives noticing changes in their husbands' and their own behaviour. Once the wives realised these changes were significant they began to reinterpret these changes as an indication that there was something wrong. This was then followed by the wives taking over their husbands' roles and developing new identities for themselves and their husbands. The last stage involved the wives organising their daily life by controlling their environment while maintaining their husbands' presence.

When we explored the subjective experience of spouse caregivers of both genders who were caring for a partner in the early stages of dementia (Quinn & Clare, 2006), we found that even though they were aware of the diagnosis, the spouses found it difficult to make sense of what was happening to their partner, and at times they tended to attribute changes in behaviour to personal traits such as laziness, rather than to dementia. They found it particularly frustrating when the partner denied having any difficulties, or minimised the impact of these. They experienced major changes in the balance of the relationship, as they had to take on more responsibility while the partner became increasingly dependent. The partner's reliance on them meant they had less and less time for themselves. They lost their outside contacts and interests, their social life became increasingly restricted, and they began to feel very isolated. At the same time, they became more and more aware of what the future would bring. The emotional consequences included feelings of frustration and irritation towards the partner, a great deal of worry and distress, depression and a sense of hopelessness. They coped by trying to make the best of things and taking one day at a time. They generally avoided talking about the situation with their partner, but were glad to meet others in a similar situation through support groups and similar networks, as this made them feel less alone. Carers varied in the way they approached the caregiving role, with some emphasising the importance of doing things together at the pace of the person with dementia, some taking over a range of tasks, and others minimising the difficulties experienced by the person with dementia. Carers also varied in their emotional response to the situation, relating this to the prior history of their relationship, to previous experiences of caregiving, and to their current expectations and goals.

To illustrate some aspects of these different responses, I will briefly describe the partners of the four people with dementia whom I introduced above.

- Ivy said she and Iain had always had a very equal relationship, and this was something she now missed, as she had taken over many of his everyday tasks and roles. Despite this, she still enjoyed doing things together with Iain, and tried to find ways in which previous activities could be adjusted to make them remain manageable. Following the initial shock of the diagnosis, she had joined the Alzheimer's Society and begun to find out as much as possible about AD. She was fighting to secure the best treatment for Iain. She had talked openly with him about the diagnosis and its implications and about plans for the future. While she did not want him to take his own life, she understood his point of view, and felt that she would support him in that decision if and when the time came.

- Ken had in effect taken over most of the household tasks from Kath, but approached this as a partnership in which they did everything together. He had found that if he told Kath what to do she would get angry with him, but if he simply got on with tasks, she felt excluded. Therefore, the best strategy was to go at her pace and accept that things would be done slowly and perhaps less than perfectly. Ken valued attending a support group and liked having the chance to exchange ideas and experiences. However, as time went on, Ken became increasingly stressed and unwell.

- Mary thought that Martin's memory was no worse than that of anyone else in their age group and could not understand why he worried so much about being forgetful. This discrepancy in viewpoints caused considerable tension. Mary was, however, concerned about how they both would manage in old age, and was keen to plan for the future insofar as was possible, given that she felt everything seemed uncertain.
- Susan said that she had spent most of her life caring for others – first her children, and then various older relatives of Steve's. She had been looking forward to some freedom and the chance to enjoy life a little, and was deeply frustrated at finding herself in the situation of having to take responsibility for Steve. It infuriated her that he now did very little around the house, so that most tasks fell on her. She confided that the marriage had not been easy and that, before his diagnosis, she had been thinking of leaving him, but now she felt obliged to stay and look after him. She was determined to keep working part-time in order to preserve something of her own life. She knew there was a support group for carers running locally, but thought this was for people who were caring for someone with severe dementia.

While support groups and networks have been available for carers for some time, it is only recently that this option has been extended to the person with dementia as well (Yale, 1995), and more recently still that interventions have attempted to address the needs of both the person with dementia and the carer in tandem (Droes, Breebaart, Ettema, Tilburg, & Mellenbergh, 2000).

Social participation in early-stage dementia

People with early-stage dementia continue to participate in a wide range of social interactions and experience varying degrees of difficulty with this. The diagnosis may bring with it the opportunity for new and additional forms of interaction, such as attendance at day care settings and involvement in various group activities or other forms of intervention. We explored the experience of attending a support group for people with early-stage dementia in a recent study (Mason, Clare, & Pistrang, 2005). Working with two different support groups, we analysed videotaped recordings of group sessions and transcripts of individual interviews with participants, deriving both a phenomenological account of participants' experience of the group and a detailed behavioural coding of interactions within sessions. Participants told us that they found the group sessions useful and enjoyable, and that the social contact and sense of belonging they derived was in contrast to the isolation they experienced in their daily lives. At the same time, they did experience some difficulties and frustrations, finding it hard to speak out, to focus on uncomfortable or painful issues, or to tolerate others' repetition and confusion. Participants appreciated the work of the professional facilitators, but clearly viewed them as essentially running, indeed controlling, the group interactions, and 'allowing' members to talk about certain topics in certain ways. Analysis of interactions during the sessions indicated that over three quarters of interactions involved a facilitator and that most of these were exchanges between a facilitator and an individual participant, with the facilitator asking a question and the participant replying, typically with a disclosure of information. Member-to-member interactions were few, and hardly any of these involved helping responses such as provision of support or advice. Thus, while participants perceived the group as supportive, there was little evidence of what might be generally considered to be mutually supportive helping interactions between members. Of course, this may not be true of all support groups, but it does raise some important issues for group facilitators to consider.

In other settings, however, people with dementia have demonstrated the possibility of genuine self-help, advocacy and mutual support, with significant implications for well-being and quality of life (Clare, Rowlands, & Quin, in press). A number of exceptional individuals with dementia have pioneered the development of a genuine self-advocacy and self-help movement, Dementia Advocacy and Support International (DASNI; see www. dasninternational.org). DASNI is a non-profit organisation founded in 2000 that aims to promote respect and dignity for persons with dementia, provide a forum for information exchange, encourage support mechanisms, advocate for services for people with dementia, and assist people in linking to local Alzheimer's groups. About one third of members have a dementia diagnosis, with the remainder being made up of supporters who endorse the goals and values of the group. DASNI espouses a more accepting and hopeful view of what it means to live with dementia. The organisation has the goal of empowering people with dementia to participate actively in their own care and treatment, and encouraging them to improve the quality of their own life by advocating for others. Members with dementia have given plenary addresses, led groups and organised exhibitions at national and international conferences around the world, published books and articles, and appeared on TV and radio. One member with dementia is on the board of Alzheimer's Disease International, and another served for a time on the executive body of the UK Alzheimer's Society. We investigated the experience of DASNI members in a collaborative approach, with participants involved at all stages from design of the study to interpretation of findings (Clare et al., in press). The results indicated that the immense emotional and practical impact of developing dementia was mitigated by participating in DASNI because this engendered a sense of collective strength and provided the opportunity to make a valued contribution. As part of the group, they offered one another information, support and encouragement, took on a range of roles essential for the group to function effectively, and worked with other members to raise public awareness and change attitudes towards dementia. This process of social identification led to enhanced individual well-being and self-efficacy (George, 1998), and increased social power and influence for the group (Turner, 2005, 2006). The resulting process of social change is mirrored in the development of new self-help networks (Pratt, Clare, & Aggarwal, 2005) and new initiatives aimed at both including and supporting people with dementia. This increased engagement of people with dementia has important implications for rehabilitation. DASNI members were the first people with dementia to advocate publicly for the relevance of rehabilitation (Friedell, 2002).

Conclusions

Attempting to understand the nature of subjective experience and interaction for people with dementia and their family carers indicates a range of coping styles, a range of specific strategies, a range of emotional responses, and a range of attributions regarding the diagnosis and the condition. These will influence the reciprocal interaction between carer and cared-for person. The results may be more or less adaptive, and if they are not adaptive, the result is likely to be elevated levels of distress for one or both, and a degree of excess disability for the person with dementia. This is the wider context within which neuropsychological decline in the person with dementia can be understood. Effective psychological intervention benefits from a clear formulation of these factors in order to identify the areas in which change is possible and how this may best be achieved. In understanding subjective experience, however, there is an additional factor that needs to be considered: the degree of awareness that the person with dementia has of his or her condition, situation and functioning. This is the focus of the next chapter.

4   Awareness and the person with dementia

The extent to which the person with dementia is aware of the developing difficulties and changes has important implications for the potential to engage in rehabilitation, and needs to be carefully considered. This chapter reviews the theoretical frameworks that are available to help in making sense of changes in awareness, and the methods that are currently used to assess awareness. Practical implications of variations in awareness, and the relationship between awareness and outcome of rehabilitation interventions, are discussed.

The way in which a person with dementia understands and responds to the condition depends crucially on that person's awareness of any changes, symptoms, or difficulties that arise as the condition develops and progresses, and of the implications of these. As we saw in the last chapter, awareness in this sense is a key element of the 'illness representation', which in turn helps to shape coping and adjustment. People with dementia, especially in the early stages, appear to vary considerably in the degree of awareness that they demonstrate. Awareness is an important concept in dementia care, with significant implications for the well-being and support needs of people with dementia and of their family members and carers. This chapter focuses on awareness and the factors that influence its development and expression in people with early-stage dementia, in order to draw out the implications for rehabilitation.

Awareness in this context can be defined as the accuracy with which people appraise aspects of their own current situation and functioning, and the impact of changes or difficulties. Often the question of just how much awareness a person has is troubling to family members and carers, and apparent fluctuations in level of awareness, or the appearance of moments of clarity following periods of confusion, can be hard to understand. With an increasing emphasis on obtaining the perspective of the person with dementia alongside that of family members and paid caregivers, the issue of awareness emerges as an important contextual factor when considering how people with dementia view their situation and perceive their own quality of life. At the same time, it has important practical implications regarding the possibility of engaging the person with dementia in a rehabilitative endeavour.

Disturbances of awareness are evident in many neurological disorders and following some kinds of brain injury, such as head injury or stroke (McGlynn & Schacter, 1989). In brain injury rehabilitation it is widely recognised that reduced awareness is associated with poorer outcomes in neurorehabilitation programmes, and that this is an important aspect to address (e.g. Ownsworth & Clare, 2006; Prigatano, 1999a, 199b).

Although awareness in dementia has attracted considerable interest among researchers, there are as yet few really clear findings to support theoretical understanding or guide practice. This is probably due partly to differing perspectives on what awareness means, and partly to the difficulty of measuring awareness. In our recent AWARE project, funded by the European Union, my colleagues and I carried out a thorough review of the area to identify the conceptual and methodological problems that needed to be addressed in order to allow us to research awareness in dementia in a way that both makes sense theoretically and offers some practical relevance to well-being for people with dementia and carers (Clare, 2004a, 2004b). Here I give an overview of the existing research evidence on awareness in dementia, explore what is meant by awareness in this context, and consider how awareness can be measured, before outlining the practical implications for rehabilitation interventions.

Empirical evidence

Research on awareness among people with dementia has most often focused on correlating levels of awareness with various clinical factors (e.g. mood, neuropsychological test scores, or severity of dementia), but results have been largely inconclusive (Aalten, van Valen, Clare, Kenny, & Verhey, 2005). One of the few findings that emerges consistently is that reduced awareness on the part of the person with dementia is linked to increased feelings of subjective burden on the part of the caregiver (DeBettignies, Mahurin, & Pirozzolo, 1990), which indicates the practical relevance of considering awareness. Apart from this, there is little conclusive evidence about the nature of awareness or its interrelationships with clinical, individual or social factors. Additionally, research in this area has focused on cross-sectional studies, although 1-year follow ups have been reported by a few groups, and consequently little is known about the way in which levels of awareness change over time as dementia progresses. As I said earlier, the lack of clear evidence arises partly because researchers adopt differing views of what is meant by awareness, and partly because awareness is difficult to measure.

Theoretical and conceptual issues

There is no one single clear definition of awareness, and researchers have adopted varying definitions, which makes it likely that studies of awareness have sometimes measured quite different things. The complexity of the awareness concept (Clare, 2004b) is reflected in the range of terminology adopted to describe states of awareness or unawareness, including 'insight', 'anosognosia', and 'denial'. Often these terms are used inconsistently, with the result that different phenomena are studied by researchers purporting to explore 'awareness'. In addition, the terms are frequently used interchangeably despite different conceptual backgrounds and underlying assumptions. This highlights the need for theoretical clarification. One of the most central conceptual and theoretical issues requiring consideration relates to whether awareness is viewed as determined solely by neurological factors or, conversely, as a product of the interaction of neurological factors, psychosocial factors and the socioenvironmental context.

Theoretical accounts of disturbances of awareness have generally tended to focus on neuroanatomical or cognitive neuropsychological explanations. While these do not consider psychosocial factors, they do offer helpful ways of making sense of some of the clinical observations. A very useful way of thinking about disturbances of awareness is by relating them to four different levels of awareness, which build on one another (Stuss, 1991a, 1991b; Stuss, Picton, & Alexander, 2001). The most basic level of awareness involves being able to take in something of what is going on around us. Pervasive disturbances of awareness reflect impairments at this basic level. A distinction is made between coma, vegetative states and minimally conscious states. In coma, as in sleep and in *effective* general anaesthesia, there is no arousal and no awareness (Laureys, Owen, & Schiff, 2004). Vegetative states, whether transitory or persisting, are characterised by a 'complete absence of behavioural evidence for awareness of self or the environment, with preserved capacity for spontaneous or stimulus-induced arousal' (Giacino & Kalmar, 2005, pp. 167–168) – that is to say, there is evidence of arousal but not awareness. People in a minimally conscious state show minimal but definite behavioural indications of awareness of self or the environment, as evidenced for example in the ability to track a moving stimulus with their eyes, respond with movement or emotional expression to an environmental stimulus, follow a simple command, or make a verbal or gestural yes/no response (Beaumont & Kenealy, 2005). These individuals show arousal along with some, albeit minimal, awareness. The next level is the ability to register changes in aspects of functioning, such as memory. Domain-specific disturbances of awareness involve lack of awareness in a specific domain of cognitive functioning. Unilateral neglect following a stroke would be an example of this. Most people with early-stage dementia describe being aware of changes in their memory, but some do not acknowledge these changes. The next level of awareness is the way in which we monitor our actions and use what we know about our current level of functioning to make decisions about how to behave in particular situations. Impairment in the ability to monitor one's own behaviour can result in behaviour that seems disinhibited, risky or inappropriate to others. For example, a person with dementia who has significant impairments in memory, concentration, perception, and problem-solving might still consider that it is safe to drive, and ignore concerns expressed by family members (Wild & Cotrell, 2003). Finally, the highest level of awareness relates to the way in which awareness at all the levels relates to the experience of self-awareness or sense of identity. A particularly dramatic example of impairments in self-awareness would be the situation where a person believes his loved ones have been replaced by identical-seeming impostors, as described by Stuss (Stuss, 1991a, 1991b; Stuss et al., 2001).

Neuroanatomical explanations for unawareness describe the contribution of different brain areas to awareness. A significant role has been proposed for the right hemisphere in general, and for right frontal and parietal areas in particular (Starkstein, Vazquez, Migliorelli, Teson, Sabe, & Leiguarda, 1995), as well as for the temporal lobes (Prigatano, 1999b). Cognitive neuropsychological models place less emphasis on localisation of function in the brain but seek to explain the cognitive processes involved in determining level of awareness, accounting for the available clinical and experimental observations. While some cognitive models propose a general impairment in metacognition or self-monitoring (Starkstein, Sabe, Chemerinski, Jason, & Leiguarda, 1996), the more influential of these models (Stuss et al., 2001) argue for changes in specific processes. One important example is Schacter's Dissociable Interactions and Conscious Experiences (DICE) model (Schacter, 1989), which proposes the operation of a conscious awareness system in interaction with other cognitive processes such as memory and executive functioning. More recently, Robin Morris and colleagues (Agnew & Morris, 1998) have developed the cognitive awareness model (CAM), which specifically aims to address limitations of previous cognitive neuropsychological models and to account for the heterogeneity of changes in awareness seen among people with dementia. The model proposes two main forms of unawareness in dementia resulting from different patterns of breakdown in cognitive processes. The first is primary anosognosia resulting from a global impairment in key higher-order mechanisms supporting the representation of conscious awareness, here termed the cognitive awareness system. The second is secondary anosognosia resulting from a failure in cognitive mechanisms that contribute to processing awareness; these include, for example, mnemonic anosognosia resulting from a failure to update the contents of semantic and/ or autobiographical memory (the 'personal knowledge base'), and executive anosognosia resulting from impairment within the executive system and leading to difficulties with making judgements and comparisons.

Cognitive neuropsychological models may constitute a complete explanation in some cases where very specific disturbances of awareness follow from focal neurological injuries or disorders. This is unlikely to be the case for the broader awareness deficits typically seen following brain injury or progressive neurological disorders of gradual onset, such as dementia, where the neurobiological changes occur in a psychosocial context that plays an important role in influencing or shaping metacognitive representations (Ownsworth, Clare, & Morris, 2006). A particular strength of the CAM is that it offers a possible link with the influence of psychosocial and contextual factors through its inclusion of the 'personal knowledge base', a store of self-relevant knowledge and information. It can therefore be related to a broader, biopsychosocial understanding of awareness, which acknowledges that a person's awareness is, at least in part, the product of a social context. Even if we consider that awareness has a biological foundation, it is still important to acknowledge that its behavioural expression, and the interpretation of that expression by others, will be influenced by social factors and psychological processes. Therefore, it is helpful to bring a person-centred approach to bear on the attempt to understand awareness in dementia alongside a neurological or neuropsychological perspective.

The role of psychological and social factors has been considered by only a few researchers. Weinstein and colleagues (Weinstein, Friedland, & Wagner, 1994) argue that neurologically based unawareness should be distinguished from denial, a psychological process whereby difficult feelings and reactions are warded-off from entering conscious awareness. Denial can be seen as an adaptive means of coping with difficult situations, and can take various forms. Explicit denial might involve denial either of the facts of the situation, or of their implications, or of their emotional impact (Caplan & Shechter, 1987). This might or might not be accompanied by implicit awareness as evidenced in behaviour that is inconsistent with the overt denial, such as accepting medical treatment despite insisting that nothing is wrong. The tendency to respond with denial to the onset of illness or disability would reflect a person's traits, values, cultural background, prior experience, and preferred ways of coping (Prigatano, 1999a).

Denial can be distinguished in turn from avoidant coping, which is a more conscious choice of response contingent on a degree of explicit awareness (Seiffer, Clare, & Harvey, 2005). Indeed, in response to the onset of illness or disability various coping mechanisms might be called into play; for example, minimising the severity of problems, selectively attending to information, or comparing oneself with people perceived to be worse off might all be used to combat the potential threats to selfhood posed by developing memory difficulties and being given a diagnosis of dementia. It is likely that the selection of coping strategies is influenced by a number of factors, including the appraisals and attributions the person makes. Using a phenomenological method, my own research (Clare, 2003a) explored the perspectives and coping styles of people with Alzheimer's disease and their spouses, highlighting the psychosocial factors that appeared to influence the expression of awareness. These included not only personal elements ranging from embarrassment to fear of being deserted or 'put away', but also responses of others in the person's social system and the nature of interactions with services. Significantly, some participants were evidently a good deal more aware than was assumed by their family members or doctors. As I described in Chapter 2, the findings suggested that as people respond to the onset of dementia their styles of coping fall along a continuum ranging from *self-maintaining* to *self-adjusting*. People with self-maintaining coping styles tend to try to normalise the situation and minimise the impact of any difficulties, thus maintaining continuity with their prior self-concept, while people with self-adjusting coping styles tend to confront the full implications of the situation head-on and thus adjust their self-concept accordingly. The 'self-adjusting' group also showed greater awareness on a standardised measure of current memory functioning than the 'self-maintaining' group (Clare, Wilson, Carter, Roth, & Hodges, 2002b); people in the latter group might be classed as 'unaware', but a self-maintaining coping style could reflect psychological and social influences, rather than brain damage.

Exploring patterns of change for individuals over time provides valuable clues about the relative contribution of neurological and psychosocial factors. For some people with dementia, awareness appears to increase over time, and this is of particular interest as it is likely to reflect the operation of psychosocial factors (Weinstein et al., 1994). The variable association with severity and duration of illness (R. Morris & Hannesdottir, 2004) suggests that changes in awareness cannot be simply explained in terms of progression of cognitive impairment. Leading on from the studies reporting the continuum model of coping and its relationship with awareness (Clare, 2003a), a 1-year follow-up of the participants (Clare, Roth, & Pratt, 2005) indicated that coping style could change in both directions, becoming either more self-adjusting or more self-maintaining over time. Self-adjusting style is associated with increased expression of explicit awareness, so the observation that people may move to a more self-adjusting style over time suggests that psychological factors such as denial do play a part here. Recently we have been investigating the way in which awareness is expressed in conversation by people with moderate to severe dementia living in residential care. Our findings highlight many aspects of retained awareness, ranging from basic awareness of sensory and perceptual experience through the ability to give accurate descriptions and make judgements about one's situation and functioning to high-level metacognitive reflection (Clare, Rowlands, Bruce, & Downs, 2006).

The extent to which an individual expresses awareness is also likely to be influenced by that person's beliefs and knowledge about dementia. Many people with dementia seem to regard their difficulties as an inevitable part of the ageing process. As I discussed in the previous chapter, relatively few choose to adopt terms such as 'dementia' or 'Alzheimer's disease' (Clare, 2003a), and indeed they may associate these only with the changes manifested in the severe stages of dementia. Additionally, practice regarding communication of the diagnosis is variable (Bamford, 2001) and professionals may use euphemistic terms such as 'accelerated ageing' or simply 'memory problems'. Therefore, it is important to distinguish between unawareness and a genuine lack of information or knowledge (Langer & Padrone, 1992).

The social context in which awareness arises and is expressed will also play a role in shaping the expression of awareness (Clare, Marková, et al., 2006). This includes the way dementia is viewed in society as a whole as well as the immediate social network and family context. The concept of the 'awareness context' (Glaser & Strauss, 1965) allows us to consider the way in which the context facilitates or hinders open discussion of sensitive issues and the expression of explicit awareness. Similarly, the extent to which it is possible to receive feedback from others on aspects of one's functioning will influence the development of awareness, so that people who live with others may receive more direct feedback than those who live alone. However, the way in which such feedback is received and the extent to which it as accepted or rejected will depend on the context of the relationship between the person with dementia and the other. Different approaches adopted by caregivers will interact with the coping style adopted by the person with dementia (de Vugt et al., 2004). Interactions with health professionals are also likely to interact with the person's beliefs and expectations to influence the expression of awareness (Clare, Marková, et al., 2006). This in turn will affect the process and indeed the possibility of engaging in cognitive rehabilitation.

Methodological issues

Measuring awareness is a difficult endeavour (Clare, Marková, Verhey, & Kenny, 2005). Many studies in this area have failed to adopt clear definitions of awareness, so that comparison of findings across studies is compromised (Clare, 2004a). First, it is likely that researchers are eliciting different phenomena under the general term of 'awareness'. Second, being aware implies being aware of something – the 'object' of awareness (Marková & Berrios, 2001). There are a large number of possible objects of awareness, and different studies focus on different objects. For example, in dementia, the object of awareness might be level of performance on a memory test, a particular symptom such as forgetfulness, a diagnostic label such as Alzheimer's disease, the experience of changes over time, alterations in sense of self, and so on. Assessment of awareness can only be made in relation to a particular 'object' (Marková, Clare, Wang, Romero, & Kenny, 2005). Thus, when assessing someone's level of awareness, it is advisable to focus on specific aspects of awareness, and target clearly defined objects of awareness.

This developing perspective on understanding and profiling awareness requires methods appropriate to capturing the range of factors involved and distinguishing between them. The choice of methods needs to be underpinned by a clear theoretical framework, and clinical assessment needs to focus on specific and clearly defined aspects of this theoretical construct (Clare, Marková, et al., 2005).

Most commonly, measures used to assess awareness are based either on discrepancy ratings or on clinician ratings. Both have limitations. Clinician ratings of a person's level of awareness (Verhey, Rozendaal, Ponds, & Jolles, 1993) are relatively quick and straightforward, but provide only global ratings, and inter-rater reliability may not be optimal (Auchus, Goldstein, Green, & Green, 1994). Furthermore, it can be argued that such measures do not take sufficient account of the complexity of individual responses or coping styles, or of the social context in which awareness is assessed. Calculation of discrepancies in ratings of functioning is one of the most frequently used methods of assessing awareness. The most common variant is the calculation of discrepancies between ratings given by the person with dementia and a carer on parallel rating scales assessing various aspects of functioning (Migliorelli et al., 1995); however, this approach is based on the assumptions that carers provide objective ratings (Jorm, 1992; Jorm, Christensen, Henderson, Korten, Mackinnon, & Scott, 1994). An alternative approach involves comparing self-ratings by people with dementia with their performance on objective tests of cognitive functioning (Anderson & Tranel, 1989). However, since the rating scales and objective tests typically do not map directly onto one another, this may be of limited value (Larrabee, West, & Crook, 1991). Another approach involves comparing actual performance on a cognitive task with an estimate of performance made either prior to or following completion of the task, the latter being preferable (Dalla Barba, Parlato, Iavarone, & Boller, 1995). This method does not take account of the possible influence of mood or situational factors on ratings of cognitive functioning; furthermore, the tasks used tend to be unfamiliar experimental laboratory tasks, which may lack ecological validity, and this in itself may make accurate performance estimates less likely.

In response to such limitations, the Memory Awareness Rating Scale (MARS) was developed and its reliability and validity was established (Clare et al., 2002b). The MARS provides both participant/informant and self-rating/objective test comparisons in relation to awareness of memory functioning. The scale is based on familiar everyday memory situations, uses equivalent situations for self-rating, informant rating and objective test, and elicits test performance ratings after completion of the task. The scale was initially developed for use with people who had early-stage Alzheimer's disease, although it is also being used with other groups, and work has been undertaken to develop an adapted version of the scale for people with moderate dementia (Hardy, Oyebode, & Clare, 2006). Alongside the MARS, as described in Chapter 3, a phenomenological method of exploring awareness has been developed based on in-depth interviews with the person with dementia and a family member (Clare et al., 2002b), which allows for a more comprehensive evaluation than the clinican rating method. The interview permits an exploration of subjective experience with regard to the participant's perception of the changes associated with the onset and progression of dementia and of his or her current situation and functioning. The phenomenological analytic method provides a coding structure for evaluating individual responses, as well as a means of rating coping styles. Similar approaches can be applied to transcripts of interviews or conversations with people who have moderate to severe dementia but are still able to communicate verbally.

All the methods discussed so far primarily involve an evaluation of explicit expressions of awareness, based in some way on the person's verbal self-report. This is important, but does not capture the full range of ways in which awareness might be expressed. Additionally, the available methods require verbal ability and may not be appropriate for assessing awareness among people with severe dementia (Clare, Marková, et al., 2005). It is important to note that in much of the research reviewed above the focus has been on demonstrating impairments of awareness, rather than providing evidence of retained aspects of awareness. However, a full assessment will need to consider the extent to which an individual is able to demonstrate or express awareness, as well as any indications of impaired awareness.

Practical implications of variations in awareness

Few studies have considered the possible practical implications of awareness. The relationship between awareness level and quality of life may be particularly salient, since maintaining or maximising quality of life is perhaps one of the most central issues in dementia care. Quality of life has not been directly considered in relation to awareness, but it appears that people with dementia who have higher levels of awareness may also tend to experience more depression and emotional distress (Clare, Wilson, Carter, Roth, & Hodges, 2004). Some recent studies have focused on awareness in particular domains of everyday functioning, such as managing financial affairs or driving (van Wielingen, Tuokko, Cramer, Mateer, & Hultsch, 2004), drawing out practical implications for supporting people with dementia and their families. This kind of approach could be helpful, both in identifying issues to work on in rehabilitation and in pinpointing areas of particular difficulty that may need extra consideration in planning an intervention.

The question of intervention does not, so far, seem to have been a major motivating factor in research on awareness in early-stage dementia, although a few studies of awareness comment briefly on the possible implications of their findings for clinical intervention and informed consent (Mullen, Howard, David, & Levy, 1996). It has been suggested (Green, Goldstein, Sirockman, & Green, 1993) that helping people with dementia to make a more accurate appraisal of their impairments might enable them to maintain their independence more effectively, and providing structured feedback to improve the accuracy of self-perceptions early in the course of the disorder is advocated. In brain-injury rehabilitation, attempts may often be made to increase awareness in order to support readjustment and enable people to return to productive activity and social engagement. However, it is perhaps unlikely that interventions for people with dementia would aim to focus directly on increasing awareness as such. Of course, some approaches might have this effect, and this could be beneficial – for example, participation in a psychotherapeutic support group (Cheston et al., 2003), engagement in a process of life review (Hirsch & Mouratoglou, 1999) or dyadic interventions designed to encourage joint planning and decision-making about the future following an early diagnosis (Whitlatch, Judge, Zarit, & Femia, 2006). In general, though, level of awareness is more likely to be seen as a factor that should be taken into account when working with people who have dementia. As noted above, it is important to distinguish between unawareness and lack of access to information, and to offer clear and accurate information where appropriate. In relation to the finding that anxiety might be linked to having good insight into one's impairments, it has been proposed that psychological interventions aimed at promoting acceptance and reducing anxiety may be beneficial (Verhey et al., 1993).

Level of awareness is likely to have implications for the kinds of psychological interventions that are most likely to prove acceptable and beneficial. This is a relatively new area of research, but there is some emerging evidence that awareness is related to outcome of cognitive rehabilitation interventions. One study (Koltai, Welsh-Bohmer, & Schmechel, 2001) reported that perceptions of gain as a result of participation in a memory training group were greater for participants with good awareness than for those with poor awareness, but this was based on retrospective classification of participants by therapist rating. The first prospective study in this area indicated that higher levels of awareness are related to better outcomes when people with dementia engage in cognitive rehabilitation interventions (Clare et al., 2004). On the basis of this finding, it was suggested that those individuals who express limited explicit awareness may benefit more from other approaches, but that taking the time to build trust and rapport might allow the possibility of finding areas that could be worked on collaboratively within a rehabilitation framework. Where there is limited expression of explicit awareness, caregivers are likely to require additional support.

It may be helpful to illustrate the implications of variations in level of awareness with some examples of people with dementia taken from my own research. Heather, Stuart and Paula have very different profiles of awareness.

- Heather had been forced to take early retirement from her job as a lecturer because she could no longer manage the work. After a range of tests, she was diagnosed with early-stage Alzheimer's disease. Her symptoms included seizures and perceptual problems, alongside difficulties with memory and problem-solving, but she insisted there was nothing really wrong with her. In her view, she had no more memory problems than anyone else of the same age. She considered that she used practical strategies like making lists to aid her memory, although her husband Harry said this did not work well. Heather would not accept any help and refused to take medication. She was often critical of and even abusive to Harry. Harry understood that this was a way of trying to maintain her self-esteem, but found it very hurtful, and was often desperate for a break from being with Heather.
- Stuart, formerly a senior army officer, was driving south on the northbound carriageway of the motorway at high speed when stopped by the police. He said he had taken the wrong slip road because the signs were confusing. His wife, Sheila, was very concerned about his increasing confusion and arranged for him to see his doctor, who referred him to the Memory Clinic. Stuart came to the Clinic on his own, refusing to allow his wife to come with him. At the start of his psychology appointment Stuart said that he did not understand why the psychologist was trying to test *him*, since he had been sent to the hospital in order to assess the staff – including the psychologist – as part of his work. Even so, following discussion, he was quite amenable to completing the psychologist's tests. He said he was certain there was nothing wrong with him, and seemed very cheerful. The Clinic team thought it was probable that he had early-stage Alzheimer's disease. When Stuart returned for a follow-up assessment 6 months later he came across very differently. He was concerned about difficulties with his memory, and felt that something was wrong with him. He seemed distressed and was rather tearful. His wife, however, said she felt much happier because Stuart had agreed not to drive, so she had fewer concerns about his safety. Because their views on Stuart's functioning were less discrepant, they were arguing less.
- Paula had worked as a nurse for many years. She initially noticed that she was 'not focusing very well and things were there that shouldn't be' when out shopping. She went to her GP, thinking that he had always viewed her as a bit of a hypochondriac, but eventually he sent her for a scan, which showed brain atrophy. She continued to get worse, and further tests eventually led to a diagnosis of Alzheimer's, although the neurologist just told her that the problem was 'premature ageing'. It was her GP who told Paula and her husband Philip the actual diagnosis. Paula said she already knew what was wrong, because of her nursing experience. She felt her memory for current and recent events was very poor indeed, although she could still recall many incidents and

experiences from the past, but at the same time she felt her personality had not changed, saying 'I'm still me'. Paula described how she was no longer able to do most of the things she had always enjoyed, such as singing, learning languages, or writing letters, and how she felt terribly slowed down, muddled and clumsy. On the other hand, she was still able to enjoy reading, listening to music and going for walks in the countryside. Philip felt very sad about what was happening to Paula, but was working hard to make plans for the future, although he was not sure about his own ability to face up to it. Philip and Paula were able to talk together about their situation, and were trying to make the most of the time they could enjoy together.

These three individuals with different awareness profiles are likely to benefit from very different intervention approaches. Heather remained insistent that although her memory was not as good as before, this was quite usual for her age, and although pleasant and welcoming to visitors was very suspicious of any professional involvement. She did not want any kind of intervention. Harry, on the other hand, felt greatly in need of both support and respite. Stuart initially lacked awareness but developed greater awareness over time, becoming more depressed as a result. Intervention for Stuart needed to start with a sensitive approach to help him come to terms with the changes he was experiencing, and talk openly with Sheila about plans for the future, before moving on to consider practical strategies. Paula, in contrast, was aware from the beginning both of her symptoms and of their possible meaning, and was able to give a very clear and accurate description of her current functioning. In intervening with Paula it was possible to address both practical and emotional issues, both individually and together with Philip.

Conclusions

Awareness is an important factor to consider when planning a rehabilitative intervention for a person with dementia. It is helpful to try to establish what the person is aware of, and to identify any limitations or disturbances in awareness. In trying to understand disturbances in awareness, we need to consider a range of factors. Certainly neurological damage will play a part for some people in the early stages, and eventually perhaps for all. However, talking with people who have dementia makes it clear that the situation is much more complex (Clare, 2002b). It is useful to take account of the person's coping style and social relationships, and to think about the information and knowledge the person has, and the impact that any contact with health or other care services may have had. It is important to remember that awareness is expressed in a particular situation at a particular time, and so we cannot assume that it is a stable trait, but instead need to consider changes over both short and longer periods of time. All of this means we need to work from a comprehensive biopsychosocial model when trying to understand a person's level of awareness. This provides a context within which to consider the neuropsychological rationale for offering cognitive rehabilitation interventions, which is the subject of the next chapter.

5 Neuropsychology, plasticity and learning in dementia

This chapter explores how theoretical models from neuropsychology combine with experimental evidence on learning, behaviour change and neural plasticity to provide a basis for cognitive rehabilitation interventions in early-stage Alzheimer's disease. Evidence suggests that people with early-stage AD may benefit from such approaches, provided they are appropriately targeted and based on a sound understanding of the profile of cognitive change and its implications for everyday functioning.

In this chapter I explore the specific rationale for offering cognitive rehabilitation to people with dementia, drawing on neuropsychological models of memory functioning and experimental evidence on learning and behaviour change. Key concepts here are the potential for learning as evidenced in behavioural changes, plasticity in terms of reorganization or reactivation at the neural level, and prevention, whether of the development of problems, or the progression of changes, or of unnecessary excess disability. I then consider how these relate to the wider psychosocial context, taking account of factors such as awareness, emotional processing, mood, coping style, social resources and support networks.

Rehabilitation offers a practical framework for conceptualising intervention approaches in dementia care (Cohen & Eisdorfer, 1986). A rehabilitative approach could be relevant to supporting well-being at any stage of dementia. For example, it might involve maintaining or rebuilding basic skills such as the ability to feed oneself so as to promote continued independence, or improving mobility to avoid pressure sores, or managing pain effectively in order to improve well-being and promote engagement. In the earlier stages, it is more likely to involve developing ways of managing memory difficulties and other cognitive difficulties, so as to remain involved in roles and activities and have the opportunity to make a valued contribution, and thus it is likely to have a cognitive emphasis. Many factors can be considered when planning interventions for people with dementia, and it is helpful if these interventions are based on an holistic understanding of the needs, abilities and difficulties of the individual. Whatever the aims of rehabilitation, in the context of progressive neurological changes it will always be important to take account of the level of cognitive functioning and of the degree to which particular abilities are retained. In some cases, especially in early-stage dementia, difficulties with aspects of cognitive functioning are one of the major issues, and addressing the impact of these in everyday settings may form the main focus of rehabilitative intervention. The aim is not to try to maintain cognitive functioning against the odds, but rather to help people with dementia to experience optimal levels of well-being and to prevent unnecessary disability.

At this point, it is crucial to note that while it is helpful to know the specific clinical diagnosis, since this offers information about the likely neuropsychological profile as well as about prognosis and needs, it is equally if not more important to be aware of the specific neuropsychological profile in each individual case, and to place this in the context of a wider formulation taking into account the relevant psychosocial factors. As discussed in Chapter 1, classification and diagnosis in the dementias are not straightforward, and the familiar categories subsume a range of heterogeneous profiles (Blacker, Albert, Bassett, Go, Harrell, & Folstein 1994). Indeed, existing distinctions such as those made between AD and vascular dementia may prove to be less clear-cut and less relevant than originally thought (Norris et al., 2003) – just as was the case previously with the now largely abandoned distinction between 'pre-senile' and 'senile' dementia (Lishman, 1994). Therefore, a diagnostic label is no substitute for a thorough psychological and neuropsychological evaluation.

Here, I aim to illustrate the relevance of neuropsychological rehabilitation with specific relevance to the development and progression of memory difficulties in early-stage Alzheimer's disease. In early-stage AD, impairment in memory and other cognitive functions is a defining feature, and problems with memory in particular tend to be a major focus of concern in terms of their impact on everyday life. Theoretical models and experimental evidence from neuropsychology and cognitive psychology provide a strong rationale for developing and providing interventions directed at supporting memory functioning in early-stage AD.

Experimental evidence of learning

Experimental studies of learning confirm that learning is possible in people with dementia. People with AD can change their behaviour in response to altered environmental contingencies (Burgess, Wearden, Cox, & Rae, 1992). They can learn or re-learn skills and procedural routines (Salmon, Heindel, & Butters, 1992), and they can learn and retain new verbal information (Little, Volans, Hemsley, & Levy, 1986). Recent studies (Fernández-Ballesteros, Zamarrón, & Tàrraga, 2005; Fernández-Ballesteros, Zamarrón, Tàrraga, Moya, & Iniguez, 2003) have compared the learning ability of people with AD, people with MCI, and healthy older people. All three groups showed evidence of improved performance, with the healthy older people improving most, followed by those with MCI and then those with AD. This evidence of 'cognitive plasticity' indicates that people with AD do have the potential to benefit from interventions targeting memory function.

While improvements in memory functioning can certainly be demonstrated, it is not reasonable to expect the person with early-stage AD to learn under the same conditions as someone without AD; extra support and adaptation of the learning environment are crucial. When the right kind of support is provided both at encoding and at retrieval, people with AD do show improvements in relevant aspects of episodic memory functioning (Bäckman, 1992), with the level of support required to produce an improvement increasing as a function of increasing severity of dementia. This provides a basis for considering the extent to which these effects might be harnessed to enhance functioning in real-life situations (Bird & Kinsella, 1996; Bird & Luszcz, 1991, 1993). In order to achieve this, it is useful to understand the way in which memory functioning and its underlying mechanisms change in early-stage AD.

Memory systems and processes

In considering how memory changes in early-stage AD, it is helpful to think about memory in terms of first, a set of dissociable systems, and second, a set of distinct processes, and to relate both systems and processes to the underlying neuroanatomical structures involved. This allows us to identify the ways in which interventions can be most appropriately targeted.

Memory can be viewed in terms of a set of interacting but dissociable systems (Squire & Knowlton, 1995), as illustrated with respect to long-term memory in Figure 5.1. Consideration of memory systems in early-stage AD shows that some subsystems are relatively preserved while others are severely impaired, and these impairments impact directly on functional ability. The greatest degree of impairment is evident in long-term memory. Declarative long-term memory is composed of episodic and semantic components. Episodic memory refers to memory for temporally and spatially defined events that are both personally relevant and context-dependent, while semantic memory refers to memory for lexical information, facts and general knowledge. Episodic memory is typically severely impaired from the early stages of AD (Overman & Becker, 2004), and episodic memory performance is already affected in the preclinical stages of the disorder (B. J. Small, Herlitz, & Bäckman, 2004). Semantic memory may be affected in the early stages to a lesser degree (Garrard, Patterson, & Hodges, 2004). Whether or not semantic memory is directly affected, impairments in episodic memory are likely to impact on the ability to acquire new semantic memories (Verfaellie, Croce, & Milberg, 1995). Bäckman and Herlitz (1996) argue that the ability to benefit from cognitive support in memory interventions relates to the way in which the person's knowledge structures are

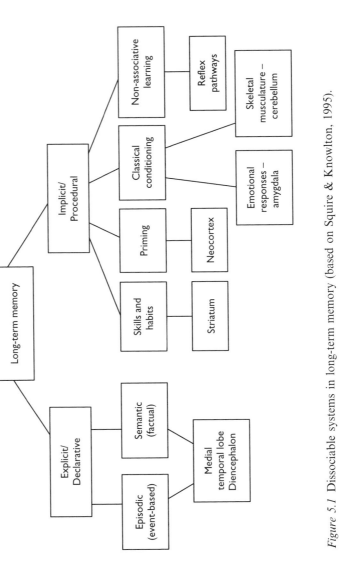

Figure 5.1 Dissociable systems in long-term memory (based on Squire & Knowlton, 1995).

able to aid encoding and retrieval of episodic information. It is hard for people with memory impairments to establish links to prior semantic knowledge at encoding, and people with AD show impairments in using their semantic knowledge as an aid for establishing episodic memories (Herlitz & Viitanen, 1991). However, if strategies are offered that perform this linking function, or if the stimuli themselves encourage appropriate semantic processing, then adequate learning can be achieved (Thoene & Glisky, 1995).

Autobiographical memory involves both episodic and semantic components (Kopelman, Wilson, & Baddeley, 1990), and is affected from the early stages of AD (Bright & Kopelman, 2004). Prospective memory, or memory for future planned events and actions, may also be impaired from the early stages of AD (Maylor, 1995). With regard to non-declarative aspects of long-term memory, procedural memory, or memory for skills and routines, is preserved in early-stage dementia, as are some aspects of priming (Salmon & Fennema-Notestine, 2004). Within working-memory systems (Baddeley, 1995, 2000), which are summarised in Figure 5.2, the central executive and visuospatial sketchpad components are typically impaired (R. G. Morris, 1996) but the phonological loop is generally unaffected (R. G. Morris & McKiernan, 1994). Impairments in the episodic buffer may also help to account for difficulties acquiring new information in early-stage Alzheimer's disease (Germano & Kinsella, 2005).

The finding that some aspects of memory are severely impaired while others are relatively unaffected, or only mildly affected, suggests that there is scope for interventions aimed at improving memory functioning. Interventions may build on relatively intact aspects of memory, or directly address areas known to be impaired, or offer ways of compensating for

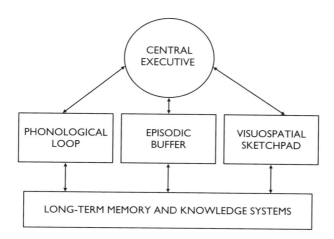

Figure 5.2 Dissociable systems in working memory (based on Baddeley, 1995).

impaired aspects of memory. Strategies for optimising memory functioning are reviewed in detail in Chapter 7.

Memory functioning, of course, interacts with other aspects of cognitive ability. Alongside memory, attention and executive function are all typically affected at an early stage in the progression of AD (Collette & Van der Linden, 2004; R. J. Perry & Hodges, 1999), and difficulties in allocating attentional resources affect dual-task performance (Baddeley, Bressi, Della Sala, Logie, & Spinnler, 1991). This has significant implications for memory functioning, as impaired executive function affects strategic aspects of encoding and retrieval (Glisky, 1998), giving rise to problems in effortful search of memory and in linking episodic memories with their source and temporal context. People with early-stage AD can be expected to have particular difficulty with some aspects of retrieval and also with implementing strategies to help themselves remember (Bäckman, 1992), so this is an area that may need to be tackled in rehabilitative interventions. Existing work in brain injury rehabilitation (e.g. Levine et al., 2000) may offer some guidance.

Memory can also be considered in terms of the processes of encoding, storage and retrieval, as summarised in Figure 5.3. These processes are closely interrelated and difficult to separate (Glisky, 1998). However, it appears that the memory problems of people with Alzheimer's disease are not primarily problems of storage, and it is not a matter of rapid or increased forgetting. While short-term forgetting, assessed within the first 30 seconds following exposure to a stimulus, is impaired in people with AD (Kopelman, 1992), rates of long-term forgetting are no greater in general than those found in healthy individuals. On most tasks where long-term forgetting is assessed at periods of between 1 minute and 1 week following stimulus presentation, forgetting rates in people with AD are equivalent to those seen in controls when the two groups are matched for initial learning (Christensen, Kopelman, Stanhope, Lorentz, & Owen, 1998). Therefore, while there can be some difficulties with memory storage (Becker, Lopez, &

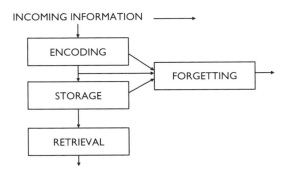

Figure 5.3 Memory processes.

Butters, 1996), this is not the major issue. Similarly, there can be some difficulties with retrieval processes (Kapur, 1994), but these are relatively subtle.

Instead, the major problem seems to lie in encoding, with the acquisition of new memories being severely affected (Christensen et al., 1998). Clearly this is not a complete explanation, because there is also a loss of some previously encoded memories, which is not the result of failure to encode (Glisky, 1998). Impairments in semantic memory, in particular, are thought to result primarily from an actual loss of knowledge (J. R. Hodges, Patterson, Graham, & Dawson, 1996). However, it does indicate that where the aim is to facilitate acquisition of new long-term memories, ensuring successful encoding is crucial. If learning is supported so that adequate encoding is achieved, and new information is incorporated into the memory store, there is a reasonable likelihood that the information will be retained. Given the impairments in episodic memory, this kind of approach should probably be reserved for small amounts of important information only. Again, therefore, consideration of evidence regarding memory processes supports the relevance of appropriately targeted rehabilitative approaches.

The behavioural findings from studies of memory functioning in early-stage AD, whether in terms of systems or processes, indicate that there is potential for rehabilitation. In order to harness this potential fully, it is also useful to consider how the behavioural evidence may relate to underlying mechanisms at the neural level.

Brain pathology and neural plasticity

The brain areas most affected in early-stage Alzheimer's disease are the medial temporal lobe, basal forebrain, thalamus and neocortex (Bauer, Tobias, & Valenstein, 1993). The impairment in episodic memory in early-stage AD results from damage in the medial temporal lobe areas, and specifically the structures of the hippocampal complex. Hippocampal structures are vital for the formation and consolidation of new episodic memories, and for linking these with existing stored knowledge, although they are not required for long-term storage (Glisky, 1998). Pathology in the medial temporal region results in a functional disconnection of the hippocampus from related areas very early in the disease process (J. R. Hodges & Patterson, 1995). Semantic memory is typically affected at a later stage when pathology extends beyond the hippocampal complex into the temporal neocortex (J. R. Hodges & Patterson, 1995). Additionally, the frontal lobes are affected. As pathology in this area affects strategic aspects of remembering and retrieval of stored information, this explains why people with early-stage AD are likely to have particular difficulty implementing strategies to help themselves remember (Bäckman, 1992).

The learning observed in behavioural studies, therefore, occurs despite what is in effect a functional disconnection of the brain areas primarily engaged in forming new episodic memories and linking new memories with existing stored knowledge. Glisky (1998) argues that other brain areas may be able to perform the function of integrating new information with existing memories, provided that strategies are offered at encoding to facilitate the linking function. It has been suggested that successful relearning of, for example, face–name associations (Clare, Wilson, Carter, Roth, & Hodges, 2002a) might be occurring independently of hippocampal function, through gradual re-establishment of links between phonological and semantic representations in neocortical regions that are less damaged in early AD than the hippocampal complex. There is growing evidence for recruitment of additional neural networks in early-stage AD (Grady, Intosh, Beig, Keightley, Burian, & Black, 2003). One functional magnetic resonance imaging (fMRI) study (Grady et al., 2003) showed that people with early-stage AD recruit different brain areas from controls when engaging in episodic and semantic memory tasks. Controls recruited left prefrontal and temporal cortical areas, while AD patients recruited bilateral dorsolateral prefrontal and posterior cortical areas; greater activation in these areas was associated with better task performance in the patient group. People with AD showed less functional activation than controls in some areas, but increased activation in others. Sperling et al. (2003) reported that AD patients show reduced activation in the hippocampus when engaging in an associative learning task, but increased activation in medial parietal and posterior cingulate areas. In an fMRI study by our own group (Parienté et al., 2005), using an event-related design to investigate performance on an associative encoding task, and comparing responses for successfully encoded face–name associations with those that were not successfully encoded, we found that AD patients showed not only reduced bilateral hippocampal activation but also bilateral hyperactivation in frontal and parietal areas, which was associated with successful encoding. Figure 5.4 shows an example of this pattern. Mean data from older controls (Figure 5.4a) demonstrate activation in the right and left hipocampus, superior colliculus, and left inferior frontal lobe during successful encoding. A single participant with AD shows less activation than controls (Figure 5.4b) in the left hippocampal area during successful encoding. However, the participant also shows greater activation than controls (Figure 5.4c) in the frontal cortex and higher visual areas during successful encoding. This recruitment of additional neural resources in AD, with greater activation in some areas and/or involvement of additional areas, may reflect a compensatory process.

For those individuals who show gains as a result of a rehabilitation intervention, it is possible that the treatment approach may have facilitated the compensatory process, and the outcome may reflect the operation of underlying mechanisms of neural plasticity. Preliminary data from our own group support this view. In an fMRI study using a blocked design to evaluate activation during associative encoding and retrieval, comparing a baseline scan with a second scan taken after an 8-week cognitive

(a) Pattern of activation associated with successful encoding in controls

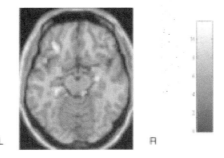

(b) Areas of reduced activation in a participant with AD

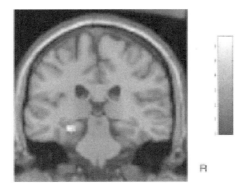

(c) Areas of increased activation in a participant with AD

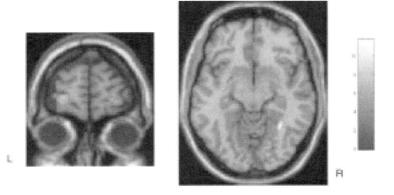

Figure 5.4 Brain activation during successful associative learning.

rehabilitation (CR) intervention, differences in activation patterns were observed following therapy. These included both increases and reductions in activation in regions of interest (Clare, van Paasschen, Evans, Parkinson, Linden, & Woods, 2006).

If there are compensatory mechanisms involved, this process could then be facilitated through targeted rehabilitation approaches. As noted above, engaging compensatory activation of other brain areas would imply that learning would be expected to be less efficient, and therefore it would be important to allow sufficient time and exposure for new learning to occur. Alternatively, of course, rehabilitation may help to strengthen compromised connections and thus provide some restoration of function in damaged areas. These two possibilities are not necessarily mutually exclusive, since different aspects of rehabilitation may reflect one or other mechanism, and indeed there may be individual variability. However, the question of whether changes reflect plasticity or restoration does have implications for the further development of rehabilitation techniques. Where gains reflect restoration of function, then practice of pre-existing knowledge and skills is likely to be helpful. Where gains reflect plasticity, there will be a need to design rehabilitation techniques that have the potential to promote activation in the targeted brain areas and support the recruitment of compensatory circuits.

In general, then, considering the brain pathology associated with memory difficulties suggests that, where the goal is retention of new information, interventions may usefully focus on ensuring effective encoding, supporting the process of linking new information with stored knowledge, and teaching and reinforcing the use of memory strategies. While new learning can be achieved, attempts to facilitate acquisition of new long-term memories will ideally be limited to information that is important and personally meaningful to the individual. Increased understanding of the mechanisms underlying behavioural changes, and the extent to which these reflect plasticity or restoration of function, will assist in targeting and refining intervention approaches in specific domains.

Possibilities for prevention

Understanding of the neural mechanisms underlying the progression of dementia is growing rapidly, and the possibilities for plasticity are increasingly being considered, but as yet relatively little is known about whether rehabilitative interventions can support plasticity, and whether cognitive and behavioural changes are mirrored in lasting changes at a neural level. If so, this would provide strong support not only for rehabilitative interventions following the observation of symptoms, but also for proactive preventive measures using similar approaches. As yet, we know relatively little about the potential for prevention in relation to dementia. Prevention in this context might mean prevention of dementia, prevention of progression from mild cognitive impairment to dementia, prevention of progression or development of functional disability within an established diagnosis of dementia, or prevention of excess disability.

As discussed in Chapter 1, we know that cognitive activity, in a general sense, seems to play a role in prevention of dementia, although the relationship between the level of cognitive activity that people report and the extent of age-related cognitive change is not clear-cut (Salthouse, Berish, & Miles, 2002). Several studies have explored the way in which reported degree of participation in cognitive and physical activity at baseline relates to later onset of dementia. There is some evidence that physical exercise plays a part in reducing the risk of developing dementia (Laurin et al., 2001), and stronger evidence that cognitive activity is important. One study (R. S. Wilson, Leon, et al., 2002) assessed participation in a range of activities including reading, puzzles and card games, and walking in a cohort of 801 older members of religious orders, who were followed up for an average of 4.5 years. Greater cognitive activity was related to reduced risk of developing AD and to better maintenance of cognitive skills, especially in the areas of working memory and perceptual speed, when controlling for age, gender and educational attainment. Similar findings were observed with a community-based sample (R. S. Wilson, Bennett, et al., 2002). Confirming that cognitive activity is related to reduced risk of developing AD or vascular dementia, a study of involvement in cognitive activity pinpointed a number of activities that appeared to be especially helpful, including reading, playing board games, playing musical instruments, and dancing (Verghese et al., 2003). While this study, like those of Wilson and colleagues, found no evidence that physical activity plays a preventive role, it should be noted that dancing combines cognitive and physical effort and skill.

The beneficial effects of general cognitive activity may derive from the contribution to building cognitive reserve capacity (Richards & Sacker, 2003), which can mitigate against the effects of age-related cognitive changes and thus offer some protection against the onset of disability. Potentially, therefore, cognitive activity might also offer some benefits for people who have already developed dementia, in terms of maintaining cognitive function and thus delaying further decline. I explore the evidence regarding the effects of interventions based on cognitive activity for people with dementia in Chapter 6. However, the impact of dementia-related cognitive changes on everyday activity and involvement, as well as on sense of self and identity, is such that once the onset of dementia has been reached, more focused interventions are likely to be required in order to optimise well-being.

Conclusions

This chapter has focused in particular on the example of early-stage Alzheimer's disease, reviewing the experimental evidence on learning and behaviour change and relating this to what is known about the profile of neuropsychological changes, as well as to emerging evidence regarding neural mechanisms and possible neural plasticity. It is quite clear that learning is possible for people with dementia, given the necessary support, and this prompts consideration of how to capitalise on the potential for new learning, relearning and behaviour change. Understanding the neuro-psychological profile allows us to determine when it is appropriate to build on preserved aspects of memory, to make better use of impaired aspects of memory, or to apply compensatory strategies that enable the person to bypass the specific difficulties. Recent findings from neuroimaging studies suggest that, with an improved understanding of the mechanisms involved, it may be possible to further refine and target intervention strategies in order to capitalise on retained potential for plasticity, although this work is in its early stages. Converging evidence from behavioural, neuropsycho-logical and neuroimaging studies offers a strong rationale for adopting a rehabilitation approach that can help to reduce the impact of disability for people with dementia, when placed in the context of a broad psychological formulation taking into account the biological, psychological and social factors that are relevant for each individual.

At this point, before going on to describe the range of specific strategies that rehabilitation therapists can employ and how these can be used to address aspects of everyday functioning that are personally relevant for the individual with dementia, it is useful to review the way in which cognition-focused interventions have traditionally been applied within dementia care. There has been a long-standing interest in interventions addressing cogni-tive function, but typically the emphasis has been substantially different from that indicated by the above review. In the next chapter, I describe these approaches and evaluate the evidence regarding their effectiveness, in order to provide a point of comparison with the cognitive rehabilitation approach.

6 Towards individualised rehabilitation interventions

Before considering how neuropsychological rehabilitation can best be put into practice in dementia care, it is useful to reflect on the history of psychological interventions in dementia, and to consider how neuro-psychological rehabilitation relates to other approaches. This chapter provides a brief history and overview of cognition-focused interventions for people with dementia in order to help clarify the distinctive aspects of neuropsychological rehabilitation in this context, and how it differs from other forms of cognition-focused intervention.

Cognition-focused approaches have traditionally been a central element of psychosocial intervention in dementia care. One of the earliest forms of psychosocial intervention for people with moderate to severe dementia was reality orientation (Woods, 1992), and there has been a continuing interest in developing approaches aimed at enhancing cognitive functioning. In recent years, following the trend towards earlier detection and diagnosis of dementia, cognition-focused approaches have been implemented for people in the earlier stages of dementia, most commonly those with a diagnosis of Alzheimer's or vascular dementia. A considerable number of studies have been reported in the research literature, and these can be difficult to classify reliably. In particular, the terminology adopted is sometimes at variance with the nature of the intervention. In previous work I have argued that, irrespective of what researchers *call* their interventions, it is possible to identify three main strands of cognition-focused approach: cognitive stimulation, cognitive training, and cognitive rehabilitation. As noted above, these terms are used somewhat interchangeably in the literature, and this can give rise to some confusion; additionally, some interventions may combine elements of more than one of these. However, the following definitions (Clare, Woods, Moniz-Cook, Spector, & Orrell, 2003) have been developed in an attempt to provide a basis for clarity:

- *Cognitive stimulation* involves engagement in a range of group activities and discussions aimed at enhancing cognitive and social functioning.

The aim is to demonstrate improvements on measures of cognition and behaviour. This definition, as currently outlined, subsumes both general cognitive stimulation and reality orientation (RO). Overall, these approaches have most often been applied with people who have moderate to severe dementia, often in day care or residential settings, although cognitive stimulation has been used with people who have early-stage dementia.

- *Cognitive training* involves guided practice on a set of standardised tasks that aim to address specific aspects of cognition, such as memory, language, attention or executive function. Within the standardised tasks, varying difficulty levels may be offered to permit a degree of adaptation to different degrees of severity of cognitive impairment. The aim is to demonstrate improved performance on cognitive tasks. This approach has been used with people who have mild to moderate dementia, as well as with healthy older people and those with mild cognitive impairment.
- *Cognitive rehabilitation* involves individually designed interventions aimed at addressing specific practical difficulties identified by the person with dementia and/or the family caregiver that are relevant to everyday life and are related in some way to cognitive impairment. The aim is to support aspects of everyday functioning and well-being rather than to improve performance on cognitive tests per se. This approach has primarily been used with people who have early-stage dementia, but could be applied to difficulties arising at all stages from mild cognitive impairment to severe dementia.

These definitions highlight the distinction between traditional cognition-based interventions, broadly termed cognitive stimulation and cognitive training, and the focus of neuropsychological or cognitive rehabilitation. Nevertheless there may be some shared elements, particularly with regard to the application of compensatory strategies or specific techniques that facilitate learning. Here I review the origins of, and current evidence regarding, cognitive stimulation and cognitive training, before outlining the ways in which cognitive rehabilitation differs from these approaches.

Reality orientation and cognitive stimulation

Reality orientation therapy for people with dementia was derived from developments in the psychosocial rehabilitation of long-term institutionalised residents of psychiatric hospitals. The RO approach offered one of the first opportunities to provide structured psychosocial intervention for people with dementia, and quickly gained widespread popularity, being adopted for use in many long-term care settings. RO therapy aims to increase the person's orientation to the present situation, and to enhance the person's cognitive and behavioural functioning through cognition-based activities, social interaction and discussion, combined with the use of cues and prompts to aid memory (Woods, 1999). It has generally been applied with people who have moderate to severe dementia. RO is usually conducted in group sessions ('classroom RO'), although in residential or day care settings cues and prompts may be generalised throughout the environment for use at all times ('24-hour RO'). Perhaps the most obvious legacy of RO in dementia care is the presence of the ubiquitous 'reality orientation board' in a dayroom or social area, sadly all too often out of date and poorly presented. This highlights one important limitation of the RO approach, as standards of implementation have sometimes been low. More importantly, the risk of RO being applied in an insensitive and confrontational manner has been widely noted. Although the stated aims of the RO approach are to provide a supportive and accepting atmosphere, there has been a strong potential for misapplication, and this has led to a great deal of criticism (Woods, 2002). Some critics have concluded that RO fails to consider the emotional needs of the person with dementia, and this observation has stimulated the development of alternative approaches, such as validation therapy (Feil, 1992). Nevertheless, the RO concept retains some influence in dementia care today, particularly, it seems, in Italy (Woods, 2002).

Evaluation of RO has typically involved assessing improvement on cognitive screening tests such as the MMSE (Folstein et al., 1975) and on staff ratings of behaviour. An early Cochrane systematic review of RO (Spector, Orrell, Davies, & Woods, 1998) evaluated traditional RO interventions for people with moderate to severe dementia, but also included a study of cognitive stimulation for people with early-stage dementia, giving a total of six randomised controlled trials in the meta-analysis. Results indicated that significant improvements on measures of cognition were evident in some, but not all, studies. There was weaker evidence for a positive effect of RO on measures of behaviour.

With the trend to earlier diagnosis of dementia, methods of general cognitive stimulation have been developed for people who have early-stage dementia (Breuil et al., 1994). The approach is not very clearly described, but seems to be based on the assumption that cognitive functions must be exercised as a whole rather than by targeting specific domains, and therefore involves tasks that are perceived as providing a general stimulus, and particularly those that involve making associations. The programme consists of activities such as joining dots to make a picture of a familiar object, naming and categorising objects, making word associations, and drawing familiar objects from different perspectives. Of course, it is inaccurate to assume that targeting specific domains of functioning leaves other aspects untouched, since most cognitive tasks involve a range of abilities and functions. For example, remembering which name belongs with a particular face clearly involves perceptual, attentional, and executive components alongside memory.

Woods (2002) proposed that this method was similar to RO and that the term 'cognitive stimulation' should be used to cover both approaches, arguing that this terminology encapsulated more effectively the aims of RO programmes. Having reported the development of an RO intervention designed to include elements taken from studies using various approaches, including not only RO but also, for example, reminiscence, that reported positive outcomes (Spector, Orrell, Davies, & Woods, 2001), the intervention was subsequently relabelled as 'cognitive stimulation' (Spector et al., 2003). This group therapy programme for people with moderate dementia in formal care settings included reminiscence, sensory stimulation, recognising people, recognising and using objects, word and number games, physical games, singing, and orientation. Evaluation indicated that improvements in cognitive function and self-rated quality of life resulted from participation, relative to a no-treatment control group. It is unclear to what extent the change of terminology was really appropriate, as this study appears to have included a much wider and more varied range of activities than those described by Breuil et al. (1994), suggesting that RO may in fact have been the more appropriate designation.

Although there are some indications that RO and cognitive stimulation can have positive effects, these methods also have significant limitations. First, it is difficult to identify a clear theoretical foundation that would help to explain the rationale for what is included and the relationship between content and outcome. Although cognitive functioning is a key outcome indicator, the approach does not seem to be based on a clear theoretical model of cognitive functioning, and there is no obvious relationship with theoretical models from neuropsychology, apart from the general assumption that mental exercise is helpful and that making links and associations between different items somehow strengthens cognitive functioning. Attempts to use theoretically derived and empirically supported methods of learning have been limited. The interventions typically incorporate a range of different elements. It is difficult, therefore, to establish the relative contribution of different intervention components to the positive outcomes that have been observed, and it has not been possible to derive a theoretical understanding of the mechanisms by which these interventions exert their positive effects (Bird, 2001). Not only do interventions incorporate various components, but the specific components chosen also vary between studies, making interpretation of results particularly difficult. In addition, the actual interventions are often poorly described, which limits the clinical usefulness of the reports. Outcome has primarily been assessed by comparing pre- and post-treatment scores on measures of impairment, mainly in the form of cognitive test scores, typically on brief and rather uninformative screening tests. It remains unclear how, if at all, any small improvements in screening test scores translate into changes in everyday functioning, and what the effects are at the level of functional disability.

In terms of the delivery of interventions, there is usually a reliance on standardised or manualised group intervention formats. Therefore, neither the overall approach nor the specific content are tailored to participants' individual needs or preferences. In consequence, this method cannot be seen as person-centred in either concept or application, and more individualised methods are required (Spector et al., 1998). While group stimulation activities may be enjoyable for some, and could offer one potentially useful element within an overall care package, it cannot be assumed that they are appropriate for everyone, and furthermore greater benefits might be achieved through a more individualised approach (Spector et al., 2001). Cohen-Mansfield and colleagues (Cohen-Mansfield et al., 2000; Cohen-Mansfield, Parpura-Gill, & Golander, 2006), in contrast, provide an example of the potential of individualised interventions for people with moderate to severe dementia in day care and residential settings. They developed a method for identifying salient role identities, covering the domains of family-social roles, professional roles, leisure time and hobbies, and personal achievements and traits. Having identified the person's currently most salient identity role, an individual activity programme was developed that was directly related to the role identity and would provide a sense of purpose or meaning, as well as being appropriate for the person's level of ability (including, of course, cognitive functioning) and needs. This experimental approach was compared in a randomised controlled trial with a control condition where participants engaged in the regular activity programme offered in the facility. Participants receiving the individualised interventions showed higher levels of pleasure, interest, involvement, orientation and identity awareness than controls, and lower levels of agitation.

One further comment on RO or cognitive stimulation groups is of particular importance. One study (Gerber, Prince, Snider, Atchison, Dubois, & Kilgour, 1991) reported that a comparison group that engaged in social activity, with equal amounts of group time and therapist attention, made equivalent gains to an RO therapy group. Both groups showed improvements in cognitive functioning, especially in the domains of orientation and language, compared with a no-treatment control group. This suggests that the benefits of RO may derive more from the social activity that is part of this approach than from any specific cognition-focused aspects. Most studies have failed to include a social activity or social support control group, so this question remains to be addressed. It is possible that RO may appear to offer benefits because it is given in the context of impoverished, non-stimulating environments and addresses the resulting under functioning, which could be viewed as a form of excess disability, rather than because of any impact on cognition as such. Clearly, addressing the deprivation that is characteristic of many formal care environments is crucially important, and is likely to have positive effects on functioning and well-being. However, a comprehensive approach to improving the care environment is undoubtedly what is required, rather than a brief group therapy intervention. In a setting that offered individualised, supported opportunities to engage in everyday activities like gardening, cooking, housework or taking care of pets, to engage in conversation about current affairs and past memories, to enjoy pastimes like games, puzzles or music, and to assume particular valued roles based on interests and abilities, there would arguably be little need for group stimulation therapy.

Cognitive training

Cognitive training (sometimes termed 'cognitive retraining' or 'cognitive remediation') involves a standardised approach, with a specific focus on exercising one or more aspects of cognitive functioning. Participants engage in guided practice on a range of standard tasks relating to particular domains of cognitive functioning, such as memory, language or attention. The specific methods used may be based on experimentally validated techniques known to enhance particular kinds of learning. In some cases tasks are offered at varying levels of difficulty, making it possible to take account of the severity of cognitive impairment. Cognitive training is implicitly based on a modular concept of cognitive functioning, and therefore can be easily related to profiles of preserved and impaired functioning in particular disorders. Cognitive training methods assume that regular or routine practice has the potential to improve or at least maintain functioning in a given domain, although of course this view has been widely criticised (Bird, 2000). Consistent with this, outcomes are typically assessed in terms of performance on cognitive or neuropsychological tests, and there is an expectation that the treatment group, in contrast to controls, will show improvement or at least maintenance of performance in the targeted domain. Cognitive training approaches, then, appear to be focusing primarily on reducing or slowing the progression of underlying impairment. There is often also an implicit assumption that any effects of practice will both transfer to related types of task and also generalise beyond the immediate training context, although generalisation is rarely formally evaluated. Experience suggests, however, that generalisation is unlikely to occur unless appropriate opportunities are built into the intervention programme itself.

Cognitive training (CT) methods for people with dementia have much in common with similar approaches used with healthy older people and those with milder forms of cognitive impairment. Therefore, in reviewing the use and efficacy of CT for people with dementia, it is helpful to begin by briefly considering the application of this approach in normal ageing, and in addressing age-related changes in memory functioning.

As I noted in Chapter 5, cognitive activity over the lifespan offers some possibility of protection against cognitive decline in later life. However, despite this observation, the effects of cognitive training for healthy older people are modest at best. A meta-analysis of 31 studies of memory training in healthy older people (Verhaeghen, Marcoen, & Goossens, 1992) indicated that training did have an effect on performance of episodic memory tasks, but the effect size was small (participants improved by 0.78 of a standard deviation unit, while controls improved by 0.38 of a standard deviation unit), and training gains were smaller as age increased. There is no evidence for generalisation of gains to everyday functioning (Verhaeghen et al., 1992). Some studies suggest that task-specific improvements following training can be maintained over substantial periods, and that the benefits can be increased by incorporating relaxation training to reduce anxiety (Ball et al., 2002). Cognitive training interventions for older people who are described as having age-associated memory impairment or age-associated cognitive decline have produced similar results (Sheikh, Hill, & Yesavage, 1986). Thus some modest gains can be derived from memory training, but they appear to be specific to the task that was trained, and do not automatically generalise. Of course, small gains in an area that is causing specific difficulty could be helpful, provided these gains can be harnessed in everyday life, but generalisation would need to be addressed. The situation has been summed up as follows: 'memory training . . . is not a powerful intervention. Most people do improve as a result of training, but the changes are neither extraordinary nor permanent' (Scogin, 1992, p. 269). This is hardly a glowing endorsement, and there is little indication as yet that cognitive training could serve a preventive function as regards development of dementia.

Recent work has begun to evaluate the effects of cognitive training with people meeting criteria for MCI. Rapp, Breenes, and Marsh (2002) reported an RCT comparing a 6-week memory training intervention with a no-treatment control condition. There were no significant differences between groups at the post-treatment assessment or at 6-month follow-up, although participants in the treatment group believed their memory had improved. At present, therefore, there is little to suggest that cognitive training is likely to be particularly beneficial for people with MCI, or to assist in preventing progression of MCI to dementia. However, as the evidence base is currently very small, it is hard to draw firm conclusions.

Despite the limited evidence for benefits of cognitive training for older people generally, and for people with mild cognitive impairments (variously defined and labelled), there has been a great deal of interest in the application of this approach for people with dementia, especially those in the mild to moderate stages. Cognitive training for people with dementia has been offered in various formats, including individual or group sessions, or as part of a wider intervention programme. Family members have some-times been involved, either joining in group sessions alongside the participants with dementia, or facilitating training in the home setting following a predefined programme and supported by therapist contact. Tasks may be presented in paper-and-pencil or computerised form, and range from abstract tasks such as learning word lists to analogues of everyday activities such as paying a bill and balancing a cheque book. Sometimes a range of difficulty levels are available within a standardised set of tasks, allowing selection of tasks according to ability. Outcome is usually assessed by comparing pre- and post-training scores on measures of impairment in the form of neuropsychological tests or cognitive screening tests. Because of the range of different modalities and the variation in domains targeted and specific tasks and methods used, it is hard to make clear comparisons across studies. For ease of understanding, therefore, I group the available studies into a number of strands for discussion: studies involving individual training sessions, including those using computerised training and those targeting activities of daily living (ADLs); studies in which family members deliver the intervention; studies involving group sessions; and studies in which cognitive training is combined with other approaches.

Individual cognitive training sessions have been evaluated in a number of studies. Beck, Heacock, Mercer, Thatcher, and Sparkman (1988) offered nursing home or hospital residents with mild or moderate AD or mixed dementia three half-hour sessions per week of individual cognitive training over 6 weeks, during which participants engaged in exercises aimed at improving attention, reading, concentration and memory. A control group received treatment as usual. No significant differences were found on cognitive test scores following treatment. Davis, Massman, and Doody (2001) compared a cognitive training intervention consisting of 5 weeks of weekly 60-minute sessions with a placebo therapy condition for people with AD. In the cognitive training sessions, participants were asked to learn face–name associations and use spaced retrieval to rehearse personal information. Performance in the trained group improved significantly compared with baseline on the specific areas trained, with better scores on recall of face–name associations and personal information, but neither the trained nor the control group showed any changes on standardised measures. The only difference between the groups following intervention was that the trained group did better on one attentional task, and there were no between-group differences in other cognitive test scores, depression or carer-rated quality of life. Clearly, one significant difference among a number of comparisons could be attributable to statistical error. While it is possible to demonstrate improvements on targeted tasks, there is no improvement in performance on tests measuring degree of impairment, and no indication that any observed gains translate into clinically meaningful benefits. Loewenstein, Acevedo, Czaja, and Duara (2004) compared 'cognitive rehabilitation training' with 'mental stimulation', delivered in 24 individual sessions over a 12- to 16-week period. The cognitive training involved practice on a range of standard tasks such as face–name association learning, giving change for a purchase and balancing a cheque book. The cognitive training group improved significantly on the trained tasks compared with the mental stimulation group, but there were no differences on standardised neuro-psychological tests. Participants in both groups reported significantly better subjective ratings of memory functioning after intervention, but informant ratings endorsed this only for the cognitive training group; there were no differences between the groups for ratings of depression, activities of daily living, or behaviour problems. Again, therefore, this study indicates that it is possible to show improvements on tasks that are specifically addressed in the intervention, but that in general these gains are not captured by standardised outcome measures, and the extent of any generalisation of gains to everyday life remains unclear.

Individual cognitive training using standardised computer packages has been explored in several studies (Butti, Buzzelli, Fiori, & Giaquinto, 1998). Schreiber and colleagues (Schreiber, Schweizer, Lutz, Kalveram, & Jaencke, 1999) engaged participants with mild to moderate dementia in 2 weeks of daily half-hour computerised cognitive training sessions involving practice on immediate and delayed recall tasks. This was compared with a social contact control group. Following training, the only observed between-group differences were that the training group performed significantly better than controls on immediate visual recall and on delayed route recall. Heiss, Kessler, Mielke, Szelies, and Herholz (1994) offered people with mild to moderate AD twice-weekly 60-minute computerised cognitive training sessions for a 26-week period. The training involved practice on memory, perceptual and motor tasks, and was compared with a social support placebo condition. No differences were found between the two groups. It appears, therefore, that computerised cognitive training has few benefits for people with early-stage dementia. This is consistent with the widespread critique of the value of computerised cognitive remediation following brain injury (Kapur, Glisky, & Wilson, 2004).

While these studies of individual training sessions targeted impaired aspects of memory along with other functions, some researchers have focused on maintaining or enhancing preserved aspects of memory by concentrating on procedural tasks. Zanetti et al. (2001) provided 3 weeks of daily, 1-hour procedural training sessions for day hospital clients with mild to moderate AD. Participants practised 13 basic and instrumental activities of daily living. Following intervention, the trained group performed the activities significantly faster than the controls. However, no attempt was made to evaluate whether any generalisation occurred to the real-life setting, and so the clinical significance of this finding remains unclear. A similar procedurally based approach was subsequently compared with cognitive training involving exercises intended to improve attention, memory, language and perceptual skills (Farina et al., 2002). At the end of training, both groups had improved significantly on ratings of functional living skills, and the procedural training group also scored significantly better on an attentional matrices task. There were no differences between the groups in ratings of ADL, memory and behaviour problems, or quality of life, or on cognitive tasks assessing memory or verbal fluency, or on MMSE score. The researchers concluded that procedural training was more beneficial than cognitive training focused on enhancing residual cognitive skills. However, given that there were few differences between the groups, this interpretation should perhaps be considered with caution. The main message from studies of procedural memory training seems to be that training on procedural tasks improves speed of execution, but whether this is practically useful remains to be seen. It may be that difficulties of initiation or independent completion are more salient in real-life situations.

In one series of studies, family members were engaged as co-therapists in providing individual cognitive training for people with mild to moderate AD within the home setting, supported by professional therapists (Quayhagen & Quayhagen, 2001; Quayhagen et al., 2000; Quayhagen, Quayhagen, Corbeil, Roth, & Rogers, 1995). The intervention was described by the researchers as 'cognitive stimulation' but appears from the descriptions available to fit the definition of cognitive training outlined above. Family members were asked to engage the person with dementia in an hour per day of practice on tasks addressing memory, problem-solving and conversational fluency, over an 8- or 12-week period. Outcomes were compared with those of participants in placebo and wait-list control conditions (Quayhagen et al., 1995). Significantly better outcomes were reported for the cognitive training group on general and non-verbal memory and verbal fluency, but not on verbal memory or problem-solving. Carer ratings of behaviour problems remained stable for the cognitive training group but declined for the other groups. In a further comparison between this programme, three other forms of psychosocial intervention and a wait-list control (Quayhagen et al., 2000), the cognitive training group were reported to perform significantly better on delayed memory, problem-solving and verbal fluency, and their carers had lower scores on a measure of depression than carers in the other conditions. While this study reports a range of positive outcomes, aggregation of measures makes the results very difficult to interpret.

Group interventions offer a range of possible benefits for the person with dementia, although these are not without associated difficulties (Scott & Clare, 2003). Groups offer the chance to make contact with others who are experiencing similar difficulties, leading to development of emotional and practical support. Group cognitive training interventions have taken a number of forms. In some cases, groups consist entirely of people with dementia, while in others, people with dementia participate together with their family caregivers. Specific cognitive training elements are augmented by group interaction and discussion, with opportunities to share ideas and to practise strategies.

Group cognitive training interventions have been offered in residential care- and community-based settings. Bernhardt, Maurer, and Frölich (2002) provided a group memory training intervention in a residential setting for people with mild to moderate dementia. This involved 1-hour sessions conducted twice-weekly for 6 weeks. Following intervention, the training group were rated as having improved cognitive functioning, while the control group were rated as having declined, although the differences between the groups were not significant. More commonly, group cognitive training interventions are offered to community-dwelling participants. Zarit, Zarit, and Reever (1982) provided group interventions for dyads consisting of the person with dementia and a family caregiver. The study compared didactic training classes, involving training in forming visual mental images and making associations, and problem-solving classes, involving discussion of practical steps that could be taken to manage everyday problems, with a wait-list control condition. Participant–carer dyads attended seven 90-minute sessions, held twice weekly. At the end of the intervention, participants in both training groups scored significantly better than controls on measures of recall. Participants in the didactic training group also showed additional learning within the sessions that was not captured in the post-intervention assessment. The effects on carers were less positive. Carers attending both types of class reported feeling more depressed at the end of the intervention, while feelings of burden and perceived severity of memory and behaviour problems did not improve. Outcomes for carers have not always been so negative, however, and other studies report more positive, or at least neutral, findings. Another group memory intervention for people with dementia and their spouses or other family carers (Moore, Kesslak, & Sandman, 1998; Moore, Sandman, McGrady, & Kesslak, 2001) involved a series of five weekly meetings in which dyads were encouraged to engage in practical memory tasks and to undertake novel, enjoyable activities together – the 'significant event' technique. Participants with dementia improved compared with baseline on measures of recall related to the trained tasks, and showed benefits from the significant event technique. In terms of standardised measures, participants with dementia improved on one of the cognitive measures used, the Kendrick digit copy task, and rated themselves as less depressed, following intervention. Carers did not report any increases in stress following participation, and their ratings of participants' memory functioning remained stable. Cahn-Weiner, Malloy, Rebok, and Ott (2003) compared a memory training programme involving six weekly small-group sessions with an educational and support programme. Following treatment, participants in the training group showed no significant benefits on neuropsychological test performance or on caregiver reports of activities of daily living and memory functioning compared with the control group.

Few studies have compared individual and group treatment. Koltai, Welsh-Bohmer, and Schmechel (1999) developed a 'memory and coping' programme that included cognitive training techniques, introduction of memory aids, and group discussion of coping strategies, with carers joining in for the last 10 to 15 minutes of each session where possible. This was offered in both individual (an average of six sessions) and group (five weekly 1-hour sessions) formats, allowing a comparison between the two. Neither intervention group improved significantly compared with a no-treatment control group, although sample sizes were small. No differences were found between the individual and group training conditions.

Some studies have combined cognitive training methods with other forms of psychosocial intervention in broad-based programmes. Focusing primarily on training and support for caregivers, Brodaty and Gresham (1989) offered a residential memory training programme either in conjunction with a carers' programme or on a 'respite' basis. Carer and patient outcomes were better where training was offered together with the carers' group. Working within a Memory Clinic setting, another group (Meier, Ermini-Fuenfschilling, & Zwick, 2000) offered weekly, hour-long, group memory training sessions for people with early-stage dementia as part of a 'milieu therapy' that includes advice and counselling, social activities, exercise, holidays, carer support and organisation of practical help. Patients were able to continue in the group for as long as needed, typically between 18 months and 3 years. In one study, patients receiving memory training showed significant benefits for mood and fluency, but not memory, while a comparison group who did not receive memory training declined. In a second study, scores on the MMSE and a quality of life measure remained stable for participants receiving memory training but declined for the control group. Arkin (2001) describes a community-based 'elder rehab' programme for people with mild to moderate Alzheimer's disease, comprising memory training, language activities, an exercise intervention, and partnered volunteering, as well as participation in other group events. Both rehabilitation and control groups improved significantly in mood, and the rehabilitation group scored significantly better on MMSE and some project-specific measures of memory and language, although not on any other standardised cognitive tests, and on measures of physical fitness. Werner (2000) describes a memory club that aimed to provide social and clinical support for older people with severe memory problems living in the community, meeting two or three times a week for 4 hours at a time. Sessions included practice on memory training exercises alongside other activities. In the context of an overall decrease in MMSE scores over the year, memory functioning was maintained, with significant improvements only in verbal fluency. However, there was no comparison group, the participants had memory difficulties for a range of reasons (61.3 per cent had a dementia diagnosis), and MMSE scores varied widely (range 0–29), so it is difficult to draw specific conclusions from these findings. Cognitive training has been offered alongside physical rehabilitation in medical settings, with the aim of reducing excess disability resulting from a hospital stay (Günther, Fuchs, Schett, Meise, & Rhomberg, 1991). Women who had an organically based memory impairment but were receiving rehabilitation for a physical condition participated in individual 45-minute cognitive training sessions daily over 9 days. Outcomes were compared with a control group who did not receive cognitive training. Participants in the training group improved significantly on the specific tasks targeted in the training, but on standardised measures of cognitive functioning they only differed from controls in object naming scores. Participants in the training group also scored better than controls on ratings of social behaviour, lethargy and affective disturbance, though not on cognitive impairment or somatic problems.

It has been suggested that cognitive training could potentiate the effects of pharmacological treatments for people with early-stage dementia (Newhouse, Potter, & Levin, 1997). Intuitively, this seems like a potentially valuable avenue to explore, and researchers have begun to consider the effects of combining individual cognitive training with medications that are thought to enhance cognitive functioning. Heiss et al. (1994) explored the effects of adding either pyritinol or phosphatidylserine to their computerised cognitive training intervention. These conditions were compared with cognitive training alone and a social support control condition (as discussed earlier). Across the range of measures assessed, there were few evident benefits, with no significant differences between groups at the 26-week point on any cognitive measure. Brinkman et al. (1982) compared the effects of lecithin (a cognitive enhancer), memory training and placebo for people with mild to moderate AD. Lecithin treatment did not produce any beneficial effects on cognitive functioning, but memory training did produce significant improvements on a memory task compared with placebo therapy. In some of the recent studies discussed above, all participants were receiving an optimal dose of an AChEI (Cahn-Weiner et al., 2003; Loewenstein et al., 2004). An Italian study (De Vreese, Belloi, Iacono, Finelli, & Neri, 1998; De Vreese, Neri, Fioravanti, Belloi, & Zanetti, 2001) compared the effects of 6 months treatment with acetylcholinesterase-inhibiting medication alone, 6 months treatment with medication coupled with 3 months cognitive training (CT) introduced after 3 months on medication (CT + AChEI), and 6 months placebo medication in an RCT with people who had a diagnosis of mild AD. Following intervention, the AChEI + CT group had significantly better scores on the MMSE and a measure of activities of daily living than the AChEI or placebo groups. Both AChEI and AChEI + CT groups improved significantly on cognitive test scores, with the greatest improvements observed for AChEI + CT. This again suggests useful possibilities for future developments.

Effectiveness

Early cognitive training studies led to the conclusion that this approach lacks efficacy and may also result in frustration or depression for participants with dementia and their family carers (Zarit et al., 1982), and this view was reflected in consensus treatment guidelines (G. W. Small et al., 1997). A number of subsequent reviews, while remaining cautions, suggested a somewhat more positive interpretation (Gatz et al., 1998). As noted above, various studies have reported at least some significant effects, usually in relation to specific tasks targeted in the training rather than on general measures of cognitive functioning. However, a Cochrane systematic review of randomised controlled trials (RCTs) of cognitive training found no evidence for clinical efficacy (Clare et al., 2003; Clare & Woods, in press).

The studies reviewed had a number of methodological limitations, many of which are shared by the wider set of studies in this area that were not included in the Cochrane review because they did not use randomised allocation. The use of neuropsychological tests as outcome measures is problematic for a number of reasons. First, improved performance on neuropsychological tests may require *transfer* of learning from trained tasks to other, related, tasks, and this would not necessarily be expected to occur unless the intervention had made some attempt to promote transfer of learning. For example, Davis et al. (2001) noted improvement on target tasks during training, but this was not captured by the outcome measures selected. Use of standardised neuropsychological tests as outcome measures in repeat testing sessions at relatively short intervals also fails to take account of the possibility that the results are contaminated by general practice effects, thus obscuring possible effects of specific treatments. Furthermore, where cognitive training is compared with other active treatments rather than placebo, this may mask potentially beneficial effects (Quayhagen et al., 2000). It remains unclear what constitutes the most appropriate format for a comparison condition, since it is difficult to design a 'placebo' condition that has face validity without activating and stimulating participants' cognitive resources (Quayhagen et al., 1995). Also relevant are the issues of limited statistical power resulting from small numbers, the possibility of statistical error accounting for observed significant effects where multiple analyses are conducted, the use of aggregated data from a range of different outcome measures in some analyses, the possible choice of insufficient frequency, intensity and duration of intervention, the absence of attempts to facilitate generalisation to everyday contexts, and the impact of heterogeneity among the participant group (Koltai et al., 2001). It is also important to note that there are few reports in this literature of any long-term follow-up to assess maintenance of any gains that were achieved as a result of intervention. To these methodological limitations it is necessary to add, of course, the general difficulties with conducting RCTs of psychosocial interventions – for example, it is impossible to blind participants to which condition they are in, and difficult to ensure complete blinding of researchers conducting assessments, since participants may describe their intervention experiences during follow-up assessment. Arguably, methods suited to trials of drugs and related interventions are not an ideal means of evaluating the effects of psychological or rehabilitative approaches, and it is important to ensure that a range of evidence is sought and considered.

It seems unlikely that failure to demonstrate significant effects can be attributed solely to methodological limitations, and it is perhaps not surprising that cognitive training does not significantly improve performance on standardised measures of impairment. However, it is possible to demonstrate some training-specific improvements on target tasks; that is to say, there could be an effect at the level of disability or handicap. If this is the case, it is possible that there could be the potential, given appropriate support, for some generalisation to the context of everyday functioning. Unfortunately, in most cases the tasks used in cognitive training do not seem to have a great deal of relevance to everyday life. Some studies have taken daily living skills as their focus, but the emphasis has often been on speed and accuracy of completion in the experimental setting. There does now seem to be a welcome trend towards including analogues of real-life tasks or utilising personal information as practice material within cognitive training settings (Loewenstein et al., 2004). In general, however, although some tasks can be personalised to a degree, the cognitive training approach tends to allow little scope for adjustment to individual needs or for attention to emotional reactions or social issues. The standardised nature of cognitive training interventions may render them unmotivating for people with dementia, and some may be reluctant to engage because they fear their deficits will be highlighted. Standardised delivery formats may not fit with individual preferences. For example, in our own work (Scott & Clare, 2003) we have found that a considerable proportion of people with early-stage dementia are reluctant to attend groups focused on addressing memory problems, but prefer individual sessions. Similarly, we have found that while it is possible to introduce and encourage familiarity with using computers (Freeman, Clare, Savitch, Royan, Litherland, & Lindsay, 2005), this is not of interest to everyone. These limitations indicate the need for an individualised rehabilitative approach that directly addresses everyday, personally relevant difficulties in order to improve well-being and quality of life.

Cognitive rehabilitation

Person-centred models in dementia care emphasise the importance of valuing people with dementia and those who care for them, treating people as individuals, looking at the world from the perspective of the person with dementia, and providing a positive social environment in which the person living with dementia can experience relative well-being (Kitwood, 1997). This strongly suggests the need to focus on improving the way in which society as a whole regards and responds to people with dementia, and especially how this is expressed through practices in the provision of care and support. As discussed above, genuine improvements in understanding and care might obviate the need for group therapies. A person with moderate to severe dementia, living in an environment that offers a range of opportunities for contact and the chance to engage in interesting activities, might have little need of group stimulation therapy or indeed of many of the pseudo-therapies described in the literature, such as 'pet therapy'. A person with early-stage dementia engaging actively in an internet-based self-help network, advocating for improved understanding of dementia, and continuing to experience a sense of self-worth and value may gain more benefit in this way than by engaging in regular practice of computer-based abstract cognitive tasks (Clare et al., in press). Even if these conditions were achieved, however, it is likely that some people would still benefit from assistance in tackling the difficulties and challenges engendered by living with dementia. In meeting this challenge, the person-centred philosophy implies a need for a more individualised approach that takes into account the perspective of the person with dementia and the personal, social and environmental context. Implicit in this is the value of selecting a focus that is directly relevant to everyday life and meaningful for the individual in terms of improving well-being. Interventions can then be targeted appropriately for each individual, depending on a careful assessment of psychological and social factors as well as neuropsychological profiles.

One example of a neuropsychologically based intervention drawing on very different principles and assumptions from cognitive training is self-maintenance therapy (*Selbsterhaltungstherapie*; Romero, 2004; Romero & Eder, 1992; Romero & Wenz, 2001). This approach, based on systemic, social cognitive and neuropsychological theory, aims to stabilise both the self and the social network to maximise well-being and support functioning for the person with dementia and the carer. It incorporates four elements: self-related knowledge training, psychotherapeutic support, encouraging satisfying everyday activities, and encouraging validating communication in caregiving. Self-related knowledge is the focus of the specific cognition-based element of the programme. The therapist assesses, in the context of understanding the full neuropsychological profile, which elements of biographical knowledge are most salient in supporting the person's sense of identity and personal continuity. These are then recorded using some form of external memory storage such as a CD-ROM or memory book, which is used as a basis for reviewing the selected components of self-relevant knowledge in a form of systematic reminiscence practice. Family members are engaged in carrying out this ongoing process of review together with the person who has dementia. Understanding of this self-relevant knowledge is used to help identify satisfying activities that are commensurate with current ability, or to adapt existing activities so that important interests can be continued. Findings from a cohort study indicated reductions in depression for both the person with dementia and the caregiver after engaging in a short-term residential treatment programme based on these principles (Romero & Wenz, 2001). This approach has clear parallels with the study of individualised activities referred to above (Cohen-Mansfield et al., 2006), although Cohen-Mansfield and colleagues do not appear to have drawn on it when designing their research.

During the past decade I have developed a model of cognitive rehabilitation for people with early-stage dementia, which integrates evidence and practice in dementia care with the concept and practice of neuropsychological or cognitive rehabilitation with brain-injured people (B. A. Wilson, 2002). In brain injury rehabilitation, understandings from neuropsychology, cognitive psychology and behavioural psychology are combined within a rehabilitation framework that takes account of personal context and emotional responses and the surrounding social networks, drawing also on perspectives from psychotherapy and systems theory (Prigatano, 1999b). Attention is paid to the way in which the person is adjusting and coping, and to emotional responses, and a family member or other carer is involved wherever possible. Interventions are usually conducted on an individual basis rather than in a group format, and where possible sessions take place in the person's home or usual setting, to promote relevance to daily life. Within this approach, intervention is aimed at enhancing participation and engagement (or countering disability and handicap) rather than reducing underlying impairment, and this determines the focus of both intervention and outcome evaluation (Wade, 2005).

I have already referred to issues of terminology in discussing cognition-focused interventions, and it is worthwhile to take a moment to consider the term 'cognitive rehabilitation' and its implications. The approach is described as 'cognitive' rather than 'neuropsychological' because, as noted above, it draws on a number of fields and not solely on neuropsychology. Cognitive rehabilitation requires an understanding of neuropsychological profiles, but also requires consideration of models of normal cognitive functioning and how these may be disrupted by injury or illness, of learning and behaviour change, of emotional responses to illness or injury, and of the effects of disability on the individual and surrounding family and social system. The term 'cognitive rehabilitation' certainly does not imply that the focus is *solely* on cognition. Sohlberg and Mateer (2001) comment that perhaps a more accurate term would be 'rehabilitation of individuals with cognitive deficits'.

Individualised cognitive rehabilitation interventions aim to tackle directly those difficulties considered most relevant by the person with dementia and his or her family members or supporters. Interventions are targeted specifically to the individual on the basis of the person's identified goals and needs and current neuropsychological profile. They target everyday situations in the real-life context, since there is no implicit assumption that changes instituted in one setting would necessarily be expected to generalise to another. Where neuropsychological tests are used as outcome measures, this is done not with the expectation of demonstrating generalised improvement, but rather in order to document the impact of any changes resulting from the trajectory of the disorder and thus assist in the evaluation of behavioural changes observed in the specific domains targeted in the intervention.

Goals for intervention are selected collaboratively wherever possible, with the intention of targeting areas in which changes in cognitive functioning are directly impacting on everyday life and consequently on well-being. Specific interventions to address these goals and promote their achievement are then designed, drawing on a range of models, methods and techniques. Interventions may involve a mixture of approaches aimed at restoration of function, implementation of compensatory strategies, or environmental modification, and the integration of these with approaches directed at emotional responses to impairment (Mateer, 2005). As I noted in Chapter 1, this rehabilitative approach can be applied at any stage of dementia, although the precise focus will necessarily differ as needs and priorities change over the course of the disorder, and may shade into a palliative care approach as end of life approaches. In the earlier, mild to moderate stages, goals are most likely to be related to overcoming practical difficulties, increasing engagement in activity, promoting adaptive behaviour and coping, reversing excess disability, combating depression and anxiety, or supporting key aspects of personal identity.

Conclusions

This review of the current evidence on cognition-focused interventions for people with dementia reminds us that people with dementia still show some capacity for learning and behaviour change, but this is often difficult to achieve. Therefore, it is important to make any attempts at intervention both personally relevant and practically useful, with an emphasis on producing clinically significant changes. It is often possible to identify within-session gains, or gains on tasks that have been specifically trained, in the absence of significant effects with standard outcome measures. We need to find ways of building on the gains that are possible. Since we cannot assume transfer and generalisation of gains to everyday life, we also need to find ways of ensuring that gains do translate into the everyday setting. If generalisation is difficult, then one option is to work in the setting where the behaviour needs to be applied – the person's own home – and to address tasks, issues or behaviours that are already a part of daily life. In so doing, it would be helpful to take a flexible approach that can identify and build on the coping strategies the person uses and adopt the methods the person finds most helpful. These observations have led to the development of the cognitive rehabilitation approach.

In the following chapters I discuss the application of this approach in detail, starting in Chapter 7 with an overview of assessment for cognitive rehabilitation. Subsequent chapters explore specific methods and techniques of memory rehabilitation that can be used in designing rehabilitative interventions for people with dementia, and describe the clinical implementation of cognitive rehabilitation.

7 Assessment for cognitive rehabilitation

Thorough assessment is the starting point for effective cognitive rehabilitation interventions, and continues as an integral part of the intervention process. This chapter briefly reviews diagnostic assessment of people with dementia before focusing in more detail on assessment for cognitive rehabilitation.

I emphasised in earlier chapters the value of gaining a sound understanding of the experience and capabilities of each individual for whom a cognitive rehabilitation approach may be relevant. Valuable information may be gained from a diagnostic assessment. However, information from the diagnostic assessment may be out of date, limited, or unavailable at the time when a cognitive rehabilitation approach is considered, and therefore additional information may be required. Here I outline the process of diagnostic assessment in dementia and then consider assessment for cognitive rehabilitation, discussing what information is needed and how this is used in planning an intervention.

Diagnostic assessment

Diagnostic assessment will aim to establish, first, whether dementia is present, or whether difficulties can be ascribed to 'normal' ageing, depression or other factors; and, second, if dementia is present, which sub-type of dementia is involved. A referral for assessment may sometimes be initiated by the individual concerned but often follows from the involvement of a family member or other health professional, or, in the case of younger persons, the identification of difficulties in the work environment. In some cases a referral may be supported by a report of the score obtained on a screening measure such as the Mini-Mental State Examination (MMSE; Folstein et al., 1975) that is indicative of likely cognitive difficulties. An overview of the process of neuropsychological assessment with older people and people who may have dementia can be found in Clare (in press) and a detailed discussion of neuropsychological assessment in relation to dementia can be found in Clare (2002a). For reviews of specific neuro-psychological tests, and information on availability of additional age-specific norms, see Spreen and Strauss (1998) and Lezak (1995).

Establishing a diagnosis of dementia requires a multidisciplinary approach. An understanding of the person's current circumstances and past experiences, education and occupation allows findings to be viewed in an appropriate context. Medical evaluation is necessary in order to rule out physical causes for observed cognitive impairment, such as heart disease, infection or vitamin deficiency; to evaluate relevant aspects of the family history, past medical history and current risk factors; and to identify any neurological or psychiatric symptoms. Neuroimaging may provide crucial evidence of focal brain lesions or vascular changes. The neuropsychological assessment provides a profile of cognitive function that helps to determine whether diagnostic criteria (for example, in the case of Alzheimer's disease, significant impairment in two domains of cognitive functioning) are met. Behavioural changes should also be considered, along with mood and well-being. Assessment of functional ability indicates the extent to which any cognitive changes impact on everyday life and what kinds of support may be required to carry out activities of daily living. A separate interview with an informant, such as a family member, provides additional information about any changes and their impact, as well as an indication of the degree of stress resulting from providing additional help and care.

A comprehensive neuropsychological assessment would cover general cognitive functioning (both current and estimated optimal IQ), long-term memory (episodic, semantic and autobiographical), working memory, attention, executive function, language (expressive and receptive) and perception, drawing together a set of tests suited to the individual's age and ability level and taking account of any difficulties with mobility, hearing or vision. This provides a profile of both strengths and limitations, and indicates whether impairments are present and in which functions. Taken together with other aspects of the assessment, this profile can assist in determining a diagnosis. For example, evidence of significant impairment in both episodic long-term memory and executive function could indicate either Alzheimer's disease, vascular dementia, mixed Alzheimer's and vascular dementia, or dementia with Lewy bodies and would need to be considered alongside information about the onset and course of the difficulties and neuroimaging findings to arrive at the most appropriate diagnosis. In vascular dementia there is a history of stepwise rather than gradual progression, and neuroimaging should provide evidence of vascular damage. In dementia with Lewy bodies the picture includes fluctuations in cognitive functioning and presence of visual hallucinations. In Alzheimer's disease there is a gradual onset and progression, without the specific features of dementia with Lewy bodies, and neuroimaging results are often inconclusive, so that Alzheimer's is essentially a diagnosis of exclusion. In contrast, evidence of marked behavioural changes with relatively preserved performance on neuropsychological tests might indicate early-stage frontal dementia, while isolated, profound semantic memory loss characterises the early stages of semantic dementia. Reaching a diagnosis is not, of course, an end in itself, but prompts consideration of any possible avenues for intervention and of what kinds of support may be available. The neuropsychological profile again can help to indicate an appropriate way forward.

Assessment for cognitive rehabilitation

Thorough assessment is the starting point for any cognitive rehabilitation intervention. In some cases much of the necessary information may be provided by a diagnostic assessment, leading to consideration of intervention strategies. It is important to note, however, that a specific diagnosis, as such, is not an essential prerequisite for cognitive rehabilitation, although it may provide some helpful guidance. What is more important is a formulation of the cognitive difficulties in relation to other psychological and social factors. Similarly, it is not essential for the person with dementia to have been informed of the diagnosis or to show explicit awareness of the diagnosis. Practice in relation to giving a diagnosis is variable (Bamford et al., 2004), and where a diagnosis is given, individuals differ in ability and willingness to acknowledge or accept it. Some acknowledgement of difficulties is, however, important. People cope in different ways, and if an individual is coping by maintaining that there are no significant changes in functioning and no problem areas, cognitive rehabilitation is probably not going to be the right approach at that time. In this kind of situation, it may be more useful to offer advice and support to family members, while remaining in contact with the person with dementia so as to build a relationship and be ready to offer support when coping strategies shift.

The most appropriate approach for any given individual will be determined through careful and comprehensive assessment. Initial assessment with neuropsychological tests and functional measures provides an indication of the person's current cognitive abilities that can be used to identify what the person can currently do and might be able to do given an appropriate intervention. This is invaluable in identifying realistic goals. Assessment of current coping strategies provides an indication of how the person prefers to respond and adjust, and thus helps to indicate how the intervention approach may best be adapted for the individual. Assessment of awareness and motivation for change permits an evaluation of the likely acceptability and success of the approach, and will help to shape the therapist's communication and interaction. Where people express limited awareness of the condition, and claim they do not have any difficulties, it may still be possible to work with them if the investment of more time spent in gaining their trust eventually allows relevant goals to be identified. If not, then providing additional support for the caregiver may be more effective than pursuing an individual rehabilitation approach. Assessment of mood may indicate that high levels of depression or anxiety need attention before any practical rehabilitation strategies are introduced. If there is a caregiver, assessment of the caregiver's well-being, needs and concerns may help to identify areas that could possibly be targeted in the intervention, and will also indicate the extent to which it is appropriate to involve the caregiver in any specific plans for carrying out the intervention. Finally, I noted in the previous chapter that individuals vary with regard to which learning strategies they find helpful, so assessing how new learning can best be facilitated will be important if the focus of rehabilitation is on supporting retained episodic memory capacity. Of course, assessment is an ongoing process that is likely to continue to some extent into the intervention phase, where plans may need to be adjusted to take account of the person's emerging reactions. In the following sections I discuss these different elements of assessment for cognitive rehabilitation in more detail.

Assessment of the neuropsychological profile

One important aim of an assessment is to achieve an understanding of the person's neuropsychological profile. This allows us to clarify the person's skills and retained abilities, as well as understanding areas of difficulty. From this, we can derive some specific pointers that can assist in devising appropriate interventions. As I suggested in Chapter 1, in establishing the neuropsychological profile for someone in the early stages of dementia, the following domains of cognitive functioning can be considered (Clare, 2002a):

- *General cognitive functioning.* Current IQ can be assessed with the Wechsler Abbreviated Scale of Intelligence (WASI; Wechsler, 1999a), Wechsler Adult Intelligence Scale (WAIS-III; Wechsler, 1999b), or Ravens Progressive Matrices (Raven, 1976, 1995). Estimated optimal level can be assessed with the National Adult Reading Test (NART; Nelson, 1982; Nelson & Willison, 1991) or Spot-the-Word Test (Baddeley, Emslie, & Nimmo-Smith, 1992).
- *Long-term memory – episodic, semantic, autobiographical and prospective.* It is useful to consider memory functions (learning, forgetting), modalities (visual, verbal, sensory), time periods affected (recent, remote), relation to onset of problems (anterograde, retrograde) and testing methods (recall vs recognition, immediate vs delayed recall). Episodic memory can be assessed via recall using subtests from the Wechsler Memory Scale (WMS-III; Wechsler, 1999c) and via recognition using the Recognition Memory Test (Warringon, 1984), Camden Memory Tests (Warrington, 1996), or Doors and People Test (Baddeley, Emslie, & Nimmo-Smith, 1994). Capacity for new episodic learning can be assessed using the WMS-III Paired Associate Learning, Doors and People Test, or California Verbal Learning Test (CVLT-II;

Delis, Kaplan, Cramer, & Ober, 2000). Semantic memory can be assessed using the Pyramids and Palm Trees Test (Howard & Patterson, 1992) and subtests from the Visual Object and Space Perception Battery (Warrington & James, 1991). Autobiographical memory can be assessed using the Autobiographical Memory Interview (Kopelman et al., 1990). Finally, everyday memory, including prospective memory, can be assessed with the Rivermead Behavioural Memory Test (RBMT-II; Wilson, Cockburn, & Baddeley, 2003).

- *Working memory* can be assessed with the digit span and visual span subtests of the WMS-III.
- *Attention* can be assessed with the Test of Everyday Attention (Robertson, Ward, Ridgeway, & Nimmo-Smith, 1994).
- *Executive function* (*abstraction, planning, organising, set-shifting, problem-solving*). Executive function can be assessed with subtests from the Behavioural Assessment of the Dysexecutive Syndrome (Wilson, Alderman, Burgess, Emslie, & Evans, 1996) or the Delis–Kaplan Executive Function System (D-KEFS; Delis et al., 2001), or via tasks such as the Trail-Making Test and Controlled Oral Word Association Test (both described in Spreen & Strauss, 1998).
- *Perception* – *object perception, spatial perception*. Perception can be assessed with the Visual Object and Space Perception Battery (Warrington & James, 1991).
- *Language* – *expressive and receptive*. Naming can be assessed using the Graded Naming Test (McKenna & Warringon, 1983). Comprehension can be evaluated with the Token Test (described in Spreen & Strauss, 1998).
- *Praxis and motor skills*. These can be evaluated with tasks such as the WAIS or WASI block design.

The Repeatable Battery for the Assessment of Neuropsychological Status (RBANS; Randolph, 1998) offers a relatively short battery sampling some of the above domains and can be useful where a brief assessment is required. For people with moderate to severe dementia, preserved areas of ability can be identified using the Severe Impairment Battery (Saxton, Swihart, McGonigle-Gibson, Miller, & Boller, 1990) or the RBMT-II (B. A. Wilson, Cockburn, et al., 2003) with adapted scoring as outlined by Cockburn and Keene (2001).

The neuropsychological assessment should provide information that is valuable in planning a cognitive rehabilitation intervention. Identifying areas of strength can assist in selecting realistic goals and identifying suitable strategies. For example, if memory performance is better in the visual than the verbal modality, visual stimuli, cues and strategies may be considered, and vice versa. If the intervention involves learning to name familiar people or objects, it is important to be sure that the ability to perceive and differentiate faces or objects is intact. If performance on tests of attention is poor, then it may be helpful to build in practice with attentional tasks to support the optimal use of remaining memory functioning. The extent to which new explicit learning is possible will influence the degree to which the intervention focuses on making the most of remaining explicit memory as opposed to developing compensatory strategies.

Assessment of everyday functioning

An assessment of everyday functioning will help to establish how the findings from the neuropsychological profile are related to performance of daily activities and tasks. For a review of functional assessment see Little (in press). Spending time with and observing the person in the home setting provides valuable information, and this can be supplemented with standardised measures of functional ability, such as the Allen Cognitive Level Screen (Allen, 2000). This will help to indicate how difficulties with memory, for example, translate into problems in the everyday setting, and what coping strategies the person employs. This in turn may highlight potential rehabilitation goals as well as possible barriers to successful intervention and ways in which the generalisation of gains to everyday life may be supported.

It is also useful to consider emotional well-being and perceived quality of life. Mood might be assessed using the Geriatric Depression Scale (Yesavage et al., 1983) or Hospital Anxiety and Depression Scale (Snaith & Zigmond, 1994). For people who are depressed or anxious, it may be advisable to begin with a focus on improving mood through practical behavioural strategies. Quality of life can be assessed using the Quality of Life in Alzheimer's Disease (QoL-AD; Logsdon, Gibbons, McCurry, & Teri, 1999). Where perceived quality of life is poor, this could suggest areas where rehabilitation goals could be identified, and where additional support might be appropriate. Understanding what kinds of activities the person may enjoy or dislike can offer valuable pointers to developing rehabilitation goals.

Assessment of coping style

One important aim of cognitive rehabilitation is to empower individuals by strengthening the sense of self and identity and enhancing feelings of being in control. Person-centred approaches in dementia care highlight the importance of individual identity and selfhood. Therefore, cognitive rehabilitation needs to be undertaken in a way that is sensitive to, and supportive of, individual coping, and this is why it is useful to start with an understanding of how people with early-stage dementia may attempt to adjust and cope with what is happening to them. As I discussed in Chapter 2, we can think of coping responses in early-stage dementia as being on a continuum (Clare, 2003a). At one end are 'self-maintaining' strategies aimed at keeping things the same as before and holding onto a past sense of self. At the other are 'self-adjusting' strategies aimed at trying to face head on the changes that are occurring and to integrate these into a developing sense of self. Individuals use a range of coping strategies that may be placed at different points along this continuum, and may draw on different strategies at different times and in different situations. Most, though, will show a preference for one or other type of approach, and therefore engage in either more self-maintaining or more self-adjusting strategies. Cognitive rehabilitation interventions can be designed to support either type of coping, and should ideally aim to be consistent with an individual's preferred coping style. Some people with early-stage dementia, especially those who adopt a self-adjusting coping style, may already be engaging in self-help activities, such as those provided in books about improving memory. This can be facilitated through provision of appropriate material or suggestions. Information about memory problems and how these may be tackled (Clare & Wilson, 1997) can be helpful for the individual and for family members, empowering them to identify their own solutions to specific issues or problems. Those who adopt a self-maintaining coping style may prefer to develop and implement simple practical strategies to avoid or deal better with problem situations.

Assessment of awareness

As I discussed in Chapter 3, the way in which the person perceives his or her difficulties is likely to be particularly important, and needs to be understood before embarking on an intervention plan. It has been shown that people who are able to express awareness of memory difficulties and their impact are likely to achieve better outcomes in cognitive rehabilitation interventions in the early stages of dementia (Clare et al., 2004). The best way to elicit this information is through discussion, but standardised measures can be used to assess the way in which the person views his or her condition and rates his or her memory functioning (Clare et al., 2002b). People who show limited awareness may do better with other approaches based more on social support, along with additional support for the family caregiver. I illustrate this with the contrasting examples of Frank and Martin and how they responded to the opportunity to participate in a cognitive rehabilitation intervention:

- Frank had only recently retired from his job as a carpenter, having been kept on despite increasing and very severe memory difficulties. He was very keen to try a rehabilitation intervention, and repeatedly asked me to persist in helping him and not give up. Consequently I spent quite some time visiting Frank and his wife to talk about their situation and what might be done to help. Despite his wish to have my help, Frank said repeatedly that he had always had a bad memory, that he did not see himself as having a problem, and that he felt it was quite appropriate to rely on his wife to remind him of things or provide him with information. Furthermore, he believed that if a problem could not be dealt with by medication then there was nothing to be done. He did try some memory strategies to help him access important information. We worked on his diary use, and he tried using visual cues by drawing small icons to represent visitors. He tried using a pager, but found it too intrusive. We tried introducing a calendar and memory board but Frank's young daughter, trying to be helpful, would alter the information rather than leaving this to Frank, so Frank lost interest. None of the strategies was very effective, because Frank really did lack awareness of the extent of his memory difficulties and the effects of these on his family, and to some extent Frank's wife was also somewhat unaware of the degree of impairment Frank was experiencing. What Frank seemed to need most of all was occupation and interaction, and the ideal solution seemed to be a voluntary work placement where he could use his carpentry skills, and where he could gain a sense that he was being productive and useful.

- Martin was not willing to accept the diagnosis of Alzheimer's that had been communicated to him, and insisted it had been a mistake. Nevertheless, he was acutely aware of his memory difficulties and he was especially concerned about continuing to manage his social commitments effectively. Martin's wife, in contrast, did not seem ready to acknowledge – at least to me – that he had any problems with his memory. Although Martin was a little wary of professionals because of the distress the diagnosis had caused him, he was keen to try the rehabilitation approach. He said his verbal memory had always been poor, and he had used strategies such as making associations in the past. His own evaluation of his current memory functioning was that his verbal memory had been affected to a much greater degree than his visual memory, which had always been stronger in any case. This provided a firm basis for working on memory strategies, which was very effective, and while doing so it was possible to explore the emotional and practical impact of the cognitive changes for Martin and his wife, and to discuss the sensitive issue of planning for the future.

As these examples illustrate, caregiver perceptions are also important.

Assessment of the family caregiver

If there is a family caregiver involved, it is useful to explore how he or she perceives the situation. It is also important to consider the needs of the caregiver and to assess whether he or she is experiencing high levels of caregiver burden (Zarit & Edwards, in press). Discussion with the caregiver may often be sufficient to establish how he or she views the situation, but if standardised measures are required, a number of appropriate ones are reviewed by Vitaliano, Young, and Russo (1991). The carer's own well-being and experience of the situation will influence the extent to which it is appropriate to involve him or her in the intervention. While some family members are keen to be involved, others see the involvement of the therapist as an opportunity to have a break from the demands and responsibilities of caregiving. This may also be related to the pre-existing quality of relationship, as well as to changes in the relationship resulting from the onset of dementia. Interventions can be adapted to take account of these preferences and any changes over time.

Conclusions

Assessment for cognitive rehabilitation involves gaining a clear understanding of the neuropsychological profile and the implications of this for practical intervention strategies, and then placing this in context by evaluating everyday functioning, coping style, awareness, and the social and interpersonal context, with consideration of the needs of the family caregiver where appropriate. Assessment does not necessarily end when the intervention begins, as a continual evaluation of progress may indicate the need for additional information or understanding in order to apply the approach in an effective way for the particular individual. Sometimes a number of strategies may need to be attempted, or additional components built in. Assessment and intervention are, therefore, not entirely separate. With this in mind, I go on to discuss the application of cognitive rehabilitation interventions in the next chapter.

8   Methods of memory rehabilitation

This chapter reviews a range of methods that can be used as the building-blocks of memory rehabilitation interventions. Methods that have been used to assist people with early-stage dementia in learning or relearning information include principles such as effortful processing and errorless learning, along with specific techniques such as spaced retrieval and mnemonic methods. The relevance and effectiveness of these methods are considered. Methods for maintenance or development of practical skills of everyday living are also discussed, along with methods of familiarising people with dementia with new memory aids and teaching the use of memory aids.

In Chapter 6, I described the development of a cognitive rehabilitation approach for people with early-stage Alzheimer's disease. In this approach, theoretical perspectives and practical techniques from neuropsychology, cognitive psychology, behavioural psychology and psychotherapy are combined within a rehabilitation framework that takes account of the personal context and surrounding social system. Within this approach intervention is aimed at disability and handicap rather than at impairment, and this determines the focus of assessment (as discussed in Chapter 7), intervention and outcome evaluation.

When applying this approach specifically to the rehabilitation of everyday difficulties arising from memory impairments for people with dementia, interventions typically fall into one of three categories. We may want to make the most of remaining aspects of memory functioning, or to enhance or maintain performance of everyday activities, or to develop the use of compensatory aids and strategies in order to reduce demands on memory. In devising interventions to address goals within each of these domains, it is possible to draw on a number of general principles and to select from a range of specific methods (Clare, 2003b). Here I review the principles and methods that apply to each of the three target categories, and describe examples of their application.

First, however, I recapitulate a number of basic features of effective interventions aimed at producing behavioural change in rehabilitation (see, for example, Sohlberg & Mateer, 2001). In summary:

- Goals and targets should be realistically achievable, and tasks should be broken down into small, manageable steps.
- Efforts should be invested in goals and targets that are relevant to daily life and are of importance to the individual – for example, attempts at new learning or relearning should focus on material the person wants and needs to know, rather than on abstract experimental tasks like word-list learning.
- At a practical level, ensuring that remembering is supported where possible by appropriate environmental cues is an obvious and simple intervention that can be applied in any situation.
- If the new learning or behaviour change needs to transfer to other similar tasks, or to generalise to different settings or situations, then attention must be given from the outset to considering how this might be achieved, and a transfer or generalisation phase should be incorporated into the intervention.

Facilitating remaining episodic memory functioning

Sometimes it is worthwhile to build on remaining episodic memory functioning to promote new learning, or the relearning of important information or associations. Experimental and clinical studies provide some guidance as to the kinds of support for learning that are likely to be helpful, in terms of both principles and specific strategies.

Guiding principles

Guiding principles that have been put forward for facilitating learning among people with dementia include dual cognitive support (Bäckman, 1992), effortful processing (Bird & Luszcz, 1993), errorless learning (Clare, Wilson, Breen, & Hodges, 1999), multimodal encoding and the use of subject-performed tasks (Karlsson, Backman, Herlitz, Nilsson, Winblad, & Osterlind, 1989).

Dual cognitive support

Early studies in which a variety of methods were used to encourage new learning produced few benefits or were interpreted negatively (see, for example, Yesavage, 1982; Zarit et al., 1982). Given that people with AD appear to have the potential to learn and retain information, this raises the question why many early experimental studies were unable to demonstrate effective facilitation of memory performance. This question has been addressed in the context of attempts to enhance performance by facilitating residual explicit memory functioning. AD affects not only episodic memory, but also the ability to make use of cognitive support for remembering (Bäckman, Josephsson, Herlitz, Stigsdotter, & Viitanen, 1991). People with AD, in contrast to healthy older adults, are impaired in their ability to use the kinds of methods that aid encoding and act as cues to facilitate retrieval. Studies that suggested that gains from memory training in AD were small or non-existent had generally required participants to use internal memory strategies such as imagery or the organisation of material, which in themselves require a considerable degree of cognitive effort and are particularly difficult for the person with AD to adopt, especially as dementia becomes more advanced. Therefore, it is important to consider how the strategies adopted can provide support at both encoding and retrieval – termed 'dual cognitive support' – and to try to ensure compatibility of cues at encoding and retrieval (Herlitz & Viitanen, 1991). Studies attempting to enhance performance by encouraging organisation of material and providing category cues have indicated that people with AD need more support than healthy older people to enhance memory, and that the level of support required to produce an improvement increases as a function of increasing severity of the disorder (Bäckman, 1992, 1996). The person may need more guidance in encoding the material, and more learning trials, as well as extra prompts and cues for retrieval, compared with healthy older adults, and the amount of help required will increase as the severity of dementia increases. Therefore, interventions should focus on achieving successful encoding, using methods that can also be carried over to generate corresponding ways of facilitating retrieval.

Error reduction during learning

The term 'errorless learning' (EL) was first used by Terrace (1963), who built on a range of teaching techniques developed in the animal learning literature, some of which had also been applied to human learners in studies of child development, in order to demonstrate that errorless stimulus fading methods were more effective than trial-and-error procedures in facilitating discrimination learning in pigeons. This concept was used to develop methods of teaching discriminations to children with learning disabilities (Sidman & Stoddard, 1967). Investigations of errorless learning later emerged in the field of brain injury rehabilitation (Glisky, Schacter, & Tulving, 1986), using methods that appeared to draw more closely on theories of programmed learning (Skinner, 1968) than on the original animal experiments.

Studies applying the principle of preventing errors during learning to teach information or skills to people with brain injury (Baddeley & Wilson, 1994) have suggested that this approach leads to superior acquisition of domain-specific knowledge than trial and error, or 'errorful', learning. Errorless learning in this context is best regarded as a principle rather than a specific technique. Subsumed under the general principle of reducing errors within the learning period are a number of specific techniques that may produce errorless learning conditions. Perhaps paradigmatic are 'study only' procedures where the participant is presented with the correct answer and asked to remember it or write it down (B. A. Wilson, Baddeley, Evans, & Shiel, 1994). Other techniques that may be applied to achieve error elimination or reduction include spaced retrieval (Landauer & Bjork, 1978) and the method of vanishing cues (Glisky et al., 1986), although with these methods it is possible that some errors may occur. A number of studies have found errorless learning more effective than errorful conditions when teaching new information and associations to people with brain injury (Hunkin, Squires, Parkin, & Tidy, 1998). However, benefits appear to be limited to certain kinds of task; for example, one study found that EL facilitated learning of face–name associations but not learning of routes or practical routines (Evans et al., 2000). Jones and Eayrs (1992) suggested that while errorless learning may work well for tasks requiring unvarying and straightforward responses, it is less effective than trial-and-error methods in facilitating acquisition of complex information or real-world skills.

Initial studies using EL principles with people who have dementia suggested that this approach can facilitate learning or relearning of information, associations and routines (Clare et al., 1999). However, there remains a need for robust direct comparisons of errorless and trial-and-error learning with this group. Additionally, there is a need to distinguish clearly between *new learning* of associations, information or skills and *relearning* of previously known associations, information, or skills, as these may require different approaches for maximum benefit. Some studies of EL in dementia have combined a number of specific techniques (e.g. mnemonic strategies, vanishing cues and spaced retrieval), making it difficult to ascertain the relative efficacy of each strategy. A study with people who had Korsakoff's dementia (Komatsu, Mimura, Kato, Wakamatsu, & Kashima, 2000) compared four methods of learning that the researchers classified as varying along the dimensions of error and effort. Errorless (paired associate and vanishing cues) conditions were superior to effortful (target selection and initial letter) conditions. Application of a similar paradigm with people who have AD, however, found no advantage for errorless learning methods over errorful methods when teaching either novel or previously familiar face–name associations to people with early-stage dementia – all methods were effective in facilitating learning, with best results achieved for previously familiar rather than novel items (Dunn, 2003; Dunn & Clare, in press). There was considerable individual variability among the participants as to which learning methods were most helpful. Haslam, Gilroy, Black, and Beesley (2006) similarly found that, while some individuals with early-stage dementia benefited to a degree from EL, others showed no benefits of EL.

Effortful processing

Other parameters may, therefore, be more important when considering the efficacy of learning methods. Clare and Wilson (2004) compared four specific errorless techniques in a single-case experimental design and concluded that those that were considered to be more effortful, requiring more active processing of the associations, were the most beneficial. Dunn and Clare (in press) found that high-effort conditions were significantly more effective than low-effort conditions in facilitating cued recall of novel associations, while error-reduction had no effect. Other issues, such as the depth of processing and the degree of cognitive effort involved, may also affect the likelihood of subsequent recall (Craik & Lockhart, 1972; Squires, Hunkin, & Parkin, 1997). Recall is facilitated by engaging in semantic elaboration at encoding (Lipinska & Bäckman, 1997). There is evidence that self-generated cues are more effective than experimenter-provided cues in assisting recall in AD (Lipinska, Bäckman, Mantyla, & Viitanen, 1994). Perlmuter and Monty (1989) emphasise that personalising a task by allowing the participant to make choices about it increases perceived control and motivation, and consequently is likely to benefit performance.

Multimodal encoding

Enriched encoding that facilitates later recall may be achieved by involving multiple sensory modalities during learning (Karlsson et al., 1989). Providing auditory and olfactory sensory cues to accompany the demonstration of an action sequence was found to improve subsequent recall of the action sequence (Rusted, Marsh, Bledski, & Sheppard, 1997).

Specific strategies

A range of specific strategies, both verbal and non-verbal, can be applied within the parameters of the guiding principles outlined above in order to facilitate learning and memory performance for people with dementia. Some of the more complex and demanding strategies for facilitating memory performance, such as visual imagery mnemonics, chunking of information, the method of loci, the story method and initial letter cueing may prove too difficult for people with cognitive impairments, for example following brain injury (B. A. Wilson, 1995), or indeed for healthy older people. There is limited evidence for the success of strategies of this kind when used with people who have Alzheimer's disease, who are likely to have difficulty both in learning an explicit mnemonic strategy and in remembering to use it appropriately (Bäckman, 1992). In some cases, however, simple strategies may be implemented to great effect. A range of specific methods such as spaced retrieval (McKitrick & Camp, 1993), vanishing cues (Glisky et al., 1986), semantic elaboration (Bird & Luszcz, 1993) and simple visual mnemonic strategies (Hill, Evankovich, Sheikh, & Yesavage, 1987) have been used to facilitate learning or relearning of relevant information. There is some evidence that treatment gains can be maintained for considerable periods (Clare, Wilson, Carter, Hodges, & Adams, 2001), which is especially significant in the context of a progressive disorder.

Spaced retrieval

Spaced retrieval, sometimes termed 'expanding rehearsal', has been used extensively with people who have dementia. The act of retrieving an item of information is a powerful aid to subsequent retention in any circumstances. In addition, the time scheduling of retrieval attempts affects the degree to which benefits are observed as a result of retrieval practice. Most benefits accrue when test trials are spaced at gradually expanding intervals (Landauer & Bjork, 1978). This pattern of retrieval at expanding intervals may be viewed as a shaping procedure for successively approximating the goal of unaided recall after a long delay (Camp & Stevens, 1990).

Experimental studies have demonstrated that spaced retrieval can aid new learning in people with memory disorders following brain injury (Schacter, Rich, & Stampp, 1985). The method has been adapted for use in Alzheimer's disease (Camp, 1989), selecting very short retrieval intervals – typically the first interval is 15 or 30 seconds long, and the length is repeatedly doubled. A series of studies has demonstrated clear benefits of spaced retrieval in teaching face–name associations, object naming (Abrahams & Camp, 1993), memory for object location, and prospective memory assignments (Camp, 1989).

An important aspect of this strategy is that it is relatively simple, but nevertheless requires the participant to make the cognitive effort necessary to retrieve the target information. Spaced retrieval per se does not rule out the possibility of errors occurring, but in practice, because the initial recall intervals are kept very short, errors are rare and may be eliminated entirely. A further advantage of the expanding rehearsal method is that it can easily be used by caregivers, with back-up support from professionals as required (Camp, Bird, & Cherry, 2000).

Cueing

Provision of a relevant cue can aid retrieval, and methods that capitalise on this have been developed for use in teaching information and associations to people with cognitive impairments (Glisky et al., 1986) Although this method is usually referred to as the 'method of vanishing cues', various specific procedures have been described. In Glisky's original work (Glisky et al., 1986), participants with amnesic syndrome were taught computer-related vocabulary by presenting the word definition for 10 seconds, followed by the initial letter only with the remaining letters represented by hyphens. If the participant could not guess or remember the word within 10 seconds, the second letter was added and so on until the participant completed the word. Subsequent trials cued completion with an initial presentation consisting of one letter fewer than had been required in the previous trial, although if the participant did not give the correct word further letters were added. Thoene and Glisky (1995) used a similar method to teach face–name associations to a group of people with memory impairments, which included one person with AD. The participant was prompted to look at a photograph of a face and shown information about the profession of the individual depicted. Then the first name was presented without the last three letters, which were represented by hyphens. If the participant could not guess the name, letters were added at the rate of one every 7 seconds until a correct response was given. The initial presentation on each subsequent trial consisted of one letter fewer than had been required on the previous trial. Riley and Heaton (2000) term this procedure 'cueing with increasing assistance'. Other studies using a vanishing cues method have adopted a procedure of 'cueing with decreasing assistance' (Riley & Heaton, 2000), where the full word or name is presented initially and then on subsequent trials the number of cues is gradually reduced. Riley, Sotiriou, and Jaspal (2004) taught word lists to people with severe memory impairments following brain injury using a four-level decreasing assistance approach where first the full word, then the full word minus 1–2 letters, then the full word minus 2–4 letters, and finally the initial letter only were shown. An incorrect response resulted in a return to the previous level. While these procedures do produce benefits, it should be noted that Hunkin and Parkin (1995) found the vanishing cues method no more effective than rote learning for teaching computer-related vocabulary to people with brain injury, and Thoene and Glisky (1995) found that a mnemonic strategy using verbal elaboration and imagery was more effective for teaching face–name associations to people with memory impairment.

A similar method has been used in teaching names to people with dementia (Clare, Wilson, Carter, Gosses, Breen, & Hodges, 2000), with one letter fewer being shown on each trial until the name was freely recalled without a letter cue. This was termed 'vanishing cues' or 'cueing with decreasing assistance'. A simplified version of the increasing assistance method, termed 'forward cueing' or 'cueing with increasing assistance', was also attempted, in which the target first name was presented along with a set of hyphens representing the letters of the family name. If the participant could not give the correct response, the initial letter of the family name was added, and on subsequent trials the number of letters was gradually increased until the participant gave a correct response. After this the letter cues were reduced one by one over the remaining trials until the participant responded correctly when cued only by the first name. Vanishing cues and forward cueing were directly compared in one single-case study (Clare, Wilson, Carter, & Hodges, 2003), where forward cueing was found to be more effective than vanishing cues, and to produce similar benefits to spaced retrieval and to a mnemonic strategy. However, in another recent study (Dunn & Clare, in press) we found no significant differences between forward cueing and vanishing cues, or between these and other learning strategies.

Mnemonics

Simple mnemonic strategies can be beneficial for some people with dementia. One report of successful use of a mnemonic strategy (Hill et al., 1987) describes a single-case experiment in which a 66-year-old man with Alzheimer's was taught to use visual imagery to extend his retention interval for names associated with photographs of faces. In an attempt to replicate the findings in a case series of eight participants, which included seven people with Alzheimer's and one with vascular dementia (Bäckman et al., 1991), only one of the participants with Alzheimer's showed a similar level of training gains, and the remaining participants failed to benefit from training. The authors conclude that the generalisability of the approach appears limited, but comment that there might be a subgroup of people with Alzheimer's disease who respond well to this form of memory training. Subsequent studies have shown that combining a simple mnemonic strategy with other methods such as vanishing cues and expanding rehearsal can result in effective learning (Clare et al., 1999, 2000, 2001, 2002a). The mnemonic strategy involved linking a feature of the person's appearance with the sound of the name. In one single-case study (Clare, Wilson, et al., 2003), a man with early-stage AD learned the names of members of his support group using a mnemonic strategy combined with either expanding rehearsal or repeated presentation at regular intervals (varying this latter component had no effect). Accuracy of naming improved from 8 per cent at baseline to 91 per cent following intervention, and this level was maintained at follow-up 3 months later.

Semantic elaboration and processing

Bäckman and Herlitz (1996) argue that people will benefit more from cognitive support if it is possible to harness their existing knowledge to help with encoding and retrieval of new episodic information. People with AD have difficulties in using semantic knowledge as an aid for episodic memory spontaneously (Herlitz & Viitanen, 1991). However, people with early-stage AD can benefit from semantic support when this is provided both at encoding and at retrieval. For example, performance is facilitated when a semantic orienting task is used at encoding (e.g. categorising an apple as a fruit) followed by provision of category cues at retrieval (e.g. asking for recall of 'a kind of fruit'; Bird & Luszcz, 1991, 1993).

Subject-performed tasks

Action-based encoding can be considerably more beneficial than verbal encoding. If people with dementia enact a task at the time of encoding, as opposed to simply receiving verbal instruction, this can result in improved subsequent recall of that task (Bird & Kinsella, 1996). Use of subject-performed tasks (SPTs) can, therefore, have beneficial effects for people in the mild to moderate stages of dementia. Following the principle of dual cognitive support, it is essential to provide appropriate cues at the time of retrieval if the benefits of SPTs are to be observed (Hutton, Sheppard, Rusted, & Ratner, 1996). However, it should be noted that while SPTs can improve recall, they may have a negative effect on prospective memory; where SPTs are used to assist with encoding for tasks that need to be repeated later, the tasks themselves may be remembered better but parti-cipants are less likely to initiate them at the appropriate time (Rusted & Clare, 2004).

Applications

A series of six single-case studies in which goals for rehabilitation were identified by the person with dementia and his or her family member (Clare et al., 2000) involved either learning or relearning information such as names of individuals important in the person's social circle, or learning to use a memory aid as an alternative to repetitive questioning of the spouse. The interventions adopted an errorless learning paradigm that incorporated techniques of known efficacy such as spaced retrieval or fading cues, as appropriate to the individual goal. Significant improvements on targeted goals were achieved in five out of six cases, with good long-term main-tenance over the following 6 to 9 months. A detailed report of one of these cases (Clare et al., 1999) demonstrated effective learning of names that the participant wished to know using a combination of mnemonics, vanishing cues and expanding rehearsal. The gains were fully maintained at follow-up 9 months after the intervention. A further study evaluated forgetting over the subsequent 2 years and found that performance remained well above initial baseline levels 3 years after the end of the intervention (Clare et al., 2001). This successful approach to learning names of familiar people was subsequently replicated in a controlled, group study (Clare et al., 2002a). Another two case studies reported in further detail explored the feasibility of different techniques in isolation (Clare, Wilson, et al., 2003). Good results were obtained for mnemonics, expanding rehearsal and forward cueing strategies, with vanishing cues proving less effective, as noted above. This is in accordance with the findings of Thoene and Glisky (1995), which showed that visual imagery was a more effective strategy than vanishing cues for the acquisition of face–name associations in memory-impaired participants (the sample included one man with dementia). The authors argued that this was because the mnemonic strategy was able to optimise the use of residual explicit memory, in addition to encouraging deep levels of processing and the development of associations with existing knowledge.

As dementia progresses, there is likely to be more emphasis on addressing behavioural issues and on enhancing well-being through maintaining interaction and engagement. An understanding of the neuropsychological profile and the possibilities for new learning can be coupled with a behavioural approach that views behaviour as having a meaning or function rather than as a symptom. This provides a framework for generating creative but highly practical rehabilitative solutions where cognitive impairments appear to play a part in producing 'problem' behaviour. This framework has been used, for example, to teach people with mild to moderate dementia to associate a cue with an adaptive behaviour, or information affecting behaviour, as a means of reducing behaviours that are regarded as problematic, such as incontinence, obsessive toileting, sexual assault and violence (Bird, 2000, 2001). Cues are only useful if they are in some way meaningful to the person with dementia, and consequently teaching the association between the cue and the relevant information or behavioural response is central in this approach. Specific strategies employed include spaced retrieval and fading cues or prompts. Bird (2001) provides an example of a successful intervention. A woman with early-stage Alzheimer's disease had given away many possessions when she moved into residential care, but having forgotten this process she concluded that staff had stolen her belongings, and became exasperated when they denied it, which led staff to view her as 'paranoid' and to fear that she would become aggressive towards them. With the help of a relative, the resident was assisted in recalling something of the process of giving away her belongings. A list was made indicating where her favourite items had gone, which she signed, and this was made into a poster that she displayed on the wall of her room. She was taught to go to the poster each time she wondered about her belongings. This was achieved by asking questions such as 'what do you do when you worry about where your things have gone?' Any incorrect or 'don't know' responses triggered a sequence of additional cues. The retrieval interval was gradually expanded with the assistance of a staff member. The intervention was effective essentially because it provided a means of allaying the resident's anxiety, by associating the behaviour of seeking out and viewing the poster with the cue provided by the internal experience of anxious thoughts (Bird, 2001).

The evidence indicates that some approaches offer promise in facilitating residual long-term memory functioning, and that these approaches can be applied in a pragmatic way to address issues that are relevant and meaningful for people with dementia and those who care for them. There is clearly scope for further development of appropriate methods that may provide assistance for people with early-stage AD.

Facilitating procedural memory functioning

Attempts to optimise procedural memory functioning have focused on maintaining or restoring the ability to carry out selected activities of daily living independently.

Specific strategies

Action-based learning

People with dementia retain the ability to draw on action-based memory to carry out individual actions, activities of daily living, and procedural skills well into the course of dementia (Hutton et al., 1996). This observation has been used to develop interventions that can support this retained procedural memory, based on carrying out the action, skill or task in question. Some performance gains on everyday tasks have been reported for people with dementia (Bird & Kinsella, 1996).

Prompting and fading

Where the capacity to carry out a task or activity is retained, but performance is affected – for example because the person does not initiate the activity – prompting methods may be used to encourage performance. Development of a prompting schedule requires a task analysis that identifies the key stages in completing the task and the actions required by the person at each stage. Prompts may be verbal (e.g. 'now pick up your spoon') or physical (e.g. guiding the person's hand to the spoon and, if necessary, assisting the person to grasp it). Once an action is well established the prompts may be gradually withdrawn ('faded out'). Sometimes, where skill performance is compromised, modelling of the skill or task may be required prior to prompting (e.g. demonstrating how to pick up the spoon).

Application

A training method based on preserved procedural memory was used in a series of studies to promote ADL skills in people with mild-to-moderate Alzheimer's (Zanetti, Binetti, Magni, Rozzini, Bianchetti, & Trabucchi, 1997; Zanetti, Magni, Binetti, Bianchetti, & Trabucchi, 1994; Zanetti et al., 2001). Training involved comprehensive prompting, with subsequent fading out of prompts. Zanetti et al. (2001) reported a significant reduction in the time taken to complete trained tasks relative to comparable untrained tasks, although Zanetti et al. (1997) included performance on a set of non-trained tasks as a control and this condition also elicited a significant (although smaller) reduction in time taken to complete the untrained tasks. This suggests non-specific effects of participation. Josephsson, Bäckman,

Borell, Bernspang, Nygard, and Ronnberg (1993) evaluated individualised training programmes for activities of daily living and showed improvements in three out of four participants, although only one maintained the gains two months later. An important and innovative feature of this study was that tasks were selected that formed part of the participants' usual routine, and that the participants were motivated to carry out.

In some situations, rehabilitation of basic skills is an important focus. Camp et al. (1997) describe the application of Montessori activities, designed to build skills in a developmental sequence in young children, to dementia care. An example here might be reinstating the ability to feed oneself with a spoon through a sequence of tasks starting with scooping beads with a large scoop, and progressing through scooping rice, sand and eventually liquids with gradually smaller scoops, and so on until a spoon can be used to drink soup. Supporting basic skills in this way can help to maintain a sense of independence, control and dignity, and this kind of intervention clearly combats the development of excess disability.

These studies show that rehabilitation strategies aimed at facilitating procedural memory offer promise in enabling people with dementia to maintain their skills and level of independence. Again, this is an area that warrants further research.

External memory aids

Providing external support for remembering in the form of compensatory memory aids can help to reduce demands on impaired aspects of memory. Compensatory memory aids may provide cognitive support in various ways. They may serve to cue and prompt actions or retrieval of information, or they may function as an external memory store that is available for consultation, or they may support knowledge acquisition or utilisation (Kapur et al., 2004). In addition, memory aids can help to promote social engagement (Bourgeois, 1990) or to reduce anxiety (Bird, 2001). Simple memory aids such as a calendar or a checklist can be very effective. However, developing technology offers increasing opportunities for identification of ingenious aids to remembering and to continuing participation and engagement. Available electronic aids used in brain-injury rehabilitation include electronic organisers, alarm and reminder systems, specially designed telephones, interactive task guidance systems, and customised systems covering a range of functions (Kapur et al., 2004). For example, a paging device sending reminder messages via a central computer can support independent functioning for people with brain injury and, in some cases, can produce new learning that is maintained when the aid is withdrawn (B. A. Wilson, Emslie, Quirk, & Evans, 2001). Currently in development is a wearable camera, SenseCam, that keeps a digital record of events experienced by the wearer, taking photographs in response to triggers such as movement or changes in lighting as well as on a fixed 30-second schedule.

This record can later be reviewed using a PC-based viewer application in order to stimulate memory for the events in question. While this could serve as a retrospective memory aid for novel or significant events for any individual, its utility as a means of improving recent autobiographical memory in a participant with amnesia has recently been reported (S. Hodges et al., 2006). Using SenseCam, the participant was able to recall 90 per cent of recent, personally experienced events, compared with only 40 per cent in a written diary control condition.

Principles

Selection of external memory aids for people with dementia needs to be considered carefully. It is likely to be more helpful if the aid provides a clear prompt to the required action or takes the person as directly as possible to the required information. Generalised reminders such as an alarm or a buzzer may be useful in certain circumstances, but only if the association with the desired response is carefully taught (Bird, 2001). An alarm clock may act as a successful reminder that something needs to be done, but this is unlikely to be sufficient on its own, since the person may not be able to remember exactly what action is required. Ideally, the aid should serve as its own cue to prompt regular use – for example, a calendar or wipe-clean memory board on display on the wall provides an inherent reminder to encourage its use. If this is not possible, then use of the aid should be supported where possible by other environmental cues. Aids need to be acceptable to the individual, accessible, and easy to use.

People with dementia are unlikely to start to use new memory aids spontaneously, and usually need training in their use, especially where the aids are relatively more complex or unfamiliar. However, we all use external memory aids in one form or another – diaries, calendars, shopping lists, and so on – and many people who develop dementia will already be used to relying on external memory aids such as diaries and lists. It is helpful to build on this and to try to ensure that these aids are used to maximum effectiveness; for example, a diary with unstructured pages might be replaced by one that has appointment times listed, or a diary allowing only a small space for each day might be replaced with one that shows one day to a page, providing more room to write clearly.

As regards learning to use a memory aid, there are two aspects to consider. Where use of the aid is already within the person's behavioural repertoire, intervention will be focused on establishing more regular or more efficient use of the aid. In cases where new learning is required in order to use the aid, this needs to be addressed before its everyday use can be established. In general, it will be easier and more effective to introduce or adapt aids when the ability to make use of them is already within the person's repertoire.

Specific strategies

Strategies for establishing or improving use of a given memory aid are similar to those involved in assisting with general skills maintenance, and are likely to emphasise prompting and fading methods and action-based learning. Learning of new behavioural repertoires can also be encouraged using modelling techniques, errorless rehearsal of a sequence of instructions (B. A. Wilson et al., 1994), and prompting methods. Explicit knowledge of the aid and its purpose may not be required, but can be taught using any of the various strategies that are helpful for facilitating new episodic learning, if necessary.

Application

A number of studies with people who have AD have demonstrated improvements resulting from the use of various external memory aids or forms of environmental support. In some cases these improvements have been maintained after the support has been withdrawn, while in other cases ongoing support has been required. In an early example, Hanley (1986) trained a resident with moderate AD to use a diary in order to find details of personal information and to keep appointments. Active training led to improvements on an individualised personal orientation questionnaire and in the proportion of appointments kept. The improvements were not maintained once prompting was withdrawn. Another in-patient who was trained to use both a reality orientation (RO) board placed on the ward and a personal notebook showed improved scores on questionnaires assessing orientation and personal information. Again, active training was necessary to develop the use of the RO board and notebook; placing the board on the ward was not enough to ensure that it would be used. The patient learnt to use the board to find the answers to continually updated orientation information, and appeared to learn and retain the items of personal information through a process of correction and rehearsal. It is unclear to what extent the improvement was maintained.

Clare et al. (2000) employed a simple prompting and fading technique to teach Evelyn, a participant with AD, to use a calendar as an alternative to repetitively questioning her husband. This produced significant reductions in repetitive questioning, and gains were maintained at follow-up 3 months later. Evelyn, who was very aware of the difficulties caused by her need to ask questions repetitively, was relieved to have an alternative strategy, and her husband commented following this intervention that things were '100 per cent better'. There was evidence of generalisation since Evelyn and her husband were subsequently able to work together to apply a similar problem-solving approach to other everyday situations. The use of a memory aid helped Evelyn to feel more in control, reduced tensions, and promoted a solution-focused approach to new challenges.

Memory aids have also been used to enhance participation and engagement. Currently, members of the internet-based self-help group DASNI (described in Chapter 3) find that communicating via email and chat rooms provides a record of group activity that serves as a form of group memory (Clare et al., in press). Bourgeois (1990, 1991, 1992) evaluated the effectiveness of memory wallets containing photographs and pictures of personally relevant events and people in enhancing conversational ability in a small sample of participants with moderate AD. People with dementia engaged in daily practice conversations with their spouse caregivers, who trained them to use the wallets as a cue for making factual statements. The benefits were maintained at 6-week follow-up in the first study, and there was evidence of generalisation to novel utterances. The second study showed that benefits were still observed when the wallets were introduced without training for three individuals, and also reported maintenance of improvements for three individuals followed up after 30 months. This finding has been replicated with people who have severe dementia (McPherson, Furniss, Sdogati, Cesaroni, Tartaglini, & Lindesay, 2001). Memory wallets or memory books do not only benefit the person with dementia but also help care staff to learn about and engage with them (Woods et al., 1992). Aids of this kind can be especially helpful at times of transition, such as during the move into residential care.

There is some evidence, therefore, that the use of compensatory aids may be beneficial. In view of the likely benefits of providing external support for remembering, there is scope for adapting existing technology to meet the needs of people with cognitive impairments. In an early example (Kurlychek, 1983), a digital watch was set to beep every hour as a cue to prompt engagement in a predetermined activity. An experimental study (Oriani et al., 2003) demonstrated that an electronic memory aid that provides an alarm and a verbal reminder improved in-session performance on a prospective memory task, in contrast to a written list, which was not beneficial. Unfortunately, however, this was not adapted to an everyday setting. Mobile phones might be complex to use, especially for older people who are not familiar with them, but they could allow people with early-stage dementia to contact a family member if they got lost or if difficulties arose while they were out alone, and thus help maintain independence. Lekeu, Wojtasik, Van der Linden, and Salmon (2002) taught two individuals with early-stage AD to use a mobile phone to contact family members. First, spaced retrieval was used to teach the participants to turn the phone over and consult an instruction card pasted on the back. Then errorless prompting methods were used during practice sessions in which the participants made calls using the phone. Both participants met criteria for success, although the individual learning patterns were markedly different.

Use of technology is now being extended beyond the realm of specific memory aids by developing a range of mechanical, electronic and computer equipment that can support independent functioning. The telephone does often provide a lifeline for people with early-stage dementia, but repeated telephone calls can be very stressful for carers. Baruch, Downs, Baldwin, and Bruce (2004) describe the case of one woman with early-stage dementia who often became disoriented during the night and phoned family members in a state of distress. This was addressed by placing a computer screen in her bedroom and another in her living room that showed the time, a photograph of her son and, during the night, a moon shape on a dark blue background to signify night-time. During this time, between 10.30 pm and 7.30 am, the screen displayed a message in large font indicating that 'It is night-time: stay in bed'. A different message and background were displayed during the day. Each day the computer system updated itself through the phone system by contacting a remote computer where her son would enter specific messages and information for the day. This intervention was highly effective in promoting orientation and reducing confusion, and the night-time phone calls reduced to almost zero. For people with more severe dementia, Mihailidis, Barbenel, and Fernie (2004) describe COACH, a cognitive orthosis for assisting activities in the home. This computer tracking system unobtrusively observes the person during an activity such as hand washing and monitors progress, providing verbal prompts to instruct or remind the participant where necessary. The caregiver is alerted via a visual reminder on the device's graphical user interface when assistance is required. In a hand-washing task, both the number of stages completed without caregiver assistance and the overall number of steps completed increased when participants used the system. A range of products designed to promote independent functioning and/or enhance safety for people with dementia have been described (Orpwood, Bjørneby, Hagen, Maki, Faulkner, & Topo, 2004), including a tap monitor, a gas cooker monitor, an automatic nightlight, a locator for lost objects (frequently used objects are tagged, and this activates a sound when a picture of the object or associated button on a control panel is pressed), a picture phone (touching a picture of the person to be called initiates a call to that person's number), and a night and day electronic calendar (time of day – morning, day, evening, night – is displayed along with time and date). Orpwood et al. (2004) emphasise the importance of user involvement in product design and development, and identify a number of key design principles. The product should require no learning, look familiar, leave control with the user, reassure the user, and require as little interaction from the user as possible.

In considering the introduction of technology in dementia care, there has been a strong emphasis on using computer and video equipment and other technology to monitor and control the environment of the person with dementia in order to promote safety (Marshall, 1999). Kinney, Kart, Murdoch, and Conley (2004) describe the development and evaluation of a web-based monitoring system that uses cameras and sensors to detect activity by the person with dementia and sends text messages to the carer's mobile phone whenever particular sensors are triggered – for example, when the front door is opened, or in relation to power or water use. While there were some difficulties associated with the use of the system, carers generally evaluated it positively, and the authors suggest that this system may be a useful resource for some families where one member has dementia. This kind of approach has generated a useful debate about ethical issues in relation to the use of technology in this context (Bjørneby et al., 2004).

Rehabilitation for people with fronto-temporal dementia

Individualised rehabilitation interventions of the kind described in this chapter may also be useful for people who are in the early stages of some of the rarer forms of dementia, such as fronto-temporal dementia, although this area of work is still in its infancy.

In a single-case study of an individual with semantic dementia (temporal variant fronto-temporal dementia), repeated rehearsal of names of concepts or items paired with pictures or exemplars dramatically improved the participant's ability to produce previously hard to retrieve words (Graham, Patterson, Pratt, & Hodges, 2001). However, constant practice was needed to maintain this improvement, and performance dropped off very rapidly when the regular practice was stopped. A similar finding was reported by Frattali (2004). Snowden and Neary (2002) found evidence for reacquisition of lost vocabulary in two individuals with semantic dementia. These experiments showed, first, that learning was more effective where the participant retained some residual semantic knowledge of the item, object or concept to be learned; and, second, that learning was more effective when it was supported by the availability of temporal and spatial contextual information relevant to the person's daily life. Thus it was possible to learn and relearn factual information, and learning extended beyond verbal labels to associated relevant knowledge, suggesting that effective learning required the material to be linked with personal experience. Reilly, Martin, and Grossman (2005) suggested that rehabilitation, especially in the early stages of semantic dementia, should focus on maintenance of current vocabulary rather than relearning of forgotten vocabulary, using repetition combined with a multimodal approach involving manipulation, naming and rich description of objects. Bozeat, Patterson, and Hodges (2004) found that a participant with advanced semantic dementia could relearn the use of objects following a brief demonstration of their use, building on relatively more preserved procedural memory. The objects used for demonstration had to be the same as those used by the participant in everyday life in order for benefits to accrue. Performance declined slowly over time when practice was discontinued. The authors suggest that repeated practice should allow improved performance to be maintained over time. These findings, taken together, indicate some possible avenues for developing cognitive rehabilitation approaches aimed at maintaining knowledge and skills in people with semantic dementia.

In frontal dementia (frontal variant fronto-temporal dementia), the early stages are typically marked by changes in personality and social behaviour, rather than by impairments on neuropsychological testing. The resulting behavioural changes are often difficult for others to manage. Behavioural approaches used in neuropsychological rehabilitation (B. A. Wilson, Herbert, & Shiel, 2003) can be applied to address these problematic behaviours while maintaining the person's quality of life. An example is provided by Lough and Hodges (2002), who successfully addressed three problem behaviours through behavioural and environmental modification. The first behaviour, obsessional checking of car suspensions by rocking the vehicle, was modified by modelling a different approach involving visual inspection only during practice sessions. The second involved entering a female-only area on the ward despite a sign saying 'do not enter'. This was altered through an environmental modification in which the sign was amended to read 'turn around' and augmented by placing a strip of black-and-yellow security tape on the floor parallel with the door. The third arose when, following regular trips into town during which the participant followed a fixed itinerary, he caught the wrong bus and ended up lost and far from home. A mobile phone keypad was adapted to highlight how to receive, but not make, calls, and the participant was taught how to use the phone to receive calls. As his schedule was very predictable, this meant that his wife or a staff member could call him at the time he would be approaching the bus station and tell him which bus to catch.

Conclusions

In this chapter I have described some of the methods that form the basic building-blocks of memory rehabilitation, and how these have been applied to assist people with dementia. In terms of facilitating new learning or reactivation of previously familiar information, approaches that encourage active, effortful processing at the time of encoding are central. On the other hand, error reduction during learning does not seem to be as important as previously thought, at least for people with early-stage dementia. Rehabilitation efforts may also be directed at improving or maintaining practical everyday skills, at modifying problematic behaviours, and at the introduction and use of compensatory aids, an area with immense possibilities for further development.

There are strong arguments in favour of an individualised rehabilitative approach that directly addresses everyday, personally relevant difficulties in order to improve well-being and quality of life, rather than a standardised cognitive training approach. The strategies described here can be used to develop interventions aimed at the individual needs and goals of people with dementia of various types and at various stages. They form the basic elements of an individualised, goal-oriented intervention. Developing this kind of comprehensive individual intervention is the subject of the next chapter.

9 Clinical application of cognitive rehabilitation

This chapter explores how the various specific methods and techniques described in the previous chapter can be linked to form a comprehensive, individualised clinical intervention for the person with dementia. The concept of personal goal setting provides a central focus for applying the available techniques creatively in a way that has the potential to enhance the person's functioning in everyday life.

Cognitive rehabilitation for people with dementia is not primarily aiming to cure or reduce impairment at the neurological level. Instead, the aim is to work together to find ways of dealing with the problems that arise as a result of cognitive changes, so as to enable people to participate in inter-actions and engage in desired activities as best they can, within their own personal and social context. Rehabilitation is essentially a collaborative endeavour. Rehabilitation is not a treatment that can be 'done to' or 'administered to' someone, but an approach that engages the person and attempts to harness the person's own resources.

Goal setting

Both during and following assessment, individual goals are identified and a strategy for addressing these is devised, drawing on the techniques and methods of memory rehabilitation outlined in Chapter 8. This in turn is integrated within a comprehensive intervention plan that considers broader factors such as well-being and emotional responses. Here I discuss the process of setting goals and devising goal-oriented interventions. Since most of the research in this area has been conducted with people who have early-stage Alzheimer's disease, I focus in particular on this group.

Individualised cognitive rehabilitation interventions aim to tackle directly those difficulties considered most relevant by the person with dementia and his or her family members or supporters. A key strength of the cognitive rehabilitation approach is that interventions are individually tailored and focus directly on real, everyday situations and difficulties. The starting point involves identifying desired outcomes in a collaborative manner. This means that interventions focus on things that are causing concern to the person with dementia and his or her family members, and goals are relevant to improving quality of life. Goals target everyday situations in the real-life context, since there is no implicit assumption that changes instituted in one setting would necessarily be expected to generalise to another. Where the goals of the person with dementia and the family are markedly discrepant, careful and sensitive negotiation is required in order to try to reach a consensus that is acceptable to both parties, acknowledging the different emotional and practical needs of all involved. Specific interventions are then devised, based on an understanding of a profile of cognitive functioning that indicates both strengths and difficulties, and taking into account the person's preferred coping styles, other psychological and emotional needs, and support system. Interventions draw on a range of principles, methods and techniques, all with demonstrated efficacy for people with dementia

Selecting rehabilitation goals

Goals may be selected quite straightforwardly through discussion, but if a more structured format is required then an occupational therapy tool, such as the Canadian Occupational Performance Measure (Law, Baptiste, Carswell, McColl, Polatajko, & Pollock, 2005), can be used. This provides an overview of potentially relevant domains, and encourages a thorough approach to considering needs and goals in various areas of life. In selecting goals, the following steps can be employed:

1 Determine whether the person is able or willing to indicate something that he or she would like to be different.
2 Identify the area to focus on – for example, memory problems, family relationships, or participation in activities.
3 Identify the specific issue to focus on – for example, remembering the names of people met during an activity.
4 Establish the baseline level of performance.
5 Identify the goal expressed in clear behavioural terms.
6 Identify the level of performance that will indicate whether the goal is (a) wholly or (b) partially achieved.
7 Plan the intervention to address the goal, using appropriate methods and techniques.
8 Implement the intervention.
9 Monitor progress and adjust the intervention if necessary.
10 Evaluate the outcome of the intervention and decide on any further steps that may be needed.

Examples of personal rehabilitation goals chosen by participants in our recent studies include the following:

- Keeping track of events that happen during the day.
- Being able to find one's glasses.
- Managing medication independently.
- Being able to talk with family members about personal memories.
- Taking up writing again.
- Starting to read books again.
- Remembering names of people encountered at social activities, such as bridge partners, indoor bowls club members or lunch club attenders.
- Remembering personal information, such as the names of one's grandchildren, or details of shared experiences to use in conversation with family members.
- Remembering to turn off lights in the house.
- Knowing what day it is and what will be happening during the day.

To take one example, in an intervention conducted by Sue Evans, an occupational therapist working in my team, Malcolm, a 64-year-old retired salesman, wanted to start reading again. This was an activity that he had previously enjoyed and was important to him, but that he had stopped doing since being diagnosed with AD. Neuropsychological assessment indicated no problems with reading and understanding information, although memory was poor. Malcolm was keen to work on this area, was not depressed or anxious, and showed good awareness of his current functioning. Prior to starting cognitive rehabilitation, Malcolm was not reading at all. The identified goal was to read for 5 minutes every day. This was addressed by placing his book in a prominent place to serve as a cue to start reading, and Malcolm's wife also prompted him to read at a set time each day. At the end of his intervention, Malcolm was reading for more than 5 minutes each day. Figure 9.1 shows the goal attainment ratings made by Malcolm and his occupational therapist. The therapist correctly rated this goal as fully achieved. Malcolm's ratings of achievement and satisfaction were more modest, indicating that in his perception the goal was partially achieved. This seemed to be because his own expectations of himself had increased, and he was keen to be reading for longer periods of time; indeed, he saw himself as gradually progressing towards this aim.

Application of specific strategies

Once a goal has been established, strategies can then be identified from among those known to be feasible and to offer possible benefits, as outlined in Chapter 8, in order to address the chosen focus of intervention. The following two examples illustrate the process of devising a goal-oriented intervention.

Evelyn, a 68-year-old former shopkeeper, was introduced in the previous chapter. Intervention with Evelyn and her husband focused on finding alternatives to repetitive questioning, since it emerged during assessment

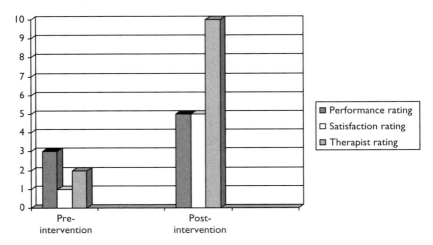

Figure 9.1 Goal attainment ratings – Malcolm.

that this was causing tensions and arguments (Clare et al., 2000). Figure 9.2a shows the goal devised for Evelyn, and Figure 9.2b summarises the results. Following intervention, Evelyn's goal was fully achieved. She was able to use a calendar to find out what day it was, and she maintained this skill at follow-up 3 months later. This very simple intervention caused her husband to remark that things were '100 per cent better'. Introducing Evelyn and her husband to a problem-solving, solution-oriented approach had additional benefits, as they were able to apply this to new situations. When Evelyn's washing machine broke down and a new one was installed, Evelyn thought she would not be able to learn how to use it, but following discussion her husband wrote a simple checklist of instructions that she was able to follow, and placed it on the wall by the machine. Evelyn found she could use the machine, but decided she could improve on the instructions, and replaced her husband's list with one she had written herself.

Alan, a 72-year-old retired builder who lived with his sister, was experiencing considerable memory difficulties (Clare et al., 1999, 2000) but otherwise continued to function quite well. Discussion with Alan and his sister revealed concerns about possible withdrawal from social activities. It emerged that Alan was embarrassed at being unable to remember names. Being a rather shy man, he liked to take on a specific role in a gathering. At his indoor bowls club, his preferred role was to call people out when it was their turn to bowl, and he was finding this increasingly difficult to maintain because of his trouble recalling names. This led him to feel he would rather not go to the meetings, but withdrawing would have meant he was isolated at home with only his sister for company. I agreed to teach Alan the names of the club members, using photographs taken for this purpose. Figure 9.3a shows the goal devised for Alan, Figure 9.3b describes the strategies that

(a) Identifying and addressing the goal

- ❑ Area: tension and arguments with husband (family relationships)
- ❑ Specific issue: tensions arise due to frequent repetitive questioning about what day it is (memory difficulty)
- ❑ Goal: to use a calendar to find out what day it is instead of asking husband
- ❑ Baseline: asking about 3 times a day (recorded by husband)
- ❑ Desired outcomes:
  wholly achieved – use a calendar regularly and ask no more than once every other day
  partially achieved – use a calendar most of the time and ask no more than once each day
- ❑ Intervention: build on retained procedural memory ability to teach use of calendar (specific techniques – prompting and fading)

(b) Results of the intervention (bl = baseline; post = post-intervention; fu = follow-up)

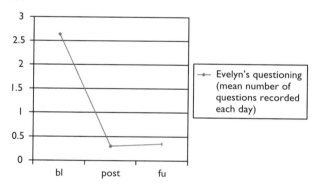

Figure 9.2 Goal setting and implementation – Evelyn.

were selected and how these were used in combination, and Figure 9.3c summarises the results. Following intervention, Alan was able to name his fellow club members accurately almost 100 per cent of the time, and maintained this ability with continued home practice up to 9 months later. When I then asked him to stop practising at home and just use his knowledge at the club, his naming ability remained stable over a further year, and then declined slowly over a third year to around 50 per cent, which was still significantly better than the 20 per cent he managed at initial baseline. At this point, he opted to resume regular practice with the photographs in order to improve his performance again. He continued to participate in his club, which was enjoyable for him and provided considerable relief to his sister.

(a) Identifying and addressing the goal

- ❑ Area: need to maintain confidence to support continued participation in a social activity group as in danger of withdrawing (participation in activities)
- ❑ Specific issue: wants to remember names of other group members to avoid embarrassment (memory difficulty)
- ❑ Goal: to remember names of key group members
- ❑ Baseline: names group members correctly 20% of the time
- ❑ Desired outcomes:
  wholly achieved – able to name group members correctly more than 90% of time during meetings
  partially achieved – able to name group members correctly more than 50% of time during meetings
- ❑ Intervention: build on residual explicit memory capacity to teach names from photographs using errorless learning principles (specific techniques – mnemonics, vanishing cues, expanding rehearsal), followed by generalisation at the group meetings

(b) Combining strategies to help Alan achieve his goal: intervention session plan

Item to be learned	Shown photograph, told name *Caroline*
Mnemonic	Discussed and agreed *Caroline with the curl*
Learning trials	Presentations with vanishing cues procedure Can you fill in her name: *CAROLIN_* *CAROLI_ _* *CAROL_ _ _* etc.
Consolidation	Recall to photograph with expanding rehearsal Tested after 30 s, 1 min , 2 min, 5 min, 10 min
Test	Free recall to photograph

(c) Results of the intervention (bl = baseline; post = post-intervention; fu = follow-up)

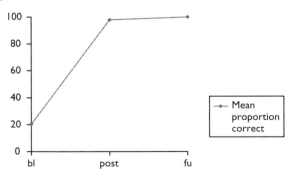

Figure 9.3 Goal setting and implementation – Alan.

While Evelyn's intervention relied on a single strategy of prompting and fading to encourage her to develop the habit of using her calendar, Alan's intervention involved combining several strategies to help him achieve his goal. He learned the names one at a time, following a procedure that began with identifying a simple mnemonic, then used a vanishing-cues procedure to elicit more and more of the name with each presentation of the photograph, after which an expanding rehearsal procedure encouraged him to recall the name on presentation of the photograph after gradually increasing intervals. He subsequently practised recalling the names at home, using the photographs as stimuli. For practical reasons, the learning sessions had to take place away from the club setting, in Alan's own home, but it was important for any new learning to generalise to the club setting. Therefore, once the face–name associations were well established, I accompanied Alan to the club on several occasions and asked him to match each photograph to a person and then recall the person's name.

Further examples come from a goal-oriented intervention conducted by assistant psychologist Susannah Cole under my guidance with six participants, all of whom had a diagnosis of early-stage AD. A modified goal attainment scaling procedure (Malec, 1999) was used to evaluate progress with personal rehabilitation goals. Using level of functioning at the beginning of the intervention as a baseline, participants were asked to rate their progress on a five-point scale where a rating of 0 indicated no improvement, a rating of 2 indicated 50 per cent goal attainment, and a rating of 4 indicated 100 per cent goal attainment. This was operationalised for each participant to give a concrete indication of what would constitute 50 per cent and 100 per cent improvement in relation to the given goal. The intention was to specify a level of improvement that would be realistically achievable with some effort and appropriate support, in the context of continuing memory difficulties. Ratings were made in each session, demonstrating progress over the course of the intervention, and the final session ratings were used as the key outcome measure for this element of the evaluation. Although each individual's goals differed, the goal attainment scaling process permits a comparison of the extent of goal attainment across participants. Table 9.1 provides brief background details about the six individuals, and below I briefly describe the goals that were selected and how they were addressed.

Elizabeth

Elizabeth wanted to remember important things that happened on a day-to-day basis. Working with her, a memory diary was designed to help Elizabeth keep track of events throughout the day. Every evening she was to review the activities of the day by looking through her memory sheet, and in this way she could check she had completed all her tasks. The operational definitions for this goal were as follows:

Table 9.1 Description of the participants

Measure	Elizabeth	Nigel	Ken	Frances	Richard	Nora
Age (years)	75	73	79	75	68	61
Education	Secondary	Secondary	Secondary	Degree	Secondary	Degree
Occupation	Clerical	Managerial	Media	Teaching	Business	Civil service
MMSE (max. 30)	27	28	24	23	26	23
QoL-AD (max. 52)	29	37	31	45	34	40
HADS Anxiety (max. 21)	7	5	3	6	10	5
HADS Depression (max. 21)	3	3	4	2	4	7
IADL (max. 14)	8	8	3	5	6	5

Notes:
MMSE: Mini-Mental State Examination (Folstein et al., 1975). Higher scores indicate better cognitive function.
QoL-AD: Quality of Life in Alzheimer's disease (Logsdon et al., 1999). Higher scores indicate better quality of life.
HADS: Hospital Anxiety and Depression Scale (Snaith & Zigmond, 1994). Higher scores indicate higher levels of anxiety or depression.
IADL: Instrumental Activities of Daily Living Scale (Lawton & Brody, 1969). Higher scores indicate greater independence.

- Achieved – Remembering important messages and activities done during the course of the day all of the time.
- Partially achieved – Remembering important messages all of the time.
- Not achieved – Forgetting important messages and activities.

Elizabeth enjoyed using the memory diary sheets and completed them in detail with information regarding her daily life. Each sheet was divided into sections relating to activities and appointments during that day, messages and other information, as well as specific problems. Writing things down became a habit for Elizabeth, and the amount of detail included on the sheets steadily increased over the 6 weeks. By the end of the 6 weeks Elizabeth felt she had made a partial improvement in reaching her goal as she was finding it useful to keep a log of what was going on, but still had instances where her memory failed. Elizabeth intended to continue using the sheets in the future with an aim to transferring the information into a large diary.

Nigel

- Goal 1. Nigel wanted to remember particular facts and events that were important to him. In order to assist with this, Nigel was helped to create a memory book containing important information, to which he could refer when necessary. Each page provided information on one topic, such as friends, family members, or holidays, and photographs and pictures were included as well as text. Nigel was prompted to refer to the book when necessary, until this habit became well established.
- Goal 2. The second goal was for Nigel to keep track of his glasses, which he was constantly losing. A designated place was identified as the place for him to keep his glasses, and he was prompted to always keep them in this particular location, until the habit became well established.

Ken

- Goal 1. Ken wanted to be able to remember what day it was and also the time sequence in which events had happened during the day. It was agreed that he would start to use a notebook to keep a detailed diary of his activities. He was encouraged to make a note of the date first thing in the morning by checking the daily newspaper, and to go over the events of the coming day by reviewing the plans for the day with his wife. This information was then transferred into his diary for reference throughout the day. His wife prompted him to use his diary rather than simply providing him with the answer.
- Goal 2. Ken wanted to take up writing again, an activity that had been important to him throughout his life and in his profession, but that he had dropped on receiving the diagnosis of AD. Building on the

previous goal, Ken was encouraged to use his notebook as a writing tool and to write about his experiences. Every week, he set himself a target for how much time he would spend writing each day. During the intervention, the amount of time spent writing was gradually increased from 5 minutes up to half an hour per day.

Frances

- Goal 1. Frances wanted to be able to find her glasses. This was tackled by identifying a special place on her bookshelf where she was to keep them. Frances's husband prompted her to put the glasses there and also to look for them there, until she had got firmly into the habit of using this strategy.
- Goal 2. Both Frances and her husband were frustrated by the extent to which she was reliant on him, so increasing her level of independence became an important goal. This was tackled by improving an existing notebook strategy that she used and making it much more organised and detailed. A new page was to be used for each day, on which activities planned and tasks to be completed were entered. Tasks and activities were ticked off once completed. Her husband prompted her to consult her book regularly and when required.

Richard

- Goal 1. Richard wanted to be able to remember to take his medication without needing to be reminded. A pill box was obtained, and Richard began to use it to manage his medication, prompted initially by his wife. This meant that once he had checked the date he could be sure whether or not he had taken his medication.
- Goal 2. Richard also wanted to be able to remember what day it was. This second problem was tackled by encouraging the use of a detailed diary. Richard worked with the therapist to devise effective ways of using the diary and was prompted by his wife to use it regularly until the habit became well established.

Nora

- Goal 1. Nora's first goal was to know what day it is and what the plans for the day were. This was tackled by asking her to use a detailed diary together with her husband. She was encouraged to orient to the day each morning and to write plans in the diary with the help of her husband, and then to review the day last thing at night and check that everything had been completed. She was to refer to the diary throughout the day and to write in extra information and messages.

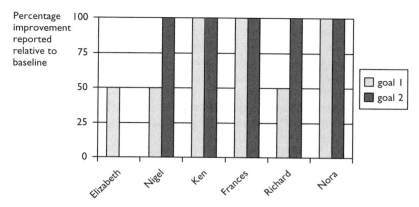

Figure 9.4 Goal attainment ratings for personal rehabilitation goals following intervention.

- Goal 2. The second goal involved keeping track of her glasses. A memory place was assigned, and this location was taught by means of a spaced retrieval intervention supplemented by prompting from her husband.

Figure 9.4 shows how these participants rated their own progress towards these goals after the final session. Out of a total of 11 goals, 8 were rated as fully achieved and 3 as partially (50 per cent) achieved, with an overall mean achievement rating of 80 per cent. As is evident, the goals were personal and individual, and different strategies were applied to achieve them, depending on the person's needs, preferences and context. Having considered the process of goal setting and goal-oriented intervention, I now consider how this kind of approach can be integrated within a comprehensive intervention plan.

Developing a comprehensive intervention plan

There is no single correct format for conducting a cognitive rehabilitation intervention. The whole point of this approach is that it is individually tailored to meet the specific needs of each person. The aim is to draw on the available evidence and guidance and on a detailed formulation of the individual's needs in order to develop a personalised approach and maximise the chances of success. Therefore, in outlining the possible format of clinical interventions in this area, it is perhaps most helpful to think in terms of areas and components that might usefully be covered. While goal-oriented approaches and the application of specific memory rehabilitation strategies form key elements in a cognitive rehabilitation intervention, and will almost certainly be included, they are not the whole story. At the neuropsychological level, for example, introduction of a range of memory strategies can allow the person to identify those that are most helpful and learn to apply these in different situations. Support for other aspects of cognition that may be affected, such as attention and concentration, may also be useful.

Cognitive rehabilitation involves engaging with the individual, and perhaps a family member or other carer, to tackle areas of difficulty. In the course of this endeavour, it is almost inevitable that emotional issues will come to the fore. Cognitive rehabilitation needs to include a focus on emotional responses, such as loss, anger, frustration, or anxiety, and to take into account the impact on the person's family or wider system, as well as identifying specific strategies for dealing with difficulties resulting from changes in memory or other cognitive domains. Throughout the rehabilitation process, there is scope for discussion of emotional responses, and specific attention can be paid to particular issues that are impacting on the intervention or on the person's general functioning, such as high levels of anxiety or embarrassment in social situations. Of course, this also offers an opportunity to build a good working relationship that provides the foundation for supporting the person and family over time as the dementia progresses. Incorporating a means of responding to emotions and feelings is discussed further in the next chapter.

While CR is an individually tailored approach, the focus is not solely at the individual level. Instead, the person with dementia is viewed within a family and social context. Needs and wishes of family carers and other key supporters are considered, first because these will impact on the person with dementia, second because they will influence the success or otherwise of the intervention, and finally because the well-being of carers is important in its own right. Therefore, alongside the identification of rehabilitation goals and associated strategies, it may be relevant to consider other cognitive needs and emotional responses, and to include and involve caregivers where possible.

While emphasising that CR needs to be applied individually in a creative way, and that there is no one single correct approach or method, it may be helpful to offer an example of a structured but flexible protocol used in our current intervention studies. The aim of developing this protocol was to allow for individual flexibility while also providing a structure that would allow outcomes for a group of participants to be compared with those of controls.

This protocol was designed to allow us to explore the efficacy of a cognitive rehabilitation intervention designed for use in real-life clinical settings with people recently diagnosed with early-stage Alzheimer's disease. The therapy is conducted by a psychologist or occupational therapist, with sessions taking place in participants' own homes. Outcome evaluation focuses on the impact of the intervention in terms of reducing disability.

The primary outcome measures are reported progress with personal rehabilitation goals, performance on associative learning tasks used within the intervention, and participants' self-ratings of quality of life.

The cognitive rehabilitation sessions take place for 1 hour a week over 8 weeks so that each participant receives eight sessions of therapy. Home practice is assigned between sessions. The aims of the intervention, for each participant, are as follows:

- To identify and work on one or two personal rehabilitation goals relevant to the person's everyday life, reflecting areas that are currently causing difficulty or worry, or are felt to require improvement. Goals might include, for example, developing and using a strategy to help remember important events during the day or to keep track of important personal effects, learning to use a memory aid such as a calendar or memory board, or learning and retaining personally relevant information. Once goals have been identified, an individual approach to addressing these is designed. To assist in identifying personal rehabilitation goals and formulating a plan for addressing these, participants are asked to complete a memory diary during the 1-week interval between sessions 1 and 2. The diary consists of 25 statements relating to particular everyday memory problems that may occur (e.g. forgetting where you have put something). Participants are asked to indicate next to each statement how often the problem happened each day for 7 days.
- To review the participant's use of memory aids and practical coping strategies, explore how it might be possible to build on these to make them more efficient, and consider the introduction of new aids or strategies where appropriate.
- To introduce techniques for learning new associations and information, provide practice in these, identify the person's preferred strategy, and encourage the wider application of this strategy in everyday life. The strategies used are simple verbal and visual mnemonics, semantic elaboration, vanishing cues and forward cueing, and expanding rehearsal. These are presented using face–name associations as an example of the kind of new learning or relearning that is relevant for everyday life. Where possible, personally relevant stimuli such as photographs of family or friends are used.
- To provide some practice in maintaining attention and concentration while processing information, drawing on rehabilitation methods devised for people with impairments of executive function (Levine et al., 2000).
- To explore the person's current ways of coping with stress and anxiety, suggest some ways of building on these, and provide relevant practice using simple relaxation techniques (Suhr, Anderson, & Tranel, 1999).

The participant's spouse or other family member or carer is invited to join the last 15 minutes of each session. This part of the session is devoted to reviewing the content of the session, agreeing the home practice to be undertaken in preparation for the next session, and discussing ways of facilitating progress with the personal rehabilitation goals.

An individualised written summary is given at the end of each session, detailing the areas covered and the particular techniques that have been used. The sheet also covers details of agreed practice to be undertaken before the next session. At the end of the intervention, the participant and carer receive a handout summarising the work done and detailing the participant's preferred strategies, along with suggested ways of extending their application in daily life.

Elizabeth, whose goal-oriented progress is described above, participated in a briefer, six-session version of this intervention protocol. She had experienced significant memory problems for 2 years prior to intervention. Despite a good score of 27 on the MMSE, detailed neuropsychological testing revealed significant memory impairment accompanied by word-finding difficulties and general cognitive decline. Elizabeth felt that her quality of life was fairly low, and she experienced a mild level of anxiety with occasional low mood. She was able to be moderately independent in terms of activities of daily living, and still drove her car. As well as making progress towards her goal of remembering daily events, Elizabeth responded well to all aspects of the intervention. Elizabeth particularly liked the mnemonic strategies, even though at first she found it quite a challenge to identify the distinctive features in each of the faces and relate them to the names in a meaningful way. She practised the homework tasks enthusiastically up to four or five times each day. Her preferred strategy was to make up a memorable sentence about the person, using either the verbal mnemonic or semantic elaboration technique. She found the visual mnemonic strategy more difficult as it was hard for her to create visual images, so she was encouraged to make use of the verbal strategy. Elizabeth did not feel that she had any specific attention or concentration problems, as she still felt able to concentrate while playing bridge and driving, and read at least one newspaper from beginning to end each day. She performed well on the attention tasks and was able to successfully sustain this performance when under time pressure. As she experienced mild levels of anxiety, the stress management component of the intervention focused on ways of dealing with this, and Elizabeth found the relaxation strategies helpful. At the start of the intervention Elizabeth had seemed somewhat apathetic and depressed, saying she felt there was not much point putting in any effort as she would only fail anyway. This changed as she began to use the mnemonic strategies and was successful in remembering the names and faces. She began to enjoy creating the associations and was able to make them humorous. At the end of the intervention Elizabeth remarked that she was feeling more positive regarding her difficulties and that she had learnt ways to help compensate.

Conclusions

Individual goal setting is a central component of cognitive rehabilitation, providing a focus for collaborative work on targets that are relevant to daily life. In this chapter I have shown that people with early-stage dementia can identify personal goals, that it is possible to devise effective interventions to address these, and that a range of methods and strategies can be applied to assist in achieving the identified goals. Goals will necessarily differ as dementia becomes more advanced, but the principle remains the same, and identification of goals that can improve well-being remains important throughout the course of dementia. For people with early-stage dementia, interventions have additionally focused on the introduction of techniques for making the most of remaining memory functioning, on the implementation of memory aids and practical strategies, on improving attention and concentration, and on finding ways of dealing with anxiety and promoting relaxation and coping. Including a family member or carer helps to ensure that progress is carried over and gains generalise beyond the sessions. This focus on emotional well-being and relationship points to the value of an holistic approach to cognitive rehabilitation, and this is the focus of the next and final chapter.

10 An holistic approach to neuropsychological rehabilitation in dementia

This chapter describes an holistic approach to neuropsychological rehabilitation for people with dementia. Interventions are considered in relation to psychotherapeutic and systemic perspectives. Service and policy contexts are briefly discussed, and methods for evaluating treatment outcome are considered. The chapter concludes by outlining current evidence for the efficacy of cognitive rehabilitation, and suggesting some future directions for the further development of this approach.

Neuropsychological rehabilitation can provide both a general framework for intervention and a means of tackling specific issues. As a general framework, it allows for a biopsychosocial formulation within which understanding and acknowledgement of the person's cognitive impairments are central. This means, for example, that explanations and advice can be provided to the person and his or her carers, helping them to make sense of some of their difficult and distressing experiences. Specific difficulties can be addressed using methods devised for people with dementia or adapted from those reported to be useful for people with brain injury or other forms of cognitive impairment. As will be evident from previous chapters, the way in which these two aspects of neuropsychological rehabilitation are implemented in practice varies according to the needs of the individual and the degree of severity of the dementia.

Theoretical models in cognitive neuropsychology allow the identification of specific patterns of impaired and preserved functions, while experimental and clinical evidence derived from learning theory provides a basis for developing appropriate intervention methods. This provides a sound basis for a behavioural approach (B. A. Wilson, Herbert, & Shiel, 2003). Prigatano (1997) argues, however, that while a behavioural approach is useful, it is necessary to take account of the patient's experiential world and emotional response to injury. Therefore, he advocates an holistic approach in which cognitive, emotional and motivational aspects of functioning are addressed together in an integrated manner, acknowledging the complex interactions between them (Prigatano, 1997, 1999b). This philosophy is equally applicable to cognitive rehabilitation in AD, and relates directly to the biopsychosocial framework and the disability model outlined in Chapter 2. As discussed in Chapters 3 and 4, cognitive rehabilitation in AD requires an understanding of the person's subjective experience, coping style, and current level of awareness in order to work in a way that encourages development of effective strategies and fosters personal adjustment and well-being for the person and his or her family carers. Involving caregivers in the intervention process is essential, and this requires sensitivity to issues in family and marital relationships that may impact on the work.

In developing a model for neuropsychological rehabilitation in dementia a range of factors need to be taken into account above and beyond the person's neuropsychological profile. Neuropsychological rehabilitation in dementia may be most beneficial if it is based on a psychotherapeutic framework, similar in concept to the 'holistic' approach in brain injury rehabilitation outlined by Prigatano (1999b). Emotional responses must be acknowledged, and coping strategies identified in order to build on existing resources. Equally, it is useful to take a systemic perspective, and to understand the context provided by the person's network of support and care. In many cases, caregivers will be essential allies if the rehabilitation process is to be effective. More broadly, it is important to consider the general impact of ageing and the ways in which this may affect the focus and process of rehabilitation (Crossley, in press), and to be sensitive to cultural, religious and linguistic diversity that may influence the way in which dementia is understood (Downs, Clare, & Mackenzie, 2006).

Psychotherapeutic and systemic perspectives

The nature of the psychotherapeutic context for rehabilitation will need to be further elaborated in future work, since the development of psychotherapeutic approaches for people who have AD is still in its early stages (Cheston, 1998). Ideas drawn from existing reports of psychotherapy in AD, from experience gained in conducting cognitive rehabilitation interventions, and from work in other areas such as brain injury, provide a preliminary framework.

Prigatano (1997, 1999a) emphasises the need to enter the phenomenological world of the cognitively impaired person and to begin from that perspective, rather than trying to describe the person's needs in terms of a pre-ordained model. Goals of therapy include facilitating psychological development, enabling the person to make appropriate decisions, and promoting adaptive coping. Cicerone (1991) notes the importance of addressing the person's beliefs about his or her situation during rehabilitation. Cognitive-behavioural approaches emphasise managing anxiety, dealing with catastrophic reactions, and reducing depression (Thompson, Wagner, Zeiss, & Gallagher, 1990). Maintaining the sense of self and personal identity is central to a number of intervention approaches described for people with early-stage AD, and is likely to be important in the context of cognitive rehabilitation. Sutton and Cheston (1997) advocate a narrative approach, in which the person with AD is able to tell his or her story and explore the meaning of what is happening within the context of an empathic relationship. Implementing cognitive rehabilitation for people with later-stage dementia requires particular attention to, and skill in, working with systems (Camp, 2001) since it will inevitably be necessary to consider the care team as well as the individual and family member.

Concepts from the application of therapeutic paradigms to the needs of older people remain relevant for people with early-stage dementia (Laidlaw, Thompson, Dick-Smith, & Gallagher-Thompson, 2003), although adaptations and adjustments should be considered. In working with people who have cognitive impairments, the structural elements of therapy require careful attention, and flexibility is essential (Hausman, 1992). The therapist's aim is to help the person learn in the most effective way, and the effects of memory difficulties can be mitigated to some degree by frequent sessions, repetition and elaboration of key issues, simplification of concepts and materials, provision of written summaries, and close involvement of a partner or significant other (Koder, 1998); additionally, the richness of interactions can be enhanced through gesture, expression and tone of voice. The working alliance may be developed by the therapist providing practical assistance (K. O'Brien & Prigatano, 1991), and discussion may take place while engaging in activities such as walking (Lewis, 1991a), or working on rehabilitation goals (Prigatano, 1999b). For some people, the provision of clear information will be an important element, but it is necessary to be sensitive to the indications the person provides about how much he or she wants to know (Husband, 1999).

As in brain-injury rehabilitation, it is helpful to try to appreciate the nature of any observed disturbances in self-awareness and to respond appropriately. Langer and Padrone (1992) suggest that, for any given person, 'not knowing' can operate at multiple levels, and that a person may both 'know' and 'not know' simultaneously, as for example in the distinction between implicit and explicit knowledge; in view of this, therapists could attempt to distinguish between the informational (knowledge-based), implicational (neurological) and integrational (psychological) elements of 'not knowing', and to respond to manifestations of each element in an appropriate way. Lewis (1991b) suggests, again with reference to brain-injury rehabilitation, that a key aim should be to help the person develop the capacity to support explicit knowledge of the situation.

For those people with early-stage AD who tend to adopt self-maintaining strategies, the aims of a therapeutic approach to cognitive rehabilitation may therefore include attempts at building trust and openness in order to provide a context in which the person feels safe to explore the meaning and impact of the situation and consider the possible usefulness of addressing practical difficulties. For people who tend to adopt more self-adjusting strategies, there is likely to be a more immediate focus on emotional issues, such as fear of disintegration and abandonment, shame, loss, anger and thoughts of suicide. The aims of therapeutic work will be to help the person negotiate the balance between hope and despair, and facilitate the development of a fighting spirit. Again, this can be approached in the context of a clearly focused practical intervention.

The focus of this psychotherapeutic approach to rehabilitation in dementia care will necessarily differ from that adopted with younger, brain-injured people. Although it has been suggested that people with early-stage AD should be confronted with their deficits so as to enhance awareness (Green et al., 1993), it is unlikely that many clinicians would support this view. Of course, some individuals with a self-adjusting coping style may be attempting to monitor their own performance and identify and correct errors, and it is possible that accurate feedback might assist in this process, helping the person to judge when tasks should not be undertaken or when help is required, and thus assisting in maintaining independence. However, for others, use of strategies such as minimisation is likely to be an adaptive way of reducing stress and managing threats to self, and it seems inappropriate that people with AD should necessarily be pushed into acknowledging deficits. Rather, it is important to understand the person's perspective and ways of coping, and to try to find ways of working together to support the person and his or her family. If lack of awareness suggests that cognitive rehabilitation is unlikely to be beneficial, then other approaches can be explored. Cognitive rehabilitation should not, therefore, be viewed as an isolated intervention. Instead, clinicians should be encouraged to view it as one element in a comprehensive, rehabilitation-oriented approach to early intervention.

This framework provides a basis for introducing attempts to facilitate memory performance or use of compensatory strategies, for matching methods and approaches to the person's needs, and for responding to emotional reactions that arise in the course of rehabilitation tasks. Further work will enable us to develop this approach in relation to people with early-stage AD in order to fully articulate a psychotherapeutic model of cognitive rehabilitation in AD that is sensitive to the emotional needs of the individual and family.

Service contexts

It is increasingly understood that care for people with dementia should ideally be 'person-centred'. That is, care should aim to meet people's psychological needs and affirm personhood, sense of self and social value (Brooker, 2004). The rehabilitative approach outlined in this book has the potential to contribute to person-centred care. It is based, first, on a collaborative relationship involving working together, and, second, on identifying individual goals, needs and preferences, with the choice of intervention strategies tailored to the individual, and it takes account of family relationships and the wider social context. This may fit more readily with some professional approaches and service settings than others.

How then can evidence and practice regarding neuropsychological rehabilitation be integrated within services for people with dementia? I believe there are three fundamental issues. First, there needs to be a belief that something can be done and that it is worthwhile to try. Second, there needs to be an understanding that what we are talking about is a set of principles, a way of thinking and approaching the situation, rather than a fixed, manualised intervention method. Third, closely related to this, there needs to be a willingness to be flexible. If these three conditions are met, then there is a good chance that a psychologist, occupational therapist or other health professional can successfully develop a rehabilitative approach that works within his or her own setting and share some of the necessary skills with other colleagues.

Many practitioners in dementia care are keen to identify and adopt new possibilities for intervention and new ways of supporting people with dementia. Although specialist expertise will sometimes be required, the principles of rehabilitation could be adopted widely and, rather than needing additional personnel, could be developed through a re-focusing of activity. This can apply to the range of provision, including Memory Clinics or specialist assessment centres, community-based services, hospital settings, and residential care homes. Consideration could be given to encouraging self-help based on rehabilitative principles. Elements of cognitive rehabilitation might, for example, be incorporated into user-led self-help initiatives (Pratt et al., 2005).

Memory Clinics have traditionally tended to focus on diagnosis with little emphasis given to intervention. However, many practitioners working within Memory Clinics do consider intervention and support as an important part of their remit. They are not satisfied with establishing the diagnosis and then waiting until impairments increase to the extent that full-time care is required. Additional emphasis on rehabilitation approaches might replace some of the time currently devoted to repeated assessment, or could be integrated into routine monitoring of medication effects. Provision of community-based mental health and support services, while often constrained by time and resources, does lend itself to the identification of clearly defined goals and attempts to address these, so a rehabilitative approach is also highly relevant here. Rehabilitative approaches could be adopted within hospital settings to promote recovery and assist in regaining independence. Similarly, rehabilitative approaches could provide a core element of basic care provision in day and residential care settings. For people with moderate to severe dementia, recent innovations have included intergenerational programming and Montessori-based activities in residential and day care contexts (Orsulic-Jeras, Judge, & Camp, 2000), while Bird

(2000) describes the application of cognitive rehabilitation methods to address problematic behaviour.

In clinical practice with people who have dementia, the methods and techniques of neuropsychological rehabilitation have so far largely been implemented through individual interventions. However, the relevant principles could perhaps be incorporated into other intervention formats as well, such as group work, which can be of benefit to some individuals with dementia and provides an opportunity to increase social contact (Scott & Clare, 2003), provided the emphasis on individually relevant goals and generalisable goals is retained.

Evaluating outcome

Rehabilitation in dementia care has tended to focus mainly on enabling the person to engage in desired activities and interactions within his or her own context, in order to enhance well-being for the individual and for his or her supporters or caregivers. Reducing underlying impairment has not usually been a primary goal. Instead, the emphasis is mainly on tackling activity limitation and participation restriction, including any excess disability. However, outcome measurement, while clearly needing to target those areas expected to be altered by the intervention, has often been conducted at the level of impairment, using alterations in performance on neuropsychological tests as the criterion by which efficacy is judged. Where neuropsychological tests are used as outcome measures, this should be done not with the expectation of demonstrating generalised improvement, but in order to document the impact of any changes resulting from the trajectory of the disorder (Gray & della Sala, 2004), and thus to assist in the evaluation of behavioural changes observed in the specific domains targeted in the intervention. Additionally, consideration must be given to practice effects where tests are repeated. Ideally, tests with parallel versions such as the Rivermead Behavioural Memory Test (B. A. Wilson, Cockburn, & Baddeley, 2003) or Test of Everyday Attention (Robertson et al., 1994) provide the best means of objective reassessment.

Evaluation of outcome will depend on the particular focus of intervention, and primary outcome measures should relate to the areas targeted in the intervention. Simple goal-attainment scaling procedures, as discussed in Chapter 9, can be used to evaluate progress with individual rehabilitation goals. Individualised measures can be developed in relation to tasks and goals. For example, if recall of names is a goal, then performance on the names can be compared for baseline and post-intervention assessment. If change in behaviour, such as, for example, using a diary is the goal, then informant ratings may be most useful. Changes in mood and perceived well-being following intervention can be captured through reassessment with standardised measures of mood and quality of life.

If outcomes are to be considered at a group level, then pre- and post-therapy assessments, and a longer-term follow-up, are required. If the aim is to present single-case data then it is essential to take repeated measurements and to gather data from each session in order to present a clear trajectory of change over time. The design of the intervention should be carefully considered to ensure that it permits clear identification of any change resulting from the intervention. Single-case designs are reviewed by Kazdin (1982, 1984), and a number of examples have been described in earlier chapters.

Clinical neuropsychologists and others engaging in cognitive rehabilitation are well placed to gather evidence regarding the efficacy of this approach in real-life clinical practice. Because cognitive rehabilitation is goal-oriented, it lends itself inherently to routine evaluation of outcome. The small effort involved in adding a few standardised outcome measures would be a worthwhile investment. Clinicians can benefit from immediate quantifiable feedback on the success of their interventions, and are in an ideal position to contribute useful evidence by collecting and publishing case series data.

Current evidence

Previous chapters have highlighted a number of specific methods that offer promise in facilitating memory functioning or promoting the development of compensatory behaviour. These include prompting and fading, expanding rehearsal, mnemonic or elaborative strategies, and effortful processing. I have argued that these can be applied to addressing individual, personally relevant rehabilitation goals as part of a comprehensive intervention plan conducted within a psychotherapeutic framework in order to maximise the chances of success.

There is a developing body of evidence to support the value of some forms of cognition-based intervention for people with early-stage AD. To date, practice guidelines have tended to pay little attention to the possibilities offered by cognition-based interventions (G. W. Small et al., 1997), but advice to practitioners will need to change in order to reflect the available findings. There is a strong theoretical and empirically derived rationale for the application of cognitive rehabilitation, and it has been argued here that an approach based on individually designed and individually targeted interventions tackling meaningful and relevant goals and situated within the context of a person-centred approach to care is likely to prove most beneficial. This will probably apply equally to people with forms of dementia other than AD. The limitations on memory rehabilitation even in early-stage AD must, however, be acknowledged (Bäckman, 1992). It is evident that the level of improvement achieved is generally modest. Individual variability is considerable; some people show no benefit from intervention even in the early stages of the disorder, while others with apparently greater difficulties may improve considerably, with factors such as awareness exerting an influence. Once again, this highlights the need to understand the phenomenological experience of the individual, and to target interventions accordingly.

There is at present no evidence to indicate whether memory rehabilitation has any long-term benefits in terms of reversing or arresting the progression of AD; at best, there may be some slowing in the progression of the disease. Nonetheless, in the context of a progressive condition such as AD, this is a worthwhile goal. A recent comprehensive review (De Vreese et al., 2001) concluded that there is sound evidence to support the effectiveness of this kind of individual approach to memory rehabilitation for people with early-stage dementia, while another review identified memory therapy as a 'probably efficacious treatment' (Gatz et al., 1998). However, a systematic review (Clare, Woods, et al., 2003) found no randomised controlled trials of individualised, goal-oriented cognitive rehabilitation and commented that at present the evidence-base is limited. Further, variability in response requires elucidation of the factors that may impact on outcome for a given individual. Therefore at present this approach can only be evaluated on the basis of currently available evidence from reports of single-case experimental designs and controlled group studies. These studies have demonstrated that people with early-stage dementia can to some extent, given appropriate support, learn or relearn important and personally relevant information, maintain this learning over time, and apply it in the everyday context; that they can develop compensatory strategies such as using a memory aid; and that they can maintain or enhance their functional skills in activities of daily living. Thus, indications from this evidence are cautiously positive.

Future directions

The evidence we currently have for cognitive rehabilitation shows we are justified in believing something can be done. Cognitive rehabilitation will not remove memory and cognitive problems, but it can make a considerable difference to quality of life and help maintain involvement and well-being.

The application of neuropsychological rehabilitation for people with progressive disorders such as dementia is a relatively recent development, and there are several issues that future research will need to address. There are a number of ways in which the quality and appropriateness of cognitive rehabilitation interventions for people with dementia might be enhanced. At a conceptual level it will be important to ensure that cognitive rehabilitation is clearly distinguished from related, but different, approaches such as reality orientation or memory training. A developing understanding of the processes involved in change at both biological and behavioural levels may allow a clearer focus in terms of impairment or disability, along with improved selection of outcome measures, and may in time provide further insights into the possibilities for slowing or preventing progression. At a practical level, it will be necessary to continue refining our knowledge of methods and techniques that may assist in achieving specific goals. Additionally, clarification of the parameters of successful intervention, in terms of intensity, duration, ongoing input to ensure maintenance, and factors that impact on outcome, will assist in developing more appropriate methods and targeting those individuals who are likely to benefit. Equally, it will be necessary to continue to situate neuropsychological rehabilitation within a coherent approach to supporting people with progressive disorders that reflects a genuinely biopsychosocial perspective and espouses the aims and values of person-centred care. In this regard, it will be important to further develop the 'holistic' framework for cognitive rehabilitation with people who have progressive disorders, ensuring that emotional needs and responses are attended to, and that the person is considered in the context of his or her social system. For people with early-stage dementia, a focus on development of 'user'-led initiatives, self-help, and mobilisation of community resources should be vigorously pursued.

Conclusions

The value of rehabilitation for people with dementia has recently been eloquently expressed by Morris Friedell, a retired professor of sociology who has a diagnosis of Alzheimer's disease and is a director of Dementia Advocacy and Support Network International (Friedell, 2003, 2005). This is how he described the situation in 1997:

> When I was diagnosed with Alzheimer's Disease . . . I started studying rehabilitation, at least tentatively. I had just assumed that, since neurologists and psychologists didn't mention it, and there were no books on rehabilitation for Alzheimer's patients, and rehabilitation institutes didn't invite them, there was nothing to be done. But one thing I learned when I was a sociological researcher is: just because no one is doing something, that doesn't mean it can't be done . . .
>
> (Friedell, 2006)

Since that time, a great deal has been achieved. The concept of cognitive rehabilitation has been established as relevant for people with dementia, and there is a growing body of evidence available. The first randomised controlled trials are now in progress. The first book on cognitive rehabilitation in dementia, an edited volume, was published in 2001 (Clare & Woods, 2001). Numerous presentations and training workshops have been given, and there has been tremendous interest in this approach from clinicians and researchers around the world.

Morris Friedell developed his own personal approach to rehabilitation, and found it offered many benefits:

I have come to believe that rehabilitation can have a powerful effect on a patient's quality of life, allowing him or her to regain much lost ground and then maintain it for years. What is needed is not some expensive institute, but some concepts which are not too complicated, the support of a good friend or psychotherapist, and lots of hope and hard work.

(Friedell, 2006)

In applying cognitive rehabilitation, we already have at our disposal a number of concepts and methods that are not too complicated, along with a developing understanding of how best to support people with dementia. This offers a strong incentive for developing the potential of cognitive rehabilitation as a means of helping people who are living with dementia.

The existing evidence provides a valuable basis for the further development of cognitive rehabilitation approaches for people with dementia. This approach offers a promising way forward that can take into account the needs and context of each person, and adapt the selection of goals and methods accordingly, with the potential for integration into a broader psychosocial intervention context. It is clear that there are grounds for optimism with regard to the possibilities offered by cognitive rehabilitation for people with dementia. Future research will undoubtedly refine and develop this approach further in an attempt to provide more effective assistance to people with dementia and their families.

References

Aalten, P., van Valen, E., Clare, L., Kenny, G., & Verhey, F. (2005). Awareness in dementia: A review of clinical correlates. *Aging and Mental Health, 9*, 414–422.

Abrahams, J. P., & Camp, C. J. (1993). Maintenance and generalisation of object naming training in anomia associated with degenerative dementia. *Clinical Gerontologist, 12*, 57–72.

Agnew, S. K., & Morris, R. G. (1998). The heterogeneity of anosognosia for memory impairment in Alzheimer's disease: A review of the literature and a proposed model. *Aging and Mental Health, 2*, 7–19.

Alladi, S., Arnold, R., Mitchell, J., Nestor, P. J., & Hodges, J. R. (2006). Mild cognitive impairment: Applicability of research criteria in a memory clinic and characterisation of cognitive profile. *Psychological Medicine, 36*, 507–515.

Allan, K. (2001). *Communication and consultation: Exploring ways for staff to involve people with dementia in developing services.* Bristol: The Policy Press.

Allen, C. (2000). *Allen Cognitive Level Screen* (4th ed.). Ormond Beach, FL: Allen Cognitive Levels.

American Psychiatric Association. (1995). *Diagnostic and statistical manual of mental disorders IV.* Washington, DC: American Psychiatric Association.

Anderson, S. W., & Tranel, D. (1989). Awareness of disease states following cerebral infarction, dementia and head trauma: Standardised assessment. *The Clinical Neuropsychologist, 3*, 327–339.

Andrén, S., & Elmståhl, S. (2005). Family caregivers' subjective experiences of satisfaction in dementia care: Aspects of burden, subjective health and sense of coherence. *Scandinavian Journal of Caring Sciences, 19*, 157–168.

Aneshensel, C. S., Pearlin, L. I., Mullan, J. T., Zarit, S. H., & Whitlatch, C. J. (1995). *Profiles in caregiving: The unexpected career.* San Diego, CA: Academic Press.

Arkin, S. M. (2001). Alzheimer rehabilitation by students: Interventions and outcomes. *Neuropsychological Rehabilitation, 11*, 273–317.

Auchus, A. P., Goldstein, F. C., Green, J., & Green, R. C. (1994). Unawareness of cognitive impairments in Alzheimer's disease. *Neuropsychiatry, Neuropsychology and Behavioral Neurology, 7*, 25–29.

Bäckman, L. (1992). Memory training and memory improvement in Alzheimer's disease: Rules and exceptions. *Acta Neurologica Scandinavica*, (Suppl. 139), 84–89.

Bäckman, L. (1996). Utilizing compensatory task conditions for episodic memory in Alzheimer's disease. *Acta Neurologica Scandinavica*, (Suppl. 165), 109–113.

Bäckman, L., & Herlitz, A. (1996). Knowledge and memory in Alzheimer's disease: A relationship that exists. In R. G. Morris (Ed.), *The cognitive neuropsychology of Alzheimer-type dementia*. Oxford: Oxford University Press.

Bäckman, L., Josephsson, S., Herlitz, A., Stigsdotter, A., & Viitanen, M. (1991). The generalisability of training gains in dementia: Effects of an imagery-based mnemonic on face–name retention duration. *Psychology and Aging, 6*, 489–492.

Baddeley, A. (1995). Working memory. In M. S. Gazzaniga (Ed.), *The cognitive neurosciences* (pp. 755–764). Cambridge, MA: MIT Press.

Baddeley, A. (2000). The episodic buffer: A new component of working memory? *Trends in Cognitive Sciences, 4*, 417–423.

Baddeley, A. D., Bressi, S., Della Sala, S., Logie, R., & Spinnler, H. (1991). The decline of working memory in Alzheimer's disease. *Brain, 114*, 2521–2542.

Baddeley, A. D., Emslie, H., & Nimmo-Smith, I. (1992). *Speed and capacity of language processing*. Bury St Edmunds: Thames Valley Test Company.

Baddeley, A. D., Emslie, H., & Nimmo-Smith, I. (1994). *Doors and People: A test of visual and verbal recall and recognition*. Bury St Edmunds: Thames Valley Test Company.

Baddeley, A. D., & Wilson, B. A. (1994). When implicit learning fails: Amnesia and the problem of error elimination. *Neuropsychologia, 32*, 53–68.

Ball, K., Berch, D. B., Helmers, K. F., Jobe, J. B., Leveck, M. D., Marsiske, M., et al. (2002). Effects of cognitive training interventions with older adults: A randomized controlled trial. *Journal of the American Medical Association, 288*, 2271–2281.

Bamford, C. (2001). Consulting older people with dementia: The value of different approaches. In C. Murphy, J. Killick, & K. Allan (Eds.), *Hearing the user's voice: Encouraging people with dementia to reflect on their experiences of services*. Stirling: Dementia Services Development Centre, University of Stirling.

Bamford, C., Lamont, S., Eccles, M., Robinson, L., May, C., & Bond, J. (2004). Disclosing a diagnosis of dementia: A systematic review. *International Journal of Geriatric Psychiatry, 19*, 151–169.

Baruch, J., Downs, M., Baldwin, C., & Bruce, E. (2004). A case study in the use of technology to reassure and support a person with dementia. *Dementia, 3*, 372–377.

Bauer, R. M., Tobias, B., & Valenstein, E. (1993). Amnesic disorders. In K. M. Heilman & E. Valenstein (Eds.), *Clinical neuropsychology* (3rd ed.). New York: Oxford University Press.

Beaumont, J. G., & Kenealy, P. M. (2005). Incidence and prevalence of the vegetative and minimally conscious states. *Neuropsychological Rehabilitation, 15*, 184–189.

Beck, C., Heacock, P., Mercer, S., Thatcher, R., & Sparkman, C. (1988). The impact of cognitive skills remediation training on persons with Alzheimer's disease or mixed dementia. *Journal of Geriatric Psychiatry, 21*, 73–88.

Becker, J. T., Lopez, O. L., & Butters, M. A. (1996). Episodic memory: Differential patterns of breakdown. In R. G. Morris (Ed.), *The cognitive neuropsychology of Alzheimer-type dementia*. Oxford: Oxford University Press.

Bender, M., Bauckham, P., & Norris, A. (1998). *The therapeutic purposes of reminiscence*. London: Sage.

Bernhardt, T., Maurer, K., & Frölich, L. (2002). Der Einfluss eines alltagsbezogenen kognitiven Trainings auf die Aufmerksamkeits- und Gedaechtnisleistung von

Personen mit Demenz [Influence of a memory training programme on attention and memory performance of patients with dementia]. *Zeitschrift fuer Gerontologie und Geriatrie, 35*, 32–38.

Bieliauskas, L. A. (1996). Practical approaches to ecological validity of neuropsychological measures in the elderly. In R. J. Sbordone & C. J. Long (Eds.), *Ecological validity of neuropsychological testing.* Delray Beach, FL: GR Press/St Lucie Press.

Bird, M. (2001). Behavioural difficulties and cued recall of adaptive behaviour in dementia: Experimental and clinical evidence. *Neuropsychological Rehabilitation, 11*, 357–375.

Bird, M., & Kinsella, G. (1996). Long-term cued recall of tasks in senile dementia. *Psychology and Aging, 11*, 45–56.

Bird, M., & Luszcz, M. (1991). Encoding specificity, depth of processing, and cued recall in Alzheimer's disease. *Journal of Clinical and Experimental Neuropsychology, 13*, 508–520.

Bird, M., & Luszcz, M. (1993). Enhancing memory performance in Alzheimer's disease: Acquisition assistance and cue effectiveness. *Journal of Clinical and Experimental Neuropsychology, 15*, 921–932.

Bird, M. (2000). Psychosocial rehabilitation for problems arising from cognitive deficits in dementia. In R. D. Hill, L. Bäckman, & A. S. Neely (Eds.), *Cognitive rehabilitation in old age.* Oxford: Oxford University Press.

Bjørneby, S., Topo, P., Cahill, S., Begley, E., Jones, K., Hagen, I., et al. (2004). Ethical considerations in the ENABLE project. *Dementia, 3*, 297–312.

Blacker, D., Albert, M. S., Bassett, S. S., Go, R. C. P., Harrell, L. E., & Folstein, M. F. (1994). Reliability and validity of NINCDS-ADRDA criteria for Alzheimer's disease. *Archives of Neurology, 51*, 1198–1204.

Bleathman, C., & Morton, I. (1994). Psychological treatments. In A. Burns & R. Levy (Eds.), *Dementia.* London: Chapman & Hall.

Bond, J., Coleman, P. G., & Peace, S. (1993). *Ageing in society* (2nd ed.). London: Sage.

Bourgeois, M. S. (1990). Enhancing conversation skills in patients with Alzheimer's disease using a prosthetic memory aid. *Journal of Applied Behavior Analysis, 23*, 29–42.

Bourgeois, M. S. (1991). Communication treatment for adults with dementia. *Journal of Speech and Hearing Research, 34*, 831–844.

Bourgeois, M. S. (1992). Evaluating memory wallets in conversations with persons with dementia. *Journal of Speech and Hearing Research, 35* (December), 1344–1357.

Bourgeois, M. S., Schulz, R., Burgio, L. D., & Beach, S. (2002). Skills training for spouses of patients with Alzheimer's disease: Outcomes of an intervention study. *Journal of Clinical Geropsychology, 8*, 53–73.

Bozeat, S., Patterson, K., & Hodges, J. R. (2004). Relearning object use in semantic dementia. *Neuropsychological Rehabilitation, 14*, 351–363.

Bradley, J. M., & Cafferty, T. P. (2001). Attachment among older adults: Current issues and directions for future research. *Attachment and Human Development, 3*, 200–221.

Brandt, J., & Rich, J. B. (1995). Memory disorders in the dementias. In A. D. Baddeley, B. A. Wilson, & F. N. Watts (Eds.), *Handbook of memory disorders.* Chichester: John Wiley & Sons Ltd.

Bråne, G., Karlsson, I., Kihlgren, M., & Norberg, A. (1989). Integrity-promoting care of demented nursing home patients: Psychological and biochemical changes. *International Journal of Geriatric Psychiatry, 4*, 165–172.

Brayne, C. (1994). How common are cognitive impairment and dementia? An epidemiological viewpoint. In F. A. Huppert, C. Brayne, & D. W. O'Connor (Eds.), *Dementia and normal aging*. Cambridge: Cambridge University Press.

Breuil, V., de Rotrou, J., Forette, F., Tortrat, D., Ganasia-Ganem, A., Frambourt, A., et al. (1994). Cognitive stimulation of patients with dementia: Preliminary results. *International Journal of Geriatric Psychiatry, 9*, 211–217.

Bright, P., & Kopelman, M. D. (2004). Remote memory in Alzheimer's disease. In R. G. Morris & J. T. Becker (Eds.), *Cognitive neuropsychology of Alzheimer's disease* (2nd ed.). Oxford: Oxford University Press.

Brinkman, S. D., Smith, R. C., Meyer, J. S., Vroulis, G., Shaw, T., Gordon, J., et al. (1982). Lecithin and memory training in suspected Alzheimer's disease. *Journals of Gerontology, 37*, 4–9.

Brodaty, H. (1992). Carers: Training informal carers. In T. Arie (Ed.), *Recent advances in psychogeriatrics* (Vol. 2). London: Churchill Livingstone.

Brodaty, H., Green, A., & Koschera, A. (2003). Meta-analysis of psychosocial interventions for caregivers of people with dementia. *Journal of the American Geriatrics Society, 51*, 657–664.

Brodaty, H., & Gresham, M. (1989). Effect of a training programme to reduce stress in carers of patients with dementia. *British Medical Journal, 299*, 1375–1379.

Brooker, D. (2004). What is person-centred care in dementia? *Reviews in Clinical Gerontology, 13*, 215–222.

Browne, C. J., & Shlosberg, E. (2005). Attachment behaviours and parent fixation in people with dementia: The role of cognitive functioning and pre-morbid attachment style. *Aging and Mental Health, 9*, 153–161.

Burgess, I. S., Wearden, J. H., Cox, T., & Rae, M. (1992). Operant conditioning with subjects suffering from dementia. *Behavioural Psychotherapy, 20*, 219–237.

Butti, G., Buzzelli, S., Fiori, M., & Giaquinto, S. (1998). Observations on mentally impaired elderly patients treated with THINKable, a computerized cognitive remediation program. *Archives of Gerontology and Geriatrics*, (Suppl. 6), 49–56.

Cahn-Weiner, D. A., Malloy, P. F., Rebok, G. W., & Ott, B. R. (2003). Results of a randomised placebo-controlled study of memory training for mildly impaired Alzheimer's disease patients. *Applied Neuropsychology, 10*, 215–223.

Camp, C. J. (1989). Facilitation of new learning in Alzheimer's disease. In G. Gilmore, P. Whitehouse, & M. Wykle (Eds.), *Memory and aging: Theory, research and practice*. New York: Springer.

Camp, C. J. (2001). From efficacy to effectiveness to diffusion: Making the transitions in dementia intervention research [Special issue]. *Neuropsychological Rehabilitation, 11*, 495–517.

Camp, C. J., Bird, M. J., & Cherry, K. E. (2000). Retrieval strategies as a rehabilitation aid for cognitive loss in pathological aging. In R. D. Hill, L. Bäckman, & A. S. Neely (Eds.), *Cognitive rehabilitation in old age*. Oxford: Oxford University Press.

Camp, C. J., Judge, K. S., Bye, C., Fox, K., Bowden, J., Bell, M., et al. (1997). An intergenerational program for persons with dementia using Montessori methods. *The Gerontologist, 37*, 688–692.

Camp, C. J., & Nasser, E. H. (2003). Psychological and nonpharmacological aspects of agitation and behavioral disorders in dementia: Assessment, intervention, and challenges to providing care. In P. A. Lichtenberg, D. L. Murman, & A. M. Mellow (Eds.), *Handbook of dementia*. Hoboken, NJ: John Wiley & Sons, Inc.

Camp, C. J., & Stevens, A. B. (1990). Spaced retrieval: A memory intervention for dementia of the Alzheimer's type (DAT). *Clinical Gerontologist, 10*, 58–61.

Caplan, B., & Shechter, J. (1987). Denial and depression in disabling illness. In B. Caplan (Ed.), *Rehabilitation psychology desk reference*. Rockville, MD: Aspen.

Cavanaugh, J. C., Dunn, N. J., Mowery, D., Feller, C., Niederehe, G., Fruge, E., et al. (1989). Problem-solving strategies in dementia patient–caregiver dyads. *The Gerontologist, 29*, 156–158.

Cheston, R. (1998). Psychotherapeutic work with people with dementia: A review of the literature. *British Journal of Medical Psychology, 71*, 211–231.

Cheston, R., Jones, K., & Gilliard, J. (2003). Group psychotherapy and people with dementia. *Aging and Mental Health, 7*, 452–461.

Christensen, H., Griffiths, K., MacKinnon, A., & Jacomb, P. (1997). A quantitative review of cognitive deficits in depression and Alzheimer-type dementia. *Journal of the International Neuropsychological Society, 3*, 631–651.

Christensen, H., Kopelman, M. D., Stanhope, N., Lorentz, L., & Owen, P. (1998). Rates of forgetting in Alzheimer dementia. *Neuropsychologia, 36*, 547–557.

Cicerone, K. D. (1991). Psychotherapy after mild traumatic brain injury: Relation to the nature and severity of subjective complaints. *Journal of Head Trauma Rehabilitation, 6*, 30–43.

Clare, L. (2002a). Assessment and intervention in Alzheimer's disease. In A. D. Baddeley, B. A. Wilson, & M. D. Kopelman (Eds.), *Handbook of memory disorders*. Chichester: Wiley.

Clare, L. (2002b). Developing awareness about awareness in early-stage dementia. *Dementia, 1*, 295–312.

Clare, L. (2002c). We'll fight it as long as we can: Coping with the onset of Alzheimer's disease. *Aging and Mental Health, 6*, 139–148.

Clare, L. (2003a). Managing threats to self: Awareness in early-stage Alzheimer's disease. *Social Science and Medicine, 57*, 1017–1029.

Clare, L. (2003b). Rehabilitation for people with dementia. In B. A. Wilson (Ed.), *Neuropsychological rehabilitation: Theory and practice* (pp. 197–215). London: Swets & Zeitlinger.

Clare, L. (2004a). Awareness in early-stage Alzheimer's disease: A review of methods and evidence. *British Journal of Clinical Psychology, 43*, 177–196.

Clare, L. (2004b). The construction of awareness in early-stage Alzheimer's disease: A review of concepts and models. *British Journal of Clinical Psychology, 43*, 155–175.

Clare, L. (in press). Neuropsychological assessment of the older person. In R. T. Woods & L. Clare (Eds.), *Handbook of the clinical psychology of ageing* (2nd ed.). Chichester: John Wiley & Sons.

Clare, L., Baddeley, A., Moniz-Cook, E. D., & Woods, R. T. (2003). A quiet revolution: Advances in the understanding of dementia. *The Psychologist, 16*, 250–254.

Clare, L., Goater, T., & Woods, R. T. (2006). Illness representations in early-stage dementia: A preliminary investigation. *International Journal of Geriatric Psychiatry, 21*, 761–767.

Clare, L., Marková, I. S., Romero, B., Verhey, F., Wang, M., Woods, R. T., et al.

(2006). Awareness and people with early-stage dementia. In B. M. M. Miesen & G. M. M. Jones (Eds.), *Caregiving in dementia: Research and application* (Vol. 4). London: Routledge.

Clare, L., Marková, I. S., Verhey, F., & Kenny, G. (2005). Awareness in dementia: A review of assessment methods and measures. *Aging and Mental Health*, *9*, 394–413.

Clare, L., Roth, I., & Pratt, R. (2005). Perceptions of change over time in early-stage Alzheimer's disease: Implications for understanding awareness and coping style. *Dementia*, *4*, 487–520.

Clare, L., Rowlands, J., Bruce, E., & Downs, M. (2006, November). *Awareness among people with moderate to severe dementia living in residential care.* Paper presented at Gerontological Society of America annual conference, Dallas, TX.

Clare, L., Rowlands, J., & Quin, R. (in press). Collective strength: The impact of developing a shared social identity in early-stage dementia. *Dementia*.

Clare, L., & Shakespeare, P. (2004). Negotiating the impact of forgetting: Dimensions of resistance in task-oriented conversations between people with early-stage dementia and their partners. *Dementia*, *3*, 211–232.

Clare, L., van Paasschen, J., Evans, S., Parkinson, C., Linden, D., & Woods, R. T. (2006). Individualised, goal-oriented cognitive rehabilitation in early-stage Alzheimer's disease: Impact on brain activation, task performance and well-being [Abstract]. *Journal of the International Neuropsychological Society*, *12*(Suppl. S2), 23.

Clare, L., & Wilson, B. A. (1997). *Coping with memory problems: A practical guide for people with memory impairments and their relatives and friends.* Bury St Edmunds: Thames Valley Test Company.

Clare, L., & Wilson, B. A. (2004). Memory rehabilitation for people with early-stage dementia: A single case comparison of four errorless learning methods. *Zeitschrift fuer Gerontopsychologie und -psychiatrie*, *17*, 109–117.

Clare, L., Wilson, B. A., Breen, K., & Hodges, J. R. (1999). Errorless learning of face–name associations in early Alzheimer's disease. *Neurocase*, *5*, 37–46.

Clare, L., Wilson, B. A., Carter, G., Gosses, A., Breen, K., & Hodges, J. R. (2000). Intervening with everyday memory problems in early Alzheimer's disease: An errorless learning approach. *Journal of Clinical and Experimental Neuropsychology*, *22*, 132–146.

Clare, L., Wilson, B. A., Carter, G., & Hodges, J. R. (2003). Cognitive rehabilitation as a component of early intervention in dementia: A single case study. *Aging and Mental Health*, *7*, 15–21.

Clare, L., Wilson, B. A., Carter, G., Hodges, J. R., & Adams, M. (2001). Long-term maintenance of treatment gains following a cognitive rehabilitation intervention in early dementia of Alzheimer type: A single case study. *Neuropsychological Rehabilitation*, *11*, 477–494.

Clare, L., Wilson, B. A., Carter, G., Roth, I., & Hodges, J. (2002a). Relearning of face–name associations in early-stage Alzheimer's disease. *Neuropsychology*, *16*, 538–547.

Clare, L., Wilson, B. A., Carter, G., Roth, I., & Hodges, J. R. (2002b). Assessing awareness in early-stage Alzheimer's disease: Development and piloting of the Memory Awareness Rating Scale. *Neuropsychological Rehabilitation*, *12*, 341–362.

Clare, L., Wilson, B. A., Carter, G., Roth, I., & Hodges, J. R. (2004). Awareness in early-stage Alzheimer's disease: Relationship to outcome of cognitive rehabilitation. *Journal of Clinical and Experimental Neuropsychology*, 26, 215–226.

Clare, L., Woods, B., Moniz-Cook, E. D., Spector, A., & Orrell, M. (2003). Cognitive rehabilitation and cognitive training for early-stage Alzheimer's disease and vascular dementia (Cochrane Review). *The Cochrane Library*, Issue 4. Chichester: John Wiley & Sons Ltd.

Clare, L., & Woods, R. T. (Eds.). (2001). *Cognitive rehabilitation in dementia*. Hove: Psychology Press.

Clare, L., & Woods, R. T. (in press). Cognitive rehabilitation and cognitive training for early-stage Alzheimer's disease and vascular dementia (Cochrane Review). *The Cochrane Library*. Chichester: John Wiley & Sons Ltd.

Clarke, C., Sheppard, L., Fillenbaum, G., Galasko, D., Morris, J., Koss, E., et al., & the CERAD Investigators (1999). Variability in annual Mini-Mental State Examination score in patients with probable Alzheimer disease. *Archives of Neurology*, 56, 857–862.

Cockburn, J., & Keene, J. (2001). Are changes in everyday memory over time in autopsy-confirmed Alzheimer's disease related to changes in reported behaviour? *Neuropsychological Rehabilitation*, 11, 201–217.

Cohen, D. (1991). The subjective experience of Alzheimer's disease: The anatomy of an illness as perceived by patients and families. *The American Journal of Alzheimer's Care and Related Disorders and Research* (May/June), 6–11.

Cohen, D., & Eisdorfer, C. (1986). *The loss of self: A family resource for the care of Alzheimer's disease and related disorders*. New York: W. W. Norton & Company.

Cohen-Mansfield, J., Golander, H., & Arnheim, G. (2000). Self-identity in older persons suffering from dementia: Preliminary results. *Social Science and Medicine*, 51, 381–394.

Cohen-Mansfield, J., Parpura-Gill, A., & Golander, H. (2006). Utilisation of self-identity roles for designing interventions for persons with dementia. *Journal of Gerontology: Psychological Sciences*, 61B, P202–P212.

Coleman, P. G., & O'Hanlon, A. (in press). Ageing and adaptation. In R. T. Woods & L. Clare (Eds.), *Handbook of the clinical psychology of ageing* (2nd ed.). Chichester: John Wiley & Sons Ltd.

Collette, F., & Van der Linden, M. (2004). Executive functions in Alzheimer's disease. In R. G. Morris & J. T. Becker (Eds.), *Cognitive neuropsychology of Alzheimer's disease* (2nd ed.). Oxford: Oxford University Press.

Collins, C. (1992). Carers: Gender and caring for dementia. In T. Arie (Ed.), *Recent advances in psychogeriatrics* (Vol. 2). London: Churchill Livingstone.

Cotrell, V., & Schulz, R. (1993). The perspective of the patient with Alzheimer's disease: A neglected dimension of dementia research. *The Gerontologist*, 33, 205–211.

Cox, S., & Keady, J. (Eds.). (1999). *Younger people with dementia: Planning, practice and development*. London: Jessica Kingsley Publishers.

Craik, F. I., & Lockhart, R. S. (1972). Levels of processing: A framework for memory research. *Journal of Verbal Learning and Verbal Behavior*, 11, 671–684.

Crook, T., Bartus, R. T., Ferris, S. H., Whitehouse, P., Cohen, G. D., & Gershon, S. (1986). Age-associated memory impairment: Proposed diagnostic criteria and measures of clinical change. *Developmental Neuropsychology*, 2, 261–276.

Crossley, M. (in press). Neuropsychological rehabilitation in later life. In R. T.

Woods & L. Clare (Eds.), *Handbook of the clinical psychology of ageing* (2nd ed.). Chichester: John Wiley & Sons.

Crossley, M., Hiscock, M., & Foreman, J. B. (2004). Dual-task performance in early-stage dementia: Differential effects for automatised and effortful processing. *Journal of Clinical and Experimental Neuropsychology, 26*, 332–346.

Curtis, E. A., & Dixon, M. S. (2005). Family therapy and systemic practice with older people: Where are we now? *Journal of Family Therapy, 27*, 43–64.

Dalla Barba, G., Parlato, V., Iavarone, A., & Boller, F. (1995). Anosognosia, intrusions and 'frontal' functions in Alzheimer's disease and depression. *Neuropsychologia, 33*, 247–259.

Davis, R. N., Massman, P. J., & Doody, R. S. (2001). Cognitive intervention in Alzheimer disease: A randomized placebo-controlled study. *Alzheimer Disease and Associated Disorders, 15*, 1–9.

De Vreese, L. P., Belloi, L., Iacono, A., Finelli, C., & Neri, M. (1998). Memory training programs in memory complainers: Efficacy on objective and subjective memory functioning. *Archives of Gerontology & Geriatrics, 26*(Suppl. 6), 141–154.

De Vreese, L. P., Neri, M., Fioravanti, M., Belloi, L., & Zanetti, O. (2001). Memory rehabilitation in Alzheimer's disease: A review of progress. *International Journal of Geriatric Psychiatry, 16*, 794–809.

de Vugt, M. E., Stevens, F., Aalten, P., Lousberg, R., Jaspers, N., Winkens, I., et al. (2004). Influence of caregiver management strategies on patient behaviour in dementia. *International Journal of Geriatric Psychiatry, 19*, 85–92.

DeBettignies, B. H., Mahurin, R. K., & Pirozzolo, F. J. (1990). Insight for impairment in independent living skills in Alzheimer's disease and multi-infarct dementia. *Journal of Clinical and Experimental Neuropsychology, 12*, 355–363.

Delis, D. C., Kaplan, E., Cramer, J. H., & Ober, B. A. (2000). *California Verbal Learning Test, 2nd UK edition (CVLT-II)*. London: Harcourt Assessment.

Delis, D. C., Kaplan, E., & Kramer, J. H. (2001). *Delis–Kaplan Executive Function System (D-KEFS)*. London: Harcourt Assessment.

Downs, M., Clare, L., & Anderson, E. (in press). Dementia as a biopsychosocial condition: Implications for practice and research In R. T. Woods & L. Clare (Eds.), *Handbook of the clinical psychology of ageing* (2nd ed.). Chichester: John Wiley & Sons Ltd.

Downs, M., Clare, L., & Mackenzie, J. (2006). Understandings of dementia: Explanatory models and their implications for the person with dementia and therapeutic effort. In J. C. Hughes, S. J. Louw, & S. R. Sabat (Eds.), *Dementia: Mind, meaning and the person.* Oxford: Oxford University Press.

Droes, R.-M., Breebaart, E., Ettema, T. P., van Tilburg, W., & Mellenbergh, G. J. (2000). Effect of integrated family support versus day care only on behavior and mood of patients with dementia. *International Psychogeriatrics, 12*, 99–115.

Dunn, J. (2003). *Learning of face–name associations using errorless and effortful methods in early-stage dementia.* Unpublished D.Clin.Psy thesis, University of London, London.

Dunn, J., & Clare, L. (in press). Learning face–name associations in early-stage dementia: Comparing the effects of errorless learning and effortful processing *Neuropsychological Rehabilitation*.

Engel, G. L. (1977). The need for a new medical model: A challenge for biomedicine. *Science, 196*, 129–136.

Evans, J. J., Wilson, B. A., Schuri, U., Andrade, J., Baddeley, A., Bruna, O., et al.

(2000). A comparison of 'errorless' and 'trial and error' learning methods for teaching individuals with acquired memory deficits. *Neuropsychological Rehabilitation, 10*, 67–101.

Farina, E., Fioravanti, R., Chiavari, L., Imbornone, E., Alberoni, M., Pomati, S., et al. (2002). Comparing two programs of cognitive training in Alzheimer's disease: A pilot study. *Acta Neurologica Scandinavica, 105*, 365–371.

Feil, N. (1992). Validation therapy with late-onset dementia populations. In G. M. M. Jones & B. M. L. Miesen (Eds.), *Care-giving in dementia: Research and applications* (Vol. 1). London: Tavistock/Routledge.

Fernández-Ballesteros, R., Zamarrón, M. D., & Tàrraga, L. (2005). Learning potential: A new method for assessing cognitive impairment. *International Psychogeriatrics, 17*, 119–128.

Fernández-Ballesteros, R., Zamarrón, M. D., Tàrraga, L., Moya, R., & Iniguez, J. (2003). Cognitive plasticity in healthy, mild cognitive impairment (MCI) subjects and Alzheimer's disease patients: A research project in Spain. *European Psychologist, 8*, 148–159.

Fisher, L., & Lieberman, M. A. (1994). Alzheimer's disease: The impact of the family on spouses, offspring and inlaws. *Family Process, 33*, 305–325.

Folstein, M. F., Folstein, S. E., & McHugh, P. R. (1975). 'Mini-mental state': A practical method for grading the cognitive state of patients for the clinician. *Journal of Psychiatric Research, 12*, 189–198.

Fortinsky, R. H. (2001). Health care triads and dementia care: Integrative framework and future directions. *Aging and Mental Health, 5*(Suppl. 1), S35–S48.

Fratiglioni, L., Paillard-Borg, S., & Winblad, B. (2004). An active and socially integrated lifestyle in late life might protect against dementia. *Lancet Neurology, 3*, 343–353.

Frattali, C. (2004). An errorless learning approach to treating dysnomia in frontotemporal dementia. *Journal of Medical Speech-Language Pathology, 12*(3), 11–24.

Freeman, E., Clare, L., Savitch, N., Royan, L., Litherland, R., & Lindsay, M. (2005). Improving the accessibility of internet-based information resources for people with dementia: A collaborative approach. *Aging and Mental Health, 9*, 442–448.

Friedell, M. (2002). Awareness: A personal memoir on the changing quality of life in Alzheimer's. *Dementia, 1*, 359–366.

Friedell, M. (2003). Dementia survival – a new vision. *Alzheimer's Care Quarterly* (April/June), 79–84.

Friedell, M. (2005). Tedious no more! In M. Marshall (Ed.), *Perspectives on rehabilitation in dementia*. London: Jessica Kingsley Publishers.

Friedell, M. (2006). Morris Friedell's home page. Retrieved August 7, 2006, from http://members.aol.com/morrisFF

Froggatt, K. A., Downs, M., & Small, N. (in press). Palliative care for people with dementia: Principles, practice and implications. In R. T. Woods & L. Clare (Eds.), *Handbook of the clinical psychology of ageing* (2nd ed.). Chichester: John Wiley & Sons Ltd.

Garrard, P., Patterson, K., & Hodges, J. R. (2004). Semantic processing in Alzheimer's disease. In R. G. Morris & J. T. Becker (Eds.), *Cognitive neuropsychology of Alzheimer's disease* (2nd ed.). Oxford: Oxford University Press.

Gatz, M., Bengtson, V. L., & Blum, M. J. (1990). Caregiving families. In J. E. Birren & K. K. Warner Schaie (Eds.), *Handbook of the psychology of aging* (3rd ed.). San Diego, CA: Academic Press.

Gatz, M., Fiske, A., Fox, L., Kaskie, B., Kasl-Godley, J. E., McCallum, T. J., et al. (1998). Empirically validated psychological treatments for older adults. *Journal of Mental Health and Aging, 4*, 9–45.

George, L. K. (1998). Self and identity in later life: Protecting and enhancing the self. *Journal of Aging and Identity, 3*, 133–152.

Gerber, G. J., Prince, P. N., Snider, H. G., Atchison, K., Dubois, L., & Kilgour, J. A. (1991). Group activity and cognitive improvement among patients with Alzheimer's disease. *Hospital and Community Psychiatry, 42*, 843–845.

Germano, C., & Kinsella, G. J. (2005). Working memory and learning in early Alzheimer's disease. *Neuropyschology Review, 15*, 1–10.

Giacino, J. T., & Kalmar, K. (2005). Diagnostic and prognostic guidelines for the vegetative and minimally conscious states. *Neuropsychological Rehabilitation, 15*, 166–174.

Gilhooly, M. L. M. (1984). The impact of care-giving on care-givers: Factors associated with the psychological well-being of people supporting a dementing relative in the community. *British Journal of Medical Psychology, 57*, 35–44.

Gilleard, C. J. (1992). Carers: Recent research findings. In T. Arie (Ed.), *Recent advances in psychogeriatrics* (Vol. 2). London: Churchill Livingstone.

Gillies, B. A. (2000). A memory like clockwork: Accounts of living through dementia. *Aging and Mental Health, 4*, 366–374.

Glaser, B. G., & Strauss, A. L. (1965). *Awareness of dying*. Chicago: Aldine.

Glisky, E. L. (1998). Differential contribution of frontal and medial temporal lobes to memory: Evidence from focal lesions and normal aging. In N. Raz (Ed.), *The other side of the error term*. Amsterdam: Elsevier.

Glisky, E. L., Schacter, D. L., & Tulving, E. (1986). Learning and retention of computer-related vocabulary in memory impaired patients: Method of vanishing cues. *Journal of Clinical and Experimental Neuropsychology, 8*, 292–312.

Goldsmith, M. (1996). *Hearing the voice of people with dementia: Opportunities and obstacles*. London: Jessica Kingsley Publishers.

Grady, C. L., Intosh, A. R. M., Beig, S., Keightley, M. L., Burian, H., & Black, S. E. (2003). Evidence from functional neuroimaging of a compensatory prefrontal network in Alzheimer's disease. *The Journal of Neuroscience, 23*, 986–993.

Graham, K. S., Patterson, K., Pratt, K. H., & Hodges, J. R. (2001). Can repeated exposure to 'forgotten' vocabulary help alleviate word-finding difficulties in semantic dementia? An illustrative case study. *Neuropsychological Rehabilitation, 11*, 429–454.

Gray, C., & della Sala, S. (2004). Measuring impairment and charting decline in Alzheimer's disease. In R. G. Morris & J. T. Becker (Eds.), *Cognitive neuropsychology of Alzheimer's disease*. Oxford: Oxford University Press.

Green, J., Goldstein, F. C., Sirockman, B. E., & Green, R. C. (1993). Variable awareness of deficits in Alzheimer's disease. *Neuropsychiatry, Neuropsychology and Behavioral Neurology, 6*, 159–165.

Günther, V., Fuchs, D., Schett, P., Meise, U., & Rhomberg, H. P. (1991). Kognitives Training bei organischem Psychosyndrom [Cognitive training in organic psychogeriatric syndromes]. *Deutsche Medizinische Wochenschrift, 116*, 846–851.

Hagberg, B. (1997). The dementias in a psychodynamic perspective. In B. M. L. Miesen & G. M. M. Jones (Eds.), *Care-giving in dementia: Research and applications* (Vol. 2). London: Routledge.

Hanley, I. (1986). Reality orientation in the care of the elderly patient with dementia – three case studies. In I. Hanley & M. Gilhooly (Eds.), *Psychological therapies for the elderly*. Beckenham: Croom Helm.

Hardy, R. M., Oyebode, J., & Clare, L. (2006). Measuring awareness in people with mild to moderate Alzheimer's disease: The development of the Memory Awareness Rating Scale – Adjusted. *Neuropsychological Rehabilitation, 16*, 178–193.

Harman, G., & Clare, L. (2006). Illness representations and lived experience in early-stage dementia. *Qualitative Health Research, 16*, 484–502.

Haslam, C., Gilroy, D., Black, S., & Beesley, T. (2006). How successful is errorless learning in supporting memory for high- and low-level knowledge in dementia? *Neuropsychological Rehabilitation, 16*, 505–536.

Hausman, C. (1992). Dynamic psychotherapy with elderly demented patients. In G. M. M. Jones & B. M. L. Miesen (Eds.), *Care-giving in dementia: Research and applications* (Vol. 1). London: Tavistock/Routledge.

Heiss, W.-D., Kessler, J., Mielke, R., Szelies, B., & Herholz, K. (1994). Long-term effects of phosphatidylserine, pyritinol, and cognitive training in Alzheimer's disease. *Dementia, 5*, 88–98.

Henderson, J., & Forbat, L. (2002). Relationship-based social policy: Personal and policy constructions of 'care'. *Critical Social Policy, 22*, 669–687.

Herlitz, A., & Viitanen, M. (1991). Semantic organisation and verbal episodic memory in patients with mild and moderate Alzheimer's disease. *Journal of Clinical and Experimental Neuropsychology, 13*, 559–574.

Hettiarachty, P., & Manthorpe, J. (1992). A carer's group for families of patients with dementia. In G. M. M. Jones & B. M. L. Miesen (Eds.), *Care-giving in dementia* (Vol. 1). London: Tavistock/Routledge.

Hill, R. D., Evankovich, K. D., Sheikh, J. I., & Yesavage, J. A. (1987). Imagery mnemonic training in a patient with primary degenerative dementia. *Psychology and Aging, 2*, 204–205.

Hirsch, C. R., & Mouratoglou, V. M. (1999). Life review of an older adult with memory difficulties. *International Journal of Geriatric Psychiatry, 14*, 261–265.

Hodges, J. R., & Patterson, K. (1995). Is semantic memory consistently impaired early in the course of Alzheimer's disease? Neuroanatomical and diagnostic implications. *Neuropsychologia, 33*, 441–459.

Hodges, J. R., Patterson, K., Graham, N., & Dawson, K. (1996). Naming and knowing in dementia of Alzheimer's type. *Brain and Language, 54*, 302–325.

Hodges, S., Williams, L., Berry, E., Izadi, S., Srinivasan, J., Butler, A., et al. (2006). SenseCam: A retrospective memory aid. In P. Dourish & A. Friday (Eds.), *Ubicomp 2006, LNCS 4206*. Heidelberg: Springer-Verlag.

Hooker, K., Frazier, L. D., & Monahan, D. J. (1994). Personality and coping among caregivers of spouses with dementia. *Gerontologist, 34*, 386–392.

Howard, D., & Patterson, K. (1992). *Pyramids and Palm Trees Test*. Bury St Edmunds: Thames Valley Test Company.

Hunkin, N. M., & Parkin, A. J. (1995). The method of vanishing cues: An evaluation of its effectiveness in teaching memory-impaired individuals. *Neuropsychologia, 33*, 1255–1279.

Hunkin, N. M., Squires, E. J., Parkin, A. J., & Tidy, J. A. (1998). Are the benefits of errorless learning dependent on implicit memory? *Neuropsychologia, 36*, 25–36.

Husband, H. J. (1999). The psychological consequences of learning a diagnosis of dementia: Three case examples. *Aging and Mental Health, 3*, 179–183.

Hutton, S., Sheppard, L., Rusted, J. M., & Ratner, H. H. (1996). Structuring the acquisition and retrieval environment to facilitate learning in individuals with dementia of the Alzheimer type. *Memory, 4*, 113–130.

Jones, R. S. P., & Eayrs, C. B. (1992). The use of errorless learning procedures in teaching people with a learning disability: A critical review. *Mental Handicap Research, 5*, 204–212.

Jorm, A. F. (1992). Use of informants' reports to study memory changes in dementia. In L. Bäckman (Ed.), *Memory functioning in dementia.* Amsterdam: Elsevier.

Jorm, A. F., Christensen, H., Henderson, A. S., Korten, A. E., Mackinnon, A. J., & Scott, R. (1994). Complaints of cognitive decline in the elderly: A comparison of reports by subjects and informants in a community survey. *Psychological Medicine, 24*, 365–374.

Josephsson, S., Bäckman, L., Borell, L., Bernspang, B., Nygard, L., & Ronnberg, L. (1993). Supporting everyday activities in dementia: An intervention study. *International Journal of Geriatric Psychiatry, 8*, 395–400.

Kahana, E., & Young, R. (1990). Theoretical questions and ethical issues in the family caregiving relationship. In D. E. Biegel & A. Blum (Eds.), *Aging and caregiving: Theory, research and policy* (pp. 76–97). Newbury Park, CA: Sage.

Kapur, N. (1994). *Memory disorders in clinical practice.* Hove: Lawrence Erlbaum Associates Ltd.

Kapur, N., Glisky, E., & Wilson, B. A. (2004). Technological memory aids for people with memory deficits. *Neuropsychological Rehabilitation, 14*, 41–60.

Karlsson, I., Bråne, G., Melin, E., Nyth, A.-L., & Rybo, E. (1988). Effects of environmental stimulation on biochemical and psychological variables in dementia. *Acta Psychiatrica Scandinavica, 77*, 207–213.

Karlsson, T., Backman, L., Herlitz, A., Nilsson, L.-G., Winblad, B., & Osterlind, P.-O. (1989). Memory improvement at different stages of Alzheimer's disease. *Neuropsychologia, 27*, 737–742.

Kasl-Godley, J., & Gatz, M. (2000). Psychosocial interventions for individuals with dementia: An integration of theory, therapy, and a clinical understanding of dementia. *Clinical Psychology Review, 20*, 755–782.

Kazdin, A. E. (1982). *Single-case research designs: Methods for clinical and applied settings.* New York: Oxford University Press.

Kazdin, A. E. (1984). Statistical analyses for single-case experimental designs. In D. H. Barlow & M. Hersen (Eds.), *Single case experimental designs* (2nd ed.). New York: Pergamon Press.

Keady, J., & Nolan, M. (1995). IMMEL 2: Working to augment coping responses in early dementia. *British Journal of Nursing, 4*, 377–380.

Keady, J., & Nolan, M. (2003). The dynamics of dementia: Working together, working separately, or working alone? In M. Nolan, U. Lundh, G. Grant, & J. Keady (Eds.), *Partnerships in family care.* Buckingham: Open University Press.

Keady, J., Nolan, M., & Gilliard, J. (1995). Listen to the voices of experience. *Journal of Dementia Care* (May/June), 15–17.

Kertesz, A. (2004). Language in Alzheimer's disease. In R. G. Morris & J. T. Becker

(Eds.), *Cognitive neuropsychology of Alzheimer's disease*. Oxford: Oxford University Press.

Kester, J. D., Benjamin, A. S., Castel, A. D., & Craik, F. I. M. (2002). Memory in elderly people. In A. D. Baddeley, M. D. Kopelman, & B. A. Wilson (Eds.), *Handbook of memory disorders* (2nd ed.). Chichester: John Wiley & Sons Ltd.

Kidron, D., & Freedman, M. (2004). Motor functioning. In R. G. Morris & J. T. Becker (Eds.), *Cognitive neuropsychology of Alzheimer's disease*. Oxford: Oxford University Press.

Kiecolt-Glaser, J. K., Dura, J. R., Speicher, C. E., Trask, J., & Glaser, R. (1991). Spousal caregivers of dementia victims: Longitudinal changes in immunity and health. *Psychosomatic Medicine, 53*, 345–362.

Killick, J., & Allan, K. (2001). *Communication and the care of people with dementia*. Buckingham: Open University Press.

Kinney, J. M., Kart, C. S., Murdoch, L. D., & Conley, C. J. (2004). Striving to provide safety assistance for families of elders: The SAFE house project. *Dementia, 3*, 351–370.

Kitwood, T. (1988). The contribution of psychology to the understanding of senile dementia. In B. Gearing, M. Johnson, & T. Heller (Eds.), *Mental health problems in old age: A reader*. Chichester: John Wiley & Sons Ltd.

Kitwood, T. (1996). A dialectical framework for dementia. In R. T. Woods (Ed.), *Handbook of the clinical psychology of ageing*. Chichester: John Wiley & Sons Ltd.

Kitwood, T. (1997). *Dementia reconsidered: The person comes first*. Buckingham: Open University Press.

Koder, D.-A. (1998). Treatment of anxiety in the cognitively impaired elderly: Can cognitive-behavior therapy help? *International Psychogeriatrics, 10*, 173–182.

Koltai, D. C., & Branch, L. G. (1999). Cognitive and affective interventions to maximise abilities and adjustment in dementia. *Annals of Psychiatry, 7*, 241–255.

Koltai, D. C., Welsh-Bohmer, K. A., & Schmechel, D. E. (1999, February). *Influence of anosognosia on treatment outcome among dementia patients*. Paper presented at the International Neuropsychological Society Annual Meeting, Boston.

Koltai, D. C., Welsh-Bohmer, K. A., & Schmechel, D. E. (2001). Influence of anosognosia on treatment outcome among dementia patients. *Neuropsychological Rehabilitation, 11*, 455–475.

Komatsu, S.-I., Mimura, M., Kato, M., Wakamatsu, N., & Kashima, H. (2000). Errorless and effortful processes involved in the learning of face–name associations by patients with alcoholic Korsakoff's syndrome. *Neuropsychological Rehabilitation, 10*, 113–208.

Kopelman, M. D. (1992). Storage, forgetting and retrieval in the anterograde and retrograde amnesia of Alzheimer dementia. In L. Bäckman (Ed.), *Memory functioning in dementia*. Amsterdam: Elsevier.

Kopelman, M. D., Wilson, B. A., & Baddeley, A. (1990). *The autobiographical memory interview*. Bury St Edmunds: Thames Valley Test Company.

Kral, V. A. (1962). Senescent forgetfulness: Benign and malignant. *Le Journal de l'Association Médicale Canadienne, 86*, 257–260.

Kurlychek, R. T. (1983). Use of a digital alarm chronograph as a memory aid in early dementia. *Clinical Gerontologist, 1*, 93–94.

Laidlaw, K., Thompson, L. W., Dick-Smith, L., & Gallagher-Thompson, D. (2003). *Cognitive behaviour therapy with older people*. Chichester: John Wiley & Sons Ltd.

Landauer, T. K., & Bjork, R. A. (1978). Optimum rehearsal patterns and name learning. In K. M. Gruneberg, P. E. Morris, & R. N. Sykes (Eds.), *Practical aspects of memory*. New York: Academic Press.

Langer, K. G., & Padrone, F. J. (1992). Psychotherapeutic treatment of awareness in acute rehabilitation of traumatic brain injury. *Neuropsychological Rehabilitation, 2*, 59–70.

Larrabee, G. J., West, R. L., & Crook, T. H. (1991). The association of memory complaint with computer-simulated everyday memory performance. *Journal of Clinical and Experimental Neuropsychology, 13*, 466–478.

Laureys, S., Owen, A. M., & Schiff, N. D. (2004). Brain function in coma, vegetative state, and related disorders. *Lancet Neurology, 3*, 537–546.

Laurin, D., Verreault, R., Lindsay, J., MacPherson, K., & Rockwood, K. (2001). Physical activity and risk of cognitive impairment and dementia in elderly persons. *Archives of Neurology, 58*, 498–504.

Law, M., Baptiste, S., Carswell, A., McColl, M. A., Polatajko, H., & Pollock, N. (2005). *Canadian Occupational Performance Measure* (4th ed.). Ottawa, ON: CAOT Publications ACE.

Lawton, M. P., & Brody, E. M. (1969). Assessment of older people: Self-maintaining and instrumental activities of daily living. *The Gerontologist, 9*, 179–186.

Lee, J. L. (2003). *Just love me: My life turned upside down by Alzheimer's*. West Lafayette, IN: Purdue University Press.

Lekeu, F., Wojtasik, V., Van der Linden, M., & Salmon, E. (2002). Training early Alzheimer patients to use a mobile phone. *Acta Neurologica Belgica, 102*, 114–121.

Leventhal, H., Benyamini, Y., Brownlee, S., Diefenbach, M., Leventhal, E. A., Patrick-Miller, L., et al. (1997). Illness representations: Theoretical foundations. In K. J. Petrie & J. A. Weinman (Eds.), *Perceptions of health and illness*. Amsterdam: Harwood Academic Publishers.

Leventhal, H., Nerenz, D., & Steele, D. J. (1984). Illness representations and coping with health threats. In S. Baum, S. E. Taylor, & J. E. Singer (Eds.), *Handbook of health psychology: Vol. IV. Social psychological aspects of health*. Hillsdale, NJ: Lawrence Erlbaum Associates, Inc.

Levine, B., Robertson, I., Clare, L., Carter, G., Hong, J., Wilson, B. A., et al. (2000). Rehabilitation of executive functioning: An experimental-clinical validation of Goal Management Training. *Journal of the International Neuropsychological Society, 6*, 299–312.

Lewis, L. (1991a). A framework for developing a psychotherapy treatment plan with brain-injured patients. *Journal of Head Trauma Rehabilitation, 6*, 22–29.

Lewis, L. (1991b). Role of psychological factors in disordered awareness. In G. P. Prigatano & D. L. Schacter (Eds.), *Awareness of deficit after brain injury: Clinical and theoretical issues*. New York: Oxford University Press.

Lezak, M. D. (1995). *Neuropsychological assessment* (3rd ed.). New York: Oxford University Press.

Lipinska, B., & Bäckman, L. (1997). Encoding–retrieval interactions in mild Alzheimer's disease: The role of access to categorical information. *Brain and Cognition, 34*, 274–286.

Lipinska, B., Bäckman, L., Mantyla, T., & Viitanen, M. (1994). Effectiveness of self-generated cues in early Alzheimer's disease. *Journal of Clinical and Experimental Neuropsychology, 16*, 809–819.

Lishman, W. A. (1994). The history of research into dementia and its relationship to current concepts. In F. A. Huppert, C. Brayne, & D. W. O'Connor (Eds.), *Dementia and normal aging*. Cambridge: Cambridge University Press.

Little, A. (in press). Assessment of functioning and behaviour. In R. T. Woods & L. Clare (Eds.), *Handbook of the clinical psychology of ageing* (2nd ed.). Chichester: John Wiley & Sons Ltd.

Little, A. G., Volans, P. J., Hemsley, D. R., & Levy, R. (1986). The retention of new information in senile dementia. *British Journal of Clinical Psychology, 25*, 71–72.

Loewenstein, D. A., Acevedo, A., Czaja, S. J., & Duara, R. (2004). Cognitive rehabilitation of mildly impaired Alzheimer disease patients on cholinesterase inhibitors. *American Journal of Geriatric Psychiatry, 12*, 395–402.

Logsdon, R. G., Gibbons, L. E., McCurry, S. M., & Teri, L. (1999). Quality of life in Alzheimer's disease: Patient and caregiver reports. *Journal of Mental Health and Aging, 5*, 21–32.

Lopez, O. L., & Bell, S. (2004). Neurobiological approaches to the treatment of Alzheimer's disease. In R. Morris & J. Becker (Eds.), *Cognitive neuropsychology of Alzheimer's disease*. Oxford: Oxford University Press.

Lough, S., & Hodges, J. R. (2002). Measuring and modifying abnormal social cognition in frontal variant frontotemporal dementia. *Journal of Psychosomatic Research, 53*, 639–646.

Malec, J. F. (1999). Goal attainment scaling in rehabilitation. *Neuropsychological Rehabilitation, 9*, 253–275.

Marková, I. S., & Berrios, G. E. (2001). The 'object' of insight assessment: Relationship with insight 'structure'. *Psychopathology, 34*, 245–252.

Marková, I. S., Clare, L., Wang, M., Romero, B., & Kenny, G. (2005). Awareness in dementia: Conceptual issues. *Aging and Mental Health, 9*, 386–393.

Marriott, A., Donaldson, C., Tarrier, N., & Burns, A. (2000). Effectiveness of cognitive-behavioural family intervention in reducing the burden of care in carers of patients with Alzheimer's disease. *British Journal of Psychiatry, 176*, 557–562.

Marshall, M. (1999). Person centred technology? *Signpost, 3*(4), 4–5.

Marshall, M. (2005). *Perspectives on rehabilitation and dementia*. London: Jessica Kingsley Publishers.

Mason, E., Clare, L., & Pistrang, N. (2005). Processes and experiences of mutual support in professionally led support groups for people with early-stage dementia. *Dementia, 4*, 87–112.

Mateer, C. (2005). Fundamentals of cognitive rehabilitation. In P. W. Halligan & D. T. Wade (Eds.), *Effectiveness of rehabilitation for cognitive deficits*. Oxford: Oxford University Press.

Maylor, E. A. (1995). Prospective memory in normal ageing and dementia. *Neurocase, 1*, 285–289.

McGlynn, S. M., & Schacter, D. L. (1989). Unawareness of deficits in neuropsychological syndromes. *Journal of Clinical and Experimental Neuropsychology, 11*, 143–205.

McKeith, I., & Fairbairn, A. (2001). Biomedical and clinical perspectives. In C. Cantley (Ed.), *Handbook of dementia care*. Buckingham: Open University Press.

McKenna, P., & Warrington, E. K. (1983). *Graded Naming Test.* Windsor: NFER-Nelson.

McKitrick, L. A., & Camp, C. J. (1993). Relearning the names of things: The spaced-retrieval intervention implemented by a caregiver. *Clinical Gerontologist, 14,* 60–62.

McLellan, D. L. (1991). Functional recovery and the principles of disability medicine. In M. Swash & J. Oxbury (Eds.), *Clinical neurology* (Vol. 1, pp. 769–790). London: Churchill Livingstone.

McLellan, D. L. (1997). Introduction to rehabilitation. In B. A. Wilson & D. L. McLellan (Eds.), *Rehabilitation studies handbook.* Cambridge: Cambridge University Press.

McPherson, A., Furniss, F. G., Sdogati, C., Cesaroni, F., Tartaglini, B., & Lindesay, J. (2001). Effects of individualised memory aids on the conversation of patients with severe dementia: A pilot study. *Aging and Mental Health, 5,* 289–294.

Meier, D., Ermini-Fuenfschilling, D., & Zwick, V. (2000). Gedaechtnistraining fuer Patienten mit beginnender Demenz. *Geriatrie Praxis, 3,* 48–51.

Miesen, B. (1992). Attachment theory and dementia. In G. M. M. Jones & B. M. L. Miesen (Eds.), *Care-giving in dementia: Research and applications.* London: Tavistock/Routledge.

Migliorelli, R., Teson, A., Sabe, L., Petracca, G., Petracchi, M., Leiguarda, R., et al. (1995). Anosognosia in Alzheimer's disease: A study of associated factors. *Journal of Neuropsychiatry and Clinical Neurosciences, 7,* 338–344.

Mihailidis, A., Barbenel, J. C., & Fernie, G. (2004). The efficacy of an intelligent cognitive orthosis to facilitate handwashing by persons with moderate to severe dementia. *Neuropsychological Rehabilitation, 14,* 135–171.

Mittelman, M. S., Roth, D. L., Coon, D. W., & Haley, W. E. (2004). Sustained benefit of supportive intervention for depressive symptoms in caregivers of patients with Alzheimer's disease. *American Journal of Psychiatry, 161,* 850–856.

Moore, S., Kesslak, P., & Sandman, C. (1998, November). *Memory retraining of patients with dementia.* Paper presented at the National Academy of Neuropsychology 18th Annual Conference, Washington, DC.

Moore, S., Sandman, C. A., McGrady, K., & Kesslak, J. P. (2001). Memory training improves cognitive ability in patients with dementia. *Neuropsychological Rehabilitation, 11,* 245–261.

Morris, J. C. (1996). Classification of dementia and Alzheimer's disease. *Acta Neurologica Scandinavica* (Suppl. 165), 41–50.

Morris, R. G. (2004). Neurobiological changes in Alzheimer's disease. In R. G. Morris & J. Becker (Eds.), *Cognitive neuropsychology of Alzheimer's disease* (pp. 299–319). Oxford: Oxford University Press.

Morris, R. G., & Becker, J. T. (2004). A cognitive neuropsychology of Alzheimer's disease. In R. G. Morris & J. T. Becker (Eds.), *Cognitive neuropsychology of Alzheimer's disease* (2nd ed., pp. 4–8). Oxford: Oxford University Press.

Morris, J. C., Storandt, M., Miller, J. P., McKeel, D. W., Price, J. L., Rubin, E. H., et al. (2001). Mild cognitive impairment represents early-stage Alzheimer's disease. *Archives of Neurology, 58,* 397–405.

Morris, R., & Hannesdottir, K. (2004). Loss of 'awareness' in Alzheimer's disease. In R. Morris & J. Becker (Eds.), *Cognitive neuropsychology of Alzheimer's disease.* Oxford: Oxford University Press.

Morris, R. G. (1996). The neuropsychology of Alzheimer's disease and related dementias. In R. T. Woods (Ed.), *Handbook of the clinical psychology of ageing*. Chichester: John Wiley & Sons Ltd.

Morris, R. G., & McKiernan, F. (1994). Neuropsychological investigations of dementia. In A. Burns & R. Levy (Eds.), *Dementia*. London: Chapman & Hall.

Mullen, R., Howard, R., David, A., & Levy, R. (1996). Insight in Alzheimer's disease. *International Journal of Geriatric Psychiatry*, *11*, 645–651.

Nelson, H. E. (1982). *National Adult Reading Test (NART)*. Windsor: NFER-Nelson.

Nelson, H. E., & Willison, J. R. (1991). *National Adult Reading Test (NART)* (2nd ed.). Windsor: NFER-Nelson.

Newhouse, P. A., Potter, A., & Levin, E. D. (1997). Nicotinic system involvement in Alzheimer's and Parkinson's diseases: Implications for therapeutics. *Drugs and Aging*, *11*, 206–228.

Norris, M. P., MacNeill, S. E., & Haines, M. E. (2003). Psychological and neuropsychological aspects of vascular and mixed dementia. In P. A. Lichtenberg, D. L. Murman, & A. M. Mellow (Eds.), *Handbook of dementia*. Hoboken, NJ: Wiley.

O'Brien, J., Ames, D., Chiu, E., Schweitzer, I., Desmond, P., & Tress, B. (1998). Severe deep white matter lesions and outcome in elderly patients with major depressive disorder: Follow up study. *British Medical Journal*, *317*, 982–984.

O'Brien, K., & Prigatano, G. P. (1991). Supportive psychotherapy for a patient exhibiting alexia without agraphia. *Journal of Head Trauma Rehabilitation*, *6*, 44–55.

O'Connor, D. (1993). The impact of dementia: A self psychological perspective. *Journal of Gerontological Social Work*, *20*, 113–128.

O'Dwyer, A. M., & Orrell, M. W. (1994). Stress, aging and dementia. *International Review of Psychiatry*, *6*, 73–83.

Oliver, C., Adams, D., & Kalsy, S. (in press). Ageing, dementia and people with intellectual disability. In R. T. Woods & L. Clare (Eds.), *Handbook of the clinical psychology of ageing* (2nd ed.). Chichester: John Wiley & Sons Ltd.

Oliver, M. (1990). *The politics of disablement*. Basingstoke: Macmillan.

Oriani, M., Moniz-Cook, E., Binetti, G., Zanieri, G., Frisoni, G. B., Geroldi, C., et al. (2003). An electronic memory aid to support prospective memory in patients in the early stages of Alzheimer's disease: A pilot study. *Aging and Mental Health*, *7*, 22–27.

Orpwood, R., Bjørneby, S., Hagen, I., Maki, O., Faulkner, R., & Topo, P. (2004). User involvement in dementia product development. *Dementia*, *3*, 263–279.

Orsulic-Jeras, S., Judge, K. S., & Camp, C. J. (2000). Montessori-based activities for long-term care residents with advanced dementia: Effects on engagement and affect. *The Gerontologist*, *40*, 107–111.

Overman, A. A., & Becker, J. T. (2004). Information processing deficits in episodic memory in Alzheimer's disease. In R. G. Morris & J. T. Becker (Eds.), *Cognitive neuropsychology of Alzheimer's disease*. Oxford: Oxford University Press.

Ownsworth, T., & Clare, L. (2006). A critical review of the association between awareness deficits and rehabilitation outcome following acquired brain injury. *Clinical Psychology Review*, *26*, 783–795.

Ownsworth, T., Clare, L., & Morris, R. (2006). A critical review of cognitive neuropsychological models of awareness: An integrated biopsychosocial approach. *Neuropsychological Rehabilitation, 16*, 415–438.

Parienté, J., Cole, S., Henson, R., Clare, L., Kennedy, A., Rossor, M., et al. (2005). Alzheimer patients engage an alternative cortical network during a memory task. *Annals of Neurology, 58*, 870–879.

Pearce, A., Clare, L., & Pistrang, N. (2002). Managing sense of self: Coping in the early stages of Alzheimer's disease. *Dementia, 1*, 173–192.

Pearlin, L. I., Mullan, J. T., Semple, S. J., & Skaff, M. M. (1990). Caregiving and the stress process: An overview of concepts and their measures. *Gerontologist, 30*, 583–594.

Perlmuter, L. C., & Monty, R. A. (1989). Motivation and aging. In L. W. Poon, D. C. Rubin, & B. A. Wilson (Eds.), *Everyday cognition in adulthood and late life*. Cambridge: Cambridge University Press.

Perry, J. (2002). Wives giving care to husbands with Alzheimer's disease: A process of interpretive caring. *Research in Nursing and Health, 25*, 307–316.

Perry, R. J., & Hodges, J. R. (1999). Attention and executive deficits in Alzheimer's disease: A critical review. *Brain, 122*, 383–404.

Petersen, R. C. (2004). Mild cognitive impairment as a diagnostic entity. *Journal of Internal Medicine, 256*, 183–194.

Petry, S., Cummings, J. L., Hill, M. A., & Shapira, J. (1989). Personality alterations in dementia of the Alzheimer type: A three-year follow-up study. *Journal of Geriatric Psychiatry and Neurology, 2*, 203–207.

Pollitt, P. A. (1994). The meaning of dementia to those involved as carers. In F. A. Huppert, C. Brayne, & D. W. O'Connor (Eds.), *Dementia and normal aging*. Cambridge: Cambridge University Press.

Pollitt, P. A. (1996). Dementia in old age: An anthropological perspective. *Psychological Medicine, 26*, 1061–1074.

Pratt, R., Clare, L., & Aggarwal, N. (2005). The 'Talking About Memory Coffee Group': A new model of support for people with early-stage dementia and their families. *Dementia, 4*, 143–148.

Prigatano, G. P. (1997). Learning from our successes and failures: Reflections and comments on 'Cognitive rehabilitation: How it is and how it might be'. *Journal of the International Neuropsychological Society, 3*, 497–499.

Prigatano, G. P. (1999a). Motivation and awareness in cognitive neurorehabilitation. In D. T. Stuss, G. Winocur, & I. H. Robertson (Eds.), *Cognitive neurorehabilitation*. Cambridge: Cambridge University Press.

Prigatano, G. P. (1999b). *Principles of neuropsychological rehabilitation*. New York: Oxford University Press.

Quayhagen, M. P., & Quayhagen, M. (2001). Testing of a cognitive stimulation intervention for dementia caregiving dyads. *Neuropsychological Rehabilitation, 11*, 319–332.

Quayhagen, M. P., Quayhagen, M., Corbeil, R. R., Hendrix, R. C., Jackson, J. E., Snyder, L., et al. (2000). Coping with dementia: Evaluation of four non-pharmacologic interventions. *International Psychogeriatrics, 12*, 249–265.

Quayhagen, M. P., Quayhagen, M., Corbeil, R. R., Roth, P. A., & Rogers, J. A. (1995). A dyadic remediation program for care recipients with dementia. *Nursing Research, 44*, 153–159.

Quinn, C., & Clare, L. (2006). Don't know what that is: The experience of partners of people with early-stage dementia [Abstract] [Special issue]. *Gerontologist*, *46*(1), 43.

Randolph, C. (1998). *Repeatable Battery for the Assessment of Neuropsychological Status (RBANS-UK)*. London: Harcourt Assessment.

Rapp, S., Breenes, G., & Marsh, A. P. (2002). Memory enhancement training for older adults with mild cognitive impairment: A preliminary study. *Aging and Mental Health*, *6*, 5–11.

Raven, J. C. (1976). *Standard Progressive Matrices*. Oxford: Oxford Psychologists Press.

Raven, J. C. (1995). *Coloured Progressive Matrices Sets A, Ab, B*. Oxford: Oxford Psychologists Press.

Reifler, B. V., & Larson, E. (1990). Excess disability in dementia of the Alzheimer's type. In E. Light & B. D. Lebowitz (Eds.), *Alzheimer's disease treatment and family stress*. New York: Hemisphere.

Reilly, J., Martin, N., & Grossman, M. (2005). Verbal learning in semantic dementia: Is repetition priming a useful strategy? *Aphasiology*, *19*, 329–339.

Richards, M., & Sacker, A. (2003). Lifetime antecedents of cognitive reserve. *Journal of Clinical and Experimental Neuropsychology*, *25*, 614–624.

Riley, G. A., & Heaton, S. (2000). Guidelines for the selection of a method of fading cues. *Neuropsychological Rehabilitation*, *10*, 133–149.

Riley, G. A., Sotiriou, D., & Jaspal, S. (2004). Which is more effective in promoting implicit and explicit memory: The method of vanishing cues or errorless learning without fading? *Neuropsychological Rehabilitation*, *14*, 257–384.

Robertson, I. H., Ward, T., Ridgeway, V., & Nimmo-Smith, I. (1994). *The Test of Everyday Attention*. Bury St Edmunds: Thames Valley Test Company.

Robinson, L., Clare, L., & Evans, K. (2005). Making sense of dementia and adjusting to loss: Psychological reactions to a diagnosis of dementia in couples. *Aging and Mental Health*, *9*, 337–347.

Rogers, S. L., Doody, R. S., Mohs, R. C., Friedhoff, L. T., & the Donepezil Study Group. (1998). Donepezil improves cognition and global function in Alzheimer disease: A 15-week, double-blind, placebo-controlled study. *Archives of Internal Medicine*, *158*, 1021–1034.

Romero, B. (2004). Selbsterhaltungstherapie: Konzept, klinische Praxis und bisherige Ergebnisse. *Zeitschrift fuer Gerontopsychologie und -psychiatrie*, *17*, 119–134.

Romero, B., & Eder, G. (1992). Selbst-Erhaltungs-Therapie (SET): Konzept einer neuropsychologischen Therapie bei Alzheimer-Kranken. *Zeitschrift fuer Gerontolopsychologie und -psychiatrie*, *5*, 267–282.

Romero, B., & Wenz, M. (2001). Self-maintenance therapy in Alzheimer's disease. *Neuropsychological Rehabilitation*, *11*, 333–355.

Ross, L. K., Arnsberger, P., & Fox, P. J. (1998). The relationship between cognitive functioning and disease severity with depression in dementia of the Alzheimer's type. *Aging and Mental Health*, *2*, 319–327.

Roth, M. (1994). The relationship between dementia and normal aging of the brain. In F. A. Huppert, C. Brayne, & D. W. O'Connor (Eds.), *Dementia and normal aging*. Cambridge: Cambridge University Press.

Rusted, J., & Clare, L. (2004). Cognitive approaches to the management of dementia. In R. G. Morris & J. Becker (Eds.), *Cognitive neuropsychology of Alzheimer's disease*. Oxford: Oxford University Press.

Rusted, J. M., Marsh, R., Bledski, L., & Sheppard, L. (1997). Alzheimer patients' use of auditory and olfactory cues to aid verbal memory. *Aging and Mental Health, 1*, 364–371.

Sabat, S. (1994). Excess disability and malignant social psychology: A case study of Alzheimer's disease. *Journal of Community and Applied Social Psychology, 4*, 157–166.

Sabat, S. (1995). The Alzheimer's disease sufferer as a semiotic subject. *Philosophy, Psychiatry, and Psychology, 1*, 145–160.

Sabat, S. (2001). *The experience of Alzheimer's disease: Life through a tangled veil.* Oxford: Blackwell.

Sabat, S. R., & Harré, R. (1992). The construction and deconstruction of self in Alzheimer's disease. *Ageing and Society, 12*, 443–461.

Sabat, S. R., Wiggs, C. L., & Pinizzotto, A. J. (1984). Alzheimer's disease: Clinical vs observational studies of cognitive ability. *Journal of Clinical and Experimental Gerontology, 6*, 337–359.

Salmon, D. P., & Fennema-Notestine, C. (2004). Implicit memory in Alzheimer's disease: Priming and skill learning. In R. G. Morris & J. T. Becker (Eds.), *Cognitive neuropsychology of Alzheimer's disease.* Oxford: Oxford University Press.

Salmon, D. P., Heindel, W. C., & Butters, N. (1992). Semantic memory, priming and skill learning in Alzheimer's disease. In L. Bäckman (Ed.), *Memory functioning in dementia.* Amsterdam: Elsevier.

Salthouse, T. A., Berish, D. E., & Miles, J. D. (2002). The role of cognitive stimulation on the relations between age and cognitive functioning. *Psychology and Aging, 17*, 548–557.

Samuelsson, A. M., Annerstedt, L., Elmståhl, S., Samuelsson, S. M., & Grafström, M. (2001). Burden of responsibility experienced by family caregivers of elderly dementia sufferers. Analyses of strain, feelings and coping strategies. *Scandinavian Journal of Caring Sciences, 15*, 25–33.

Saxton, J., Swihart, A., McGonigle-Gibson, K., Miller, V., & Boller, F. (1990). Assessment of the severely impaired patient: Description and validation of a new neuropsychological test battery. *Psychological Assessment, 2*, 298–303.

Schacter, D. L. (1989). On the relation between memory and consciousness: Dissociable interactions and conscious experience. In H. L. Roediger III & F. I. M. Craik (Eds.), *Varieties of memory and consciousness: Essays in honour of Endel Tulving.* Hillsdale, NJ: Lawrence Erlbaum Associates, Inc.

Schacter, D. L., Rich, S. A., & Stampp, M. S. (1985). Remediation of memory disorders: Experimental evaluation of the spaced-retrieval technique. *Journal of Clinical and Experimental Neuropsychology, 7*, 79–96.

Schreiber, M., Schweizer, A., Lutz, K., Kalveram, K. T., & Jaencke, L. (1999). Potential of an interactive computer-based training in the rehabilitation of dementia: An initial study. *Neuropsychological Rehabilitation, 9*, 155–167.

Scogin, F. (1992). Memory training for older adults. In G. M. M. Jones & B. M. L. Miesen (Eds.), *Care-giving in dementia: Research and applications.* London: Routledge.

Scott, J., & Clare, L. (2003). Do people with dementia benefit from psychological interventions offered on a group basis? *Clinical Psychology and Psychotherapy, 10*, 186–196.

Seiffer, A., Clare, L., & Harvey, R. (2005). The role of personality and coping in relation to awareness of current functioning in early-stage dementia. *Aging and Mental Health, 9*, 535–541.

Shakespeare, P. (1993). Performing. In P. Shakespeare, D. Atkinson, & S. French (Eds.), *Reflecting on research practice: Issues in health and social welfare.* Buckingham: Open University Press.

Shakespeare, P. (1998). *Aspects of confused speech: A study of verbal interaction between confused and normal speakers.* Mahwah, NJ: Lawrence Erlbaum Associates, Inc.

Shakespeare, P., & Clare, L. (2005). Focusing on task oriented talk as a way of exploring the interaction between people with early onset dementia and their carers. *Qualitative Research in Psychology, 2*, 327–340.

Sheikh, J. I., Hill, R. D., & Yesavage, J. A. (1986). Long-term efficacy of cognitive training for age-associated memory impairment: A six-month follow-up study. *Developmental Neuropsychology, 2*, 413–421.

Shifflett, P. A., & Blieszner, R. (1988). Stigma and Alzheimer's disease: Behavioural consequences for support groups. *The Journal of Applied Gerontology, 7*, 147–160.

Sidman, M., & Stoddard, L. T. (1967). The effectiveness of fading in programming a simultaneous form discrimination for retarded children. *Journal of the Experimental Analysis of Behavior, 10*, 3–15.

Sixsmith, A., Stilwell, J., & Copeland, J. (1993). 'Rementia': Challenging the limits of dementia care. *International Journal of Geriatric Psychiatry, 8*, 993–1000.

Skinner, B. F. (1968). *Technology of teaching.* Englewood Cliffs, NJ: Prentice Hall.

Small, B. J., Herlitz, A., & Bäckman, L. (2004). Preclinical Alzheimer's disease: Cognitive and memory functioning. In R. G. Morris & J. T. Becker (Eds.), *Cognitive neuropsychology of Alzheimer's disease.* Oxford: Oxford University Press.

Small, G. W., Rabins, P. V., Barry, P. P., Buckholtz, N. S., DeKosky, S. T., Ferris, S. H., et al. (1997). Diagnosis and treatment of Alzheimer disease and related disorders: Consensus statement of the American Association for Geriatric Psychiatry, the Alzheimer's Association and the American Geriatric Society. *Journal of the American Medical Association, 278*, 1363–1371.

Snaith, R. P., & Zigmond, A. S. (1994). *The Hospital Anxiety and Depression Scale.* Windsor: NFER-Nelson.

Snowden, J., & Neary, D. S. (2002). Relearning of verbal labels in semantic dementia. *Neuropsychologia, 40*, 1715–1728.

Snowdon, D. A. (2003). Healthy aging and dementia: Findings from the Nun Study. *Annals of Internal Medicine, 139*, 450–454.

Sohlberg, M. M., & Mateer, C. (2001). *Cognitive rehabilitation: An integrative neuropsychological approach.* New York: Guilford.

Spector, A., Orrell, M., Davies, S., & Woods, B. (2001). Can reality orientation be rehabilitated? Development and piloting of an evidence-based programme of cognition-based therapies for people with dementia. *Neuropsychological Rehabilitation, 11*, 377–397.

Spector, A., Orrell, M., Davies, S., & Woods, R. T. (1998). Reality orientation for dementia: A review of the evidence for its effectiveness. *The Cochrane Library*, Issue 4. Chichester: John Wiley & Sons Ltd.

Spector, A., Thorgrimsen, L., Woods, B., Royan, L., Davies, S., Butterworth, M., et al. (2003). Efficacy of an evidence-based stimulation therapy programme for people with dementia. *British Journal of Psychiatry, 183*, 248–254.

Sperling, R. A., Bates, J. F., Chua, E. F., Cocchiarella, A. J., Rentz, D. M., Rosen, B. R., et al. (2003). fMRI studies of associative encoding in young and elderly controls and mild Alzheimer's disease. *Journal of Neurology, Neurosurgery and Psychiatry, 74*, 44–50.

Spreen, O., & Strauss, E. (1998). *A compendium of neuropsychological tests: Administration, norms and commentary* (2nd ed.). Oxford: Oxford University Press.

Squire, L. R., & Knowlton, B. J. (1995). Memory, hippocampus, and brain systems. In M. Gazzaniga (Ed.), *The cognitive neurosciences*. Boston: MIT Press.

Squires, E. J., Hunkin, N. M., & Parkin, A. J. (1997). Errorless learning of novel associations in amnesia. *Neuropsychologia, 35*, 1103–1111.

Starkstein, S. E., Sabe, L., Chemerinski, E., Jason, L., & Leiguarda, R. (1996). Two domains of anosognosia in Alzheimer's disease. *Journal of Neurology, Neurosurgery and Psychiatry, 61*, 485–490.

Starkstein, S. E., Vazquez, S., Migliorelli, R., Teson, A., Sabe, L., & Leiguarda, R. (1995). A single-photon emission computed tomographic study of anosognosia in Alzheimer's disease. *Archives of Neurology, 52*, 415–420.

Stern, Y., Zarahn, E., Hilton, H. J., Flynn, J., De La Paz, R., & Rakitin, B. (2003). Exploring the neural basis of cognitive reserve. *Journal of Clinical and Experimental Neuropsychology, 25*, 691–701.

Stuss, D. T. (1991a). Disturbance of self-awareness after frontal system damage. In G. P. Prigatano & D. L. Schacter (Eds.), *Awareness of deficit after brain injury: Clinical and theoretical issues*. New York: Oxford University Press.

Stuss, D. T. (1991b). Self, awareness and the frontal lobes: A neuropsychological perspective. In J. Strauss & G. R. Goethals (Eds.), *The self: Interdisciplinary approaches*. New York: Springer-Verlag.

Stuss, D. T., Picton, T. W., & Alexander, M. P. (2001). Consciousness, self-awareness and the frontal lobes. In S. Salloway, P. Malloy, & J. Duffy (Eds.), *The frontal lobes and neuropsychiatric illness*. Washington, DC: American Psychiatric Press.

Suhr, J., Anderson, S., & Tranel, D. (1999). Progressive muscle relaxation in the management of behavioural disturbance in Alzheimer's disease. *Neuropsychological Rehabilitation, 9*, 31–44.

Sutton, L. J., & Cheston, R. (1997). Rewriting the story of dementia: A narrative approach to psychotherapy with people with dementia. In M. Marshall (Ed.), *State of the art in dementia care*. London: Centre for Policy on Ageing.

Teasdale, J., & Barnard, P. (1993). *Affect, cognition and change*. Hove: Lawrence Erlbaum Associates.

Terrace, H. S. (1963). Discrimination learning with and without 'errors'. *Journal of the Experimental Analysis of Behavior, 6*, 1–27.

Thoene, A. I. T., & Glisky, E. L. (1995). Learning of face–name associations in memory impaired patients: A comparison of different training procedures. *Journal of the International Neuropsychological Society, 1*, 29–38.

Thompson, L. W., Wagner, B., Zeiss, A., & Gallagher, D. (1990). Cognitive/behavioral therapy with early stage Alzheimer's patients: An exploratory view of the utility of this approach. In E. Light & B. D. Lebowitz (Eds.), *Alzheimer's disease treatment and family stress*. New York: Hemisphere.

Turner, J. C. (2005). Explaining the nature of power: A three-process theory. *European Journal of Social Psychology, 35*, 1–22.

Turner, J. C. (2006). Tyranny, freedom and social structure: Escaping our theoretical prisons. *British Journal of Social Psychology, 45*, 41–46.

Turner, R. S. (2003). Neurologic aspects of Alzheimer's disease. In P. A. Lichtenberg, D. L. Murman, & A. M. Mellow (Eds.), *Handbook of dementia: Psychological, neurological and psychiatric perspectives*. Hoboken, NJ: John Wiley & Sons, Inc.

van Dijkhuizen, M., Clare, L., & A Pearce. (2006). Striving for connection: Appraisal and coping among women with early-stage Alzheimer's disease. *Dementia, 5*, 73–94.

van Wielingen, L. E., Tuokko, H. A., Cramer, K., Mateer, C. A., & Hultsch, D. F. (2004). Awareness of financial skills in dementia. *Aging and Mental Health, 8*, 374–380.

Verfaellie, M., Croce, P., & Milberg, W. P. (1995). The role of episodic memory in semantic learning: An examination of vocabulary acquisition in a patient with amnesia due to encephalitis. *Neurocase, 1*, 291–304.

Verghese, J., Lipton, R. B., Katz, M. J., Hall, C. B., Derby, C. A., Kuslansky, G., et al. (2003). Leisure activities and the risk of dementia in the elderly. *New England Journal of Medicine, 348*, 2508–2516.

Verhaeghen, P., Marcoen, A., & Goossens, L. (1992). Improving memory performance in the aged through mnemonic training: A meta-analytic study. *Psychology and Aging, 7*, 242–251.

Verhey, F. R. J., Rozendaal, N., Ponds, R. W. H. M., & Jolles, J. (1993). Dementia, awareness and depression. *International Journal of Geriatric Psychiatry, 8*, 851–856.

Vitaliano, P. P., Young, H. M., & Russo, J. (1991). Burden: A review of measures used among caregivers of individuals with dementia. *The Gerontologist, 31*, 67–75.

Wade, D. T. (2005). Applying the WHO ICF framework to the rehabilitation of patients with cognitive deficits. In P. W. Halligan & D. T. Wade (Eds.), *Effectiveness of rehabilitation for cognitive deficits*. Oxford: Oxford University Press.

Wands, K., Merskey, H., Hachinski, V., Fisman, M., Fox, H., & Boniferro, M. (1990). A questionnaire investigation of anxiety and depression in early dementia. *Journal of the American Geriatrics Society, 38*, 535–538.

Warringon, E. (1996). *Camden Memory Tests*. London: Psychology Press.

Warrington, E. (1984). *Recognition Memory Test*. Windsor: NFER-Nelson.

Warrington, E., & James, M. (1991). *Visual Object and Space Perception Battery*. Bury St Edmunds: Thames Valley Test Company.

Wechsler, D. (1999a). *Wechsler Abbreviated Scale of Adult Intelligence (WASI)*. London: Harcourt Assessment.

Wechsler, D. (1999b). *Wechsler Adult Intelligence Scale, 3rd UK edition (WAIS-III)*. London: Harcourt Assessment.

Wechsler, D. (1999c). *Wechsler Memory Scale, 3rd UK edition (WMS-III)*. London: Harcourt Assessment.

Weinstein, E. A., Friedland, R. P., & Wagner, E. E. (1994). Denial/unawareness of impairment and symbolic behavior in Alzheimer's disease. *Neuropsychiatry, Neuropsychology and Behavioral Neurology, 7*, 176–184.

Werner, P. (2000). Assessing the effectiveness of a memory club for persons suffering from mild cognitive deterioriation. *Clinical Gerontologist, 22*, 3–14.

Whitehouse, P. J., Lerner, A., & Hedera, P. (1993). Dementia. In K. M. Heilman & E. Valenstein (Eds.), *Clinical neuropsychology*. Oxford: Oxford University Press.

Whitlatch, C., Judge, K., Zarit, S. H., & Femia, E. (2006). Dyadic interventions for family caregivers and care receivers in early-stage dementia. *The Gerontologist, 46*, 688–694.

WHO. (1980). *International classification of impairments, disabilities, and handicaps.* Geneva: World Health Organisation.

WHO. (1998). *International classification of impairments, disabilities and handicaps: 2.* Geneva: World Health Organisation. Available from www.who.int/msa/mnh/ems/icidh/introduction.htm

Wild, K., & Cotrell, V. (2003). Identifying driving impairment in Alzheimer disease: A comparison of self and observer reports versus driving evaluation. *Alzheimer Disease and Associated Disorders, 17*, 27–34.

Wilson, B. A. (1995). Management and remediation of memory problems in brain-injured adults. In A. D. Baddeley, B. A. Wilson, & F. N. Watts (Eds.), *Handbook of memory disorders*. Chichester: John Wiley & Sons.

Wilson, B. A. (1997). Cognitive rehabilitation: How it is and how it might be. *Journal of the International Neuropsychological Society, 3*, 487–496.

Wilson, B. A. (2002). Towards a comprehensive model of cognitive rehabilitation. *Neuropsychological Rehabilitation, 12*, 97–110.

Wilson, B. A., Alderman, N., Burgess, P. W., Emslie, H., & Evans, J. J. (1996). *Behavioural Assessment of the Dysexecutive Syndrome (BADS)*. Bury St Edmunds: Thames Valley Test Company.

Wilson, B. A., Baddeley, A., Evans, J. J., & Shiel, A. (1994). Errorless learning in the rehabilitation of memory impaired people. *Neuropsychological Rehabilitation, 4*, 307–326.

Wilson, B. A., Cockburn, J., & Baddeley, A. (2003). *Rivermead Behavioural Memory Test, 2nd edition (RBMT-II)*. London: Harcourt Assessment.

Wilson, B. A., Emslie, H. C., Quirk, K., & Evans, J. J. (2001). Reducing everyday memory and planning problems by means of a paging system: A randomised control crossover study. *Journal of Neurology, Neurosurgery and Psychiatry, 70*, 477–482.

Wilson, B. A., Herbert, C. M., & Shiel, A. (2003). *Behavioural approaches in neuropsychological rehabilitation: Optimising rehabilitation procedures*. Hove: Psychology Press.

Wilson, R. S., Bennett, D. A., Bienias, J. L., Aggarwal, N. T., de Leon, C. F. M., Morris, M. C., et al. (2002). Cognitive activity and incident AD in a population-based sample of older persons. *Neurology, 59*, 1910–1914.

Wilson, R. S., de Leon, C. F. M., Barnes, L. L., Schneider, J. A., Bienias, J. L., Evans, D. A., et al. (2002). Participation in cognitively stimulating activities and risk of incident Alzheimer disease. *Journal of the American Medical Association, 287*, 742–748.

Woods, R. T. (1992). What can be learned from studies on reality orientation? In G. M. M. Jones & B. M. L. Miesen (Eds.), *Care-giving in dementia: Research and applications*. London: Tavistock/Routledge.

Woods, R. T. (1999). Psychological 'therapies' in dementia. In R. T. Woods (Ed.),

Psychological problems of aging: Assessment, treatment and care. Chichester: John Wiley & Sons Ltd.

Woods, R. T. (2002). Reality orientation: A welcome return? [Editorial]. *Age and Ageing, 31*, 155–156.

Woods, R. T., & Britton, P. G. (1985). *Clinical psychology with the elderly*. London: Croom Helm.

Woods, R. T., & Clare, L. (2006). Cognition-based therapies and mild cognitive impairment. In H. Tuokko & D. Hultsch (Eds.), *Mild cognitive impairment: International perspectives*. New York: Taylor & Francis.

Woods, R. T., Portnoy, S., Head, D., & Jones, G. (1992). Reminiscence and life review with persons with dementia: Which way forward? In G. M. M. Jones & B. M. L. Miesen (Eds.), *Care-giving in dementia: Research and applications*. London: Tavistock/Routledge.

Woods, R. T., Wills, W., Higginson, I. J., Hobbins, J., & Whitby, M. (2003). Support in the community for people with dementia and their carers: A comparative outcome study of specialist mental health service interventions. *International Journal of Geriatric Psychiatry, 18*, 298–307.

Yale, R. (1995). *Developing support groups for individuals with early-stage Alzheimer's disease*. Baltimore: Health Professions Press.

Yesavage, J. A. (1982). Degree of dementia and improvement with memory training. *Clinical Gerontology, 1*, 77–81.

Yesavage, J. A., Brink, T. L., Rose, T. L., Lum, O., Huang, V., Adey, M., et al. (1983). Development and validation of a geriatric depression screening scale: A preliminary report. *Journal of Psychiatric Research, 17*, 37–49.

Zaitchik, D., & Albert, M. S. (2004). Cognition and emotion. In R. G. Morris & J. T. Becker (Eds.), *Cognitive neuropsychology of Alzheimer's disease*. Oxford: Oxford University Press.

Zanetti, O., Binetti, G., Magni, E., Rozzini, L., Bianchetti, A., & Trabucchi, M. (1997). Procedural memory stimulation in Alzheimer's disease: Impact of a training programme. *Acta Neurologica Scandinavica, 95*, 152–157.

Zanetti, O., Magni, E., Binetti, G., Bianchetti, A., & Trabucchi, M. (1994). Is procedural memory stimulation effective in Alzheimer's disease? *International Journal of Geriatric Psychiatry, 9*, 1006–1007.

Zanetti, O., Zanieri, G., di Giovanni, G., de Vreese, L. P., Pezzini, A., Metitieri, T., et al. (2001). Effectiveness of procedural memory stimulation in mild Alzheimer's disease patients: A controlled study. *Neuropsychological Rehabilitation, 11*, 263–272.

Zarit, S. H., & Edwards, A. B. (in press). Family caregiving: Research and clinical intervention. In R. T. Woods & L. Clare (Eds.), *Handbook of the clinical psychology of ageing* (2nd ed.). Chichester: John Wiley & Sons Ltd.

Zarit, S. H., Zarit, J. M., & Reever, K. E. (1982). Memory training for severe memory loss: Effects on senile dementia patients and their families. *The Gerontologist, 22*, 373–377.

Author index

Subject index